'A Treasure Hou

San Francisco Chronicle:
"An incredible source of information about . . . what tourist traps to avoid and where to find the best values."

Los Angeles Times:
". . . filled with information on beaches, restaurants and things to do and see. Lenore Horowitz's love for Kauai comes through in her writing."

"A fabulous book! We saw places we've ignored because we didn't know they existed!"
– *EW, Milwaukie, OR*

"I found beautiful beaches that showed me what Hawaii was like years ago..." – *DC, Coos Bay, OR*

"You've been our valued companion, through your book, on all our trips since 1988."
– *TM, El Cerito, CA*

"the best investment I made!"
– *GM, Freeport, TX*

Los Angeles Times:
"Our vacation became an adventure the day we discovered the *Kauai Underground Guide!*"

Seattle Post Intelligencer:
"I can't imagine riding around the island without this book resting on the dash of my rental car."

Vancouver Courier:
"A little gem of a book that each and every traveler should have in hand!"

Travel-Age West:
"A downhome commentary on the best beaches, restaurants, and activities..."

San Francisco Chronicle:
"Our constant companion! This book opened our eyes to delights we would otherwise have missed."

"our passport to Kauai!"
– *LB, Durango, CO*

"A distinctive, thorough, & helpful guide to Kauai"

—Jeff Phillips, Senior Travel Writer, **Sunset Magazine**

Special thanks to Mirah, Jeremy, Mike, Lauren,
& Larry Horowitz
for their invaluable help
with the research, writing,
illustration, and design of this
fourteenth edition.

& thanks to Robin
for the expertise, support, & friendship
that brought this book from screen to press,
& to David E. Kendall & Ervin Klein
for solving problems no matter when, where or at what hour!

Kauai Underground Guide

Lenore W. Horowitz

fourteenth edition

PAPALOA PRESS

©1997 by Papaloa Press, a Division of LCH Enterprises Inc.

First edition:	1980
Second edition:	1981
Third Edition:	1982
Fourth edition:	1983
Fifth edition:	1984
Sixth edition:	1985
Seventh edition:	1986
Eighth edition:	1987
Ninth edition:	1988
Tenth edition:	1989
Eleventh edition:	1990
Twelfth edition:	1992
Thirteenth edition:	1995
Fourteenth edition:	1996
2nd printing with revisions	1997

ISBN 0-9615498-7-4
ISSN 1045-1358
Library of Congress Catalog card 82-643643

Printed in U.S.A.
by House of Printing, Mountain View CA

Color Production by Graphic Express, Saratoga, CA
Maps by Schema Design, and Reineck & Reineck
Original Line Drawings by Pat Bergeron
& Lauren, Mirah, Jeremy & Mike Horowitz & Devon Davey
Historic Petroglyph Drawings by Likeke R. McBride
Petroglyph art by Lauren Horowitz

Photographs by Lenore W. Horowitz

http://www.hshawaii.com/kvp/best_kauai_guide/

Contents

Preface

Planning Ahead

Beach Adventures

Activities

Kauai Specialties

Adventures

Restaurants

Maps

Preface

Kauai shows few traces of
Hurricane Iniki, which struck the
island in September, 1992.
Beaches sparkle gold in the sun,
some even wider and more sandy
than before. Papayas and bananas
are bountiful; flame trees, heliconia, plumeria and hibiscus stretch
up to the sky in brilliant splashes
of color, fragrant in gentle
breezes. Kauai is once again a
garden, and as if it had been
pruned, the island has the lush
bright greenness of a burst of new

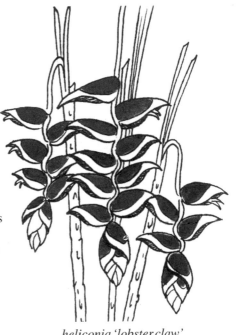

heliconia 'lobster claw'

growth. New roofs and paint give the houses a sparkle they never had
before, even in Poipu, hardest hit of all, as man catches up with nature
in the island's restoration. Thanks to the tireless efforts of Mayor
Maryanne Kusaka, the island's beach parks once again welcome visitors
and *kamainas* alike. As you fly in over beautiful Kalapaki Bay, you'll
see a Kauai more lush and lovely than ever.

This is the Kauai we will try to describe to you in our *Guide*— not
what you would see from a tour bus, but the rare and special place we
have discovered during more than twenty years as vacationers and
homeowners. We want to share with you our favorite adventures—at the
beaches, in restaurants, and on tours and shopping expeditions. We do
not describe every restaurant and shop, only those we have visited, and
our opinions are shaped by personal preference. We look for peace and
quiet, privacy and natural beauty.

In many ways our *Guide* is unique. As a family of six, we can offer
advice on beaches and activities based on having taken children to
Kauai at all ages! For adults with that enviable freedom to go off by
themselves, we describe in detail what one can expect to find in many

island restaurants. Even a single year brings dramatic change to this island, and our working vacations keep us busy tracking what's new, what's different, and what's still as lovely as ever. You may find that in some cases prices, policies, even managements may be changed, so do your research carefully when making decisions and keep us posted about what you find out. It's been great fun hearing from people all over the country who have enjoyed discovering Kauai with our *Guide,* and who want to help update the next one. We hope you enjoy our newest addition — our favorite family photographs!

So as we go to press with this 14th edition, we want to thank all the readers who have helped make our *Guide* a storybook success. Who would have thought that our first edition of sixteen pages would grow into a book which has sold close to 100,000 copies! Or that our oldest child, Mirah, would arrange such a spectacular send-off by handing our first edition to a friend she made on the beach. He turned out to be Chandler Forman of the *Chicago Sun-Times*, and when his story about Kauai—and our book—was syndicated nationwide, more than 700 letters arrived at our door, and we had to rush to press with a new edition!

When she arranged this PR spectacular, Mirah was a gregarious six-year-old with two baby brothers. Today, our youngest child, Lauren, is thirteen, and Mirah at twenty flies to Kauai by herself, fitting our family vacation into her own agenda. Our boys are changing too, their love for sandcrabs and rainbow shells giving way to a passion for surf. When they were small, we hoped one day to escape from all their clutter. Today, toy cars and crayons are off the floor at last, but now Jeremy and Michael each bring friends, and each of the friends is bigger! We seem to be spending quite a bit of time at the airport picking up arriving friends or sending suntanned friends back home!

Watching our children change so dramatically over twenty years helps put the development of Kauai in perspective. With children and with islands, change brings the excitement of new opportunities and at the same time the loss of what was precious. The roads we travel today are certainly more congested, but our destinations are also far more interesting. Once perfect for our family with small children, Kauai is also perfect for a family with teenagers, with definite and sometimes contradictory interests. And as we explore their newest horizons, we see this wonderful island unfold in fascinating new possibilities.

Like an old friend, Kauai gets better with each visit. New adventures take us to new places, and at the same time we rediscover with deeper affection what we have loved in the past. We hope you will feel the same way about this special place and return again soon!

Exploring Kauai

Kauai is like an America in miniature, with rolling hills and valleys to the east and majestic mountains to the west. On the eastern shore, sand as fine as sugar rings half-moon bays fringed with stately ironwood trees. These are the best beaches for walking and hunting for shells and driftwood. On the south shore, the island's flat, leeward side offers protected swimming almost all year round under sunny skies and gentle breezes. We love the north shore, where magnificent cliffs reach to touch the sky, and the foaming, churning surf crashes against the rocks. Here, rain showers freshen the air, dance among the flowers, and make the coastline sparkle. Or go west to Polihale Beach, and find cliffs like the exotic towers of some lost civilization, with golden sand stretching as far as the eye can see. Kauai will never bore you, because a half–hour drive, at the most, can take you to a beach that almost seems to belong to another island.

Different as they are, the beaches also change their moods with the seasons. In summer, the sea may be so calm and clear that bubbles on the surface cast shadows on the sandy bottom. But winter tides can turn a peaceful lagoon to a roaring, raging caldron; and ocean spray can drape the northern valleys with salty mist. In winter, some north shore beaches disappear entirely under crashing surf, and may even be officially closed for safety reasons. Boats which anchor peacefully in Hanalei Bay for half the year take shelter in Nawiliwili to the south. Even north shore sunsets change with the shifting angle of the sun. In winter months, when the sun rides lower in the sky, you'll see the sunset in burnished clouds over the mountains, while in summer, the sun sinks into the sea in a torrent of gold.

Almost circular in shape, Kauai has three main tourist areas: Princeville & Hanalei to the north, Poipu to the south, and the 'Coconut Coast' between Lihue and Kapa'a to the east. Each of Kauai's three major tourist areas has a unique character. **The north shore**, which includes Kilauea, Kalihiwai, Anini, Princeville, Hanalei, and Ha'ena, is the most spectacular— its rugged mountains, beautiful beaches, and green vistas are the Kauai of postcards. As the windward shore, the north also gets the most rainfall, particularly in winter months when the surf at the beaches is also stronger. Despite its rainfall, many people love the north for its rural peacefulness and magnificent beauty. Princeville, once a cattle ranch high on an ocean bluff, is now a resort complex featuring the spectacular Princeville Golf Course and the even more spectacular *Princeville Hotel*, as well as a wide range of condos and homes. These accommodations offer astonishing ocean views, particularly at sunset. Getting to the beach may be difficult for most people, however, requiring a hike down the cliff to one of the small beaches — except for hotel guests who can take an elevator! A short drive away is magnificent Hanalei Bay, one of Kauai's finest beaches. You can stay in the town of Hanalei itself, and rent a private home or apartment on the beach or, at the most, a block or two away. Or you can travel further west, towards Ha'ena, and rent a house, B&B, or a *Hanalei Colony Resort* condo.

The south shore, at Poipu, on the leeward side of the island, has drier weather and generally calmer swimming conditions year round. It's also generally flatter, with vegetation more dry. For swimming, there is wonderful Poipu Beach, and for sheer beauty, spectacular Maha'ulepu. You have many choices for lodgings, from a beautiful luxury resort hotel—*The Hyatt Regency*— to a host of condos and B&B's, many within walking distance of Poipu Beach Park, which offers excellent protected swimming and snorkeling all year round. The best beachfront location is at *Kiahuna*, a luxury condominium resort.

The eastern shore, from Lihue (where the airport is located) to Wailua and Kapa'a—the "Coconut Coast"— has location as its main advantage. It's about midway between Poipu and Hanalei and about a half hour drive from each, so you can explore the island in either direction, depending on the weather and your inclinations. You'll find hotels, condo developments and B&B's, and many can accurately be described as beachfront. You should ask careful questions, however, because eastern shore beaches often have tricky currents, and swimmers must be very cautious. Some excellent beachfront condos are in the Wailua area (*Lae Nani, Wailua Bay View, Lanikai, Kapa'a Sands*) and the *Kauai Resort Hotel* near Lydgate Park. The best beachfront location is the magnificent sandy swimming beach at Kalapaki Bay, home to the *Kauai Marriott*.

No matter where you decide to stay, you can easily explore the rest of the island by car. Except for the wilderness area in the northwest quadrant, Kauai is nearly encircled by a main two-lane highway, with sequentially numbered 'mile markers' to make tracking easy. You can drive from Lihue to Kapa'a in about 10 minutes, from Kapa'a to Hanalei in about 30 minutes, or from Lihue to Poipu in about 20 minutes, and from Poipu to Polihale in about 35 minutes.

While Kauai has recovered almost entirely from Hurricane Iniki, which struck the island in fall, 1992, the south shore still shows some scars. Brennecke's beach, beloved by so many surfers, has disappeared, the seawall broken and the sand washed away. Some sand seems to have shifted to Poipu Beach, now wider and more lovely than ever, to Shipwreck Beach in front of the Hyatt Regency Hotel, and to Maha'ulepu, our favorite (almost) hidden beach on the south shore, nestled in fields of sugar cane tipped with silken tassels shimmering in the sunshine. Away from Poipu, you will see only traces of Iniki, and once you travel north of Kapa'a, the main effect is the absence of crowds!

Planning Ahead: Kauai by Mail

A few quick phone calls can yield a lot of planning information!

*Call the Kauai Visitor's Bureau at 800-262-1400 and request the *Kauai Vacation Planner,* which includes a descriptive directory of hotels, condos, B&B's, and rental agencies, and activities (no prices, however). Or send a FAX to 800-637-5762. Ask also for a free book of discount coupons, and illustrated island map.

*Contact Resort associations on Kauai for a mini-guide. The *Poipu Beach Resort Association* publishes a full listing of south shore accommodations and activities, including rates, and a handy map. PO Box 730 Koloa, HI 96756 (808-742-7444). (E-mail at *info@poipu-beach.org*). For the eastern shore region, contact *Coconut Coast Resort Association* at 808-822-7610 or write to 4-241 Kuhio Hwy., Kapa'a HI 96746. For Princeville information on the north shore, contact *Princeville Resort,* PO Box 3069, Princeville HI 96722 or call 800- 826-4400.

Check out discounts. The *Entertainment Club Hawaii* coupon book ($40 plus $3 shipping) has discount coupons for hotels, car rentals restaurants, and activities on all Hawaiian islands. The newest edition has only a few Kauai listings, so call (800-477-3234) and ask what they are. Order direct from the Hawaii office (808-737-3252) to receive a 'companion flies free' coupon on Aloha Airlines (holidays excluded).

Order a catalog of books & maps from *Basically Books* (800-903-6277) 46 Waianuenue, Hilo HI 96720 or *Island Bookshelf* 800-967-5944. If you're on the internet, visit *www.amazon.com*—an internet bookstore.

Virtual Kauai

Visit these INTERNET web sites for information and virtual tours.

Discover Kauai	http://www.kauai-hawaii.com/
Kauai Vacation Planner	http://www.hshawaii.com/kvp/
Kauai Underground Guide	http://www.hshawaii.com/kvp/
	best_kauai_guide/
Planet Hawaii	http://planet-hawaii.com/
Poipu Beach Association	http://poipu-beach.org/poipu/
Hawaii Visitors Bureau	http://www.visit.hawaii.org/
Hawaii Link	http://hawaiilink.com/

Where to Stay: Resort Hotels

Kauai has three wonderful—and very different luxury resort hotels. On the north shore, *The Princeville Hotel* combines a magnificent cliffside setting overlooking Hanalei Bay with elegant rooms and gourmet dining. A small beach at the base of the cliff, which you reach by elevator, offers marvelous views and, when seas are calm, swimming and snorkeling. Rates from $300/nite (800-826-4400). On the south shore in Poipu, *The Hyatt Regency* is another architectural marvel with spacious rooms and elegant dining. The major drawback is the beach, where strong surf and currents can be intimidating, but the Hyatt offers guests an elaborate swimming waterway, complete with waterfalls and waterslide, as well as a 5 acre saltwater lagoon. Rates from $200 (800-233-1234). In Lihue, on the eastern shore, the spectacular *Marriott at Kauai Lagoons*, with 880 acres of golf courses and waterways, fronts beautiful Kalapaki Beach. While the rooms are relatively smaller than the other two luxury resorts, the Marriott offers one of the island's best swimming beaches and a circular pool ringed by jaccuzzis — one of the largest in the state, and you can walk to excellent dining. Rates from $200 (800-228-9290). Of the dozen smaller hotels offering more reasonable rates and fewer amenities, *Kauai Resort Hotel* is walking distance to an excellent swimming beach at Lydgate Beach Park in Wailua. (800-272-5275). Most of the best beaches on Kauai are (like 'early Monopoly') without hotels — protected in the parks, or in residential areas, or near undeveloped land.

Luxury condominium hotels offer the extra space of an apartment along the many amenities of a hotel. Embassy Resorts operates *The Point at Poipu* on the south shore, adjacent to the Hyatt Regency, and on the north shore, Princeville's *Hanalei Bay Resort*, overlooking Hanalei Bay. Neither fronts a safe swimming beach. Rates from $200/nite. Embassy has a coupon in the 1996 *Entertainment Club Hawaii Book*.

When inquiring about rates, mention your memberships. Hotels often give discounts to members of auto clubs, the American Association of Retired Persons, and other groups.

spotted puffer fish

Condominiums & Homes

For renting a condominium or home, you have several choices. You can contact the condo complex through its reservation desk (*The Kauai Vacation Planner* contains a descriptive listing with phone numbers), or you can rent directly from an individual apartment owner, many of whom advertise in local newspapers or in major magazines like *Hawaii Magazine* or *Sunset Magazine*. You can also deal with a rental agency which handles individually owned units in various condo complexes. By comparing the different properties, the staff can help you find the one best suited to your special needs. *Hawaiian Apartment Leasing Enterprises (HALE)* offers condos and homes on all islands (800-854-8843). *Kauai Vacation Rentals* (800-367-5025) represents condos and homes on Kauai. Some agencies specialize. For a complete listing of the Poipu area rental agencies, as well as detailed rate and amenity information on all accommodations in Poipu, contact the *Poipu Beach Association* at P.O. Box 730, Koloa, HI 96756 or call (808) 742-7444. (E-mail at *info@poipu-beach.org*). Poipu rental agencies include *R & R Realty (800) 367-8022, Poipu Connection* (800-742-2260), *Poipu Beach Travel* (800-3-ALOHA-3) *Garden Island Rentals* (800-247-5599) or *Suite Paradise* (800-367-8020). For the north shore, call *North Shore Properties* (800-488-3336), *Harrington's Paradise Properties* (808-826-6114), *Blue Water Rentals* (800-628-5533), *Hanalei Aloha*

Management (800-487-9833), or *Oceanfront Realty* (800-222-5541). Request brochures. Expect to pay at least $100 per night, and at least $150 for a resort condo at or near a swimming beach. Many agencies require advance deposits and one week minimum stays (for shorter stays, try the condo's front desk). Popular months (December through March, and also August) book up quickly, so plan ahead!

Readers' favorites: *Lae Nani, Kapa'a Sands, Wailua Bay View* (eastern shore, Wailua). *Kiahuna, Poipu Kai* (south shore, Poipu). *Hanalei Bay Resort, Hanalei Colony Resort* (north shore). On the west side, the *Waimea Plantation Cottages* is a unique resort set in a restored sugar plantation camp.

Where to Stay: Bed & Breakfasts

B & B's are plentiful on Kauai, one result of the small boomlet resulting from post-Iniki insurance money. They come at all prices (from $45, with $60 as the average) and types, from a beachfront cottage to the spare room-with-bath in a home with gregarious host. You can contact individual owners, but an agency will save you time. Two excellent agencies on Kauai represent most of the individual owners, as well as some small hotels, inns and condos. *Bed & Breakfast Hawaii* (800-733-1632) has listings on all the islands, and will send you a short list (free) or a guidebook-style directory ($13). *Bed & Breakfast Kauai* (800-822-1176) is smaller with an exclusive focus on Kauai. Disabled or single travelers receive special consideration from both agencies, and can also call Edee Seymour in Lawai, proprietress of Victoria's Place, for advice (808-332-9300). *Poipu Bed & Breakfast* (800-552-0095) specializes in south shore properties. Questions to ask: What's for breakfast (continental, full meal, or stocked kitchen?) What kind of beds (length, width, etc.?) What degree of interaction with host and other guests? Most require a deposit and a minimum stay. Ask about weekly discounts and the cancellation policy. Many B&B's are booked 2 to 3 months in advance, so plan ahead!

Where to Stay: Rustic Kauai

If you like hiking and camping (yet amid relative comfort), you can rent cabins in some of Kauai's loveliest wilderness areas. In the beautiful Koke'e forest region, you can rent a cabin containing a stove, refrigerator, hot shower, cooking and eating utensils, linens, bedding, and wood burning stove at bargain rates, only $35-$45/night (maximum stay of 5 nights during a 30 day period). Contact *Koke'e Lodge,* Box 819, Waimea HI 96796 (808-335-606). Closer to 'civilization' and conveniently located between Lihue and Koloa, *Kahili Mountain Park* offers reasonably priced, rustic cabins ($44 -$55 for two) and even more rustic one room 'cabinettes' ($33 for two) in a serene meadow setting backed by mountains with a view of the sea. Contact Kahili Mountain Park, Box 298, Koloa HI 96756 (808-742-9921) Map: 3.

Near road's end on the north shore, *YMCA Camp Naue* in Ha'ena offers beachfront camping in bunk houses (or your own tent). Contact YMCA of Kauai, Box 1786, Lihue HI 96766. Kapa'a has an *International Hostel* (800-858-2295). A bunk costs $16/nite.

Beachfront & Oceanfront

As you investigate accommodations, become a connoisseur of words, especially if you want to be located on or close to a swimming beach. 'Ocean front' probably means a rocky place, or at least marginal swimming, but even 'beachfront' can be a misleading term. The so-called 'beach' could be rocky or unswimmable due to dangerous currents and strong surf. A property as a whole may be accurately described as 'beachfront,' but shaped like a pie wedge, with the tip on the beach and the wide end back on the road! Or it may be technically adjacent to a beach, but with a building, a swimming pool (or even a road!) in between.

We have learned to ask two key questions: What will I see when I open up my sliding glass door? And how far do I have to walk (or drive) to get to the nearest sandy swimming beach? If you have children, ask where the closest "child-safe" swimming beach is. Inquire carefully about the swimming pool, because pools vary in size and location, and yours may end up being a tiny kidney next to the parking lot! Ask how far you have to walk to reach it, a key question if you have toddlers and all their paraphernalia to carry — and then find out you have left their favorite toys back in the room!

Weather & Seasons

If you dial 245-6001 for the weather report on Kauai, you will probably hear this 'forecast': 'Mostly fair today, with occasional windward and mauka (mountain) showers. Tonight, mostly fair, with showers varying from time to time and from place to place." Except for storms, Kauai's normal weather pattern is mostly sunny, with showers passing over the ocean, crossing the coastline and backing up against the island's mountainous interior. Normal trade winds come from the north and northeast, bringing rainfall to these 'windward' shores and creating the 'lee' of the island in the south, at Poipu, and west, at Kekaha and Polihale. Occasionally the winds come from the south, and these 'Kona winds' create the lee on the north shore. At these times, Kilauea, Hanalei and Ha'ena can be absolutely spectacular! So plan your adventures with an eye to the weather. If it's clear up north, visit the north shore's spectacular beaches, for if your stay is only for a few days, you may not get another chance!

The seasons on Kauai follow the usual pattern of the mainland: precipitation is more frequent in winter and spring, while summer months are warmer and more humid, fall months clearer and more dry. Normal temperatures are between 60's & mid-80's, and in summer can reach the 90's. Careful planning can make the most of any weather, however, since Kauai has 'micro climates' and a 20 minute drive can take you from rain to sun. Flexibility is the key! If your base is on the north shore, getting to Poipu can take you more than an hour, depending on traffic. The same is true if you are traveling from Poipu to the north shore. From Wailua and Kapa'a, on the eastern shore, you can drive north in 40 minutes or south in 25. On Kauai, no matter where you stay, be prepared to be an active vacationer and drive to the sun—all the way west to Polihale if necessary! Only an island-wide storm should send you indoors to rent a movie.

Flying to Kauai

The typical travel plan involves a flight first to Honolulu International Airport on Oahu and then a connecting flight to Kauai's Lihue Airport. This can turn into a full day of travel, particularly on the return trip to the mainland, when the clock moves ahead of you. You can gain back some vacation time on that return trip if you take the latest evening flight out of Honolulu, thus leaving Kauai around dinner time to make the connection.

Charter companies offering discount fares may save you money, especially for a family. Occasionally they can cost you time — if there's a problem with your flight, for example, you have no way to change carriers. Major airlines with frequent daily flights give you more options if have to make a change — in case someone gets sick, for example, or you need to go home earlier, or (even better) later!

After you land in Honolulu, you will take a connecting flight on Hawaiian, Aloha, or Mahalo Airlines for your twenty-minute flight to Kauai. Airline regulations require a minimum 70 minute layover in Honolulu to allow passengers and baggage to be transferred to inter-island

connecting flights. However, there is a way to beat the system and minimize time wasted in the airport. After landing in Honolulu, proceed directly to the Inter-island Terminal, a ten-minute walk or short bus ride. Go to your airline's ticket counter, ask if there's an earlier flight to Lihue, and try to get on, even as a stand-by if necessary (The computer data is often wrong, and stand-bys can usually get seats). Your luggage will remain on your originally scheduled flight, but you will be in Lihue with a head start, which you can use for filling out the forms on your rental car. Then you can drop someone off at the grocery store or leave the family at McDonald's while you go back for the baggage. On long travel days, especially with young children, this saved time can be a lifesaver!

When you're getting ready to board your inter-island flight, you might be told that your carry-on luggage will have to go under the plane, because some inter-island aircraft have very small overhead bins. Keep your jewelry, camera, prescription drugs, and favorite stuffed animals in a small bag inside your larger one, just in case!

Aloha Island Air offers flights between Honolulu and Kauai's Princeville Airport, which is too small for an agricultural inspection station. This means that on your trip back to the mainland, you won't be able to check your luggage straight through to your final destination. Instead, you'll have to collect it in Honolulu and have it inspected there.

Entertainment Club (808-737-3252) offers a Hawaii coupon book for about $40, including two-dinners-for-the-price-of-one offers for a half-dozen Kauai restaurants and one companion-flies-free coupon on Aloha Airlines (holidays excluded). Note: This Aloha Airlines coupon is not available on Entertainment Club books sold at the 800-374-4464 number.

What to Pack

When two suitcases disappeared during our flight home in 1982, we learned some lessons the hard way about packing. Now we pack a change of clothes, bathing suit, and toilet articles for each family member, as well as any prescription drugs, in a carry-on bag just in case someone's suitcase is lost temporarily. We also distribute everybody's belongings in every suitcase, so that no one person is left without clothes if a suitcase is lost permanently. And we label each bag clearly *inside* where the label can't be accidentally detached. Since one of our missing suitcases contained all our exposed film, a heartbreaking loss, we now use mailers and send each roll off as we finish it. Incredibly, lightning struck twice, and two more suitcases disappeared three years later. A replacement-cost rider on our Homeowner's insurance policy has turned out to be a wise investment, for the airline's insurance limit is $1,250 per passenger, although the Department of Transportation has proposed to Congress to increase the limit to $1,850. Airlines typically subtract 10% of the purchase price for each year you have owned an item, exclude cameras and jewelry, and may take up to six months to process a claim. If your luggage is missing or damaged, save all baggage-claim stubs, boarding passes, and tickets, and be sure to fill out an official claim form at the baggage supervisor's office *before* you leave the airport. Most clearly tagged luggage makes its way to the owner within 24 hours. If your luggage is orphaned longer and you are out of town, most airlines offer emergency funds of $25 a day if you present receipts. Call daily for an update on your bags!

Vacation days are too precious to spend on line in stores. We try to cut down on clothes (except for swim suits and T-shirts) and use space for other essentials— beach sandals, walking shoes, snorkel gear (that fits!), extra film, sunscreen, hat with brim, sunglasses, beach bag or back pack, tennis ball or beach ball, frisbee. Most island restaurants are informal— no tie or jacket— but a sweater or long sleeved shirt is great for cool evenings!

Traveling with Children

If you are traveling with babies or toddlers, you can request bulkhead seating (but not exit rows, which can be assigned only to adults) in advance. Be sure to get your boarding passes in advance too, so that your seats have priority if the flight is overbooked. Don't forget to enroll the kids in the airline's Frequent Flyer Program.   Be sure to bring along your child's car seat, which goes into the baggage compartment with your luggage, as Hawaii state law requires them for children under three. A new ruling allows airlines to permit use of the child's restraint seat on board the aircraft, but that requires the child to have a paid seat!

Families who fly to Kauai from the east coast might consider staying overnight in California to help children make the difficult time adjustment in stages, particularly on the long trip home. After flying from Kauai to California, the kids can run around in the hotel, have some ice cream, and stay up as late as possible in order to push their body clocks ahead three hours while they sleep. If you book a late morning flight out of California the next day, the kids can sleep late in the morning, and if you're lucky, they will wake up fresh for the second day's flight and be ready to adjust their body clocks another three hours. Traveling through two time zones is no snap, but this plan can make it a bit easier.

On that journey home, bad weather might delay your connecting flight from Lihue to Honolulu, and so you might consider taking a flight earlier in the day, before the inter-island flights get backed up. In fact, it's a good idea to see if you can get on as a stand-by on *any* earlier flight to Honolulu once you're in the Lihue airport. This plan is well worth it if you are traveling with young children, when the consequences of missing your flight to the mainland are too awful to consider!

To amuse little ones during the long flight, pack lots of small toys, crayons, books, paper dolls, and an "airplane present" to be unwrapped when the seatbelt sign goes off! Ask the cabin attendants for "kiddie packs" or cards right away as supplies are often limited. Pack a secret snack or toy for those awful moments when one child spills coke on another! Keep chewing gum handy to help children relieve the ear-clogging which can be so uncomfortable, even painful, during the last twenty minutes of the descent when cabin pressure changes. Sucking on a bottle will help a baby or toddler.

To save shopping time, we pack as many beach and swimming toys as we can. "Swimmies" (arm floats) are great for small children to use in the pool, as are goggles and masks (that fit!). Toy trucks for sand-dozing, frisbees, inflatable beach balls, and floats can be stuffed into suitcase corners! Boogie boards, by far the best swimming toy, are expensive, but can be brought home in the baggage compartment after your vacation (packed in a pillowcase!). Best choices are at the M. Miura store (Kapaʻa) Progressive Expressions (Koloa); cheapest ones at K-Mart and WalMart. Boogie boards are better balanced than the cheaper imitations, and even small children enjoy trying to ride them. Caution: they can be hazardous in a pool; a small child who tips over in deep water can be trapped underneath.

You can rent all kinds of children's equipment at *Baby's Away* on Kauai (800) 996-9030. For babies, bring a hat with a large brim to protect delicate skin, socks for feet, Tylenol and Desitin, for those problems that occur *only* in the middle of the night, and a strong, waterproof sunblock!!

Driving Kauai

Kauai is still rural as far as the infrastructure goes—just two-lanes, all around the island! Increasing traffic has prompted the creation of three 'bypass roads' to alleviate back-ups in congested areas. You'll see the first one as you leave the airport; it merges with Rt. 56 or Kuhio Highway, the island's main two-lane road, just north of Hanama'ulu. Traffic moves easily as you continue north — until you reach the town of Wailua, where three little traffic lights can cause unbelievable congestion during rush hour. A new 'bypass road' goes behind Wailua and winds through cane fields, then comes out near the center of Kapa'a, offering you a view of sugar cane rather than the rear bumper of the car in front of you! You'll see the turnoff on the left just north of Sizzler and south of the Coconut Plantation Marketplace. Sometimes, however, the sugar harvest closes the road, and traffic on Rt. 56 reverts to a crawl! At those times, polish your left hand turn skills, try not to drive between 4 and 6:30, and be patient. Remember, you're on vacation! A third 'bypass' road connects the center of Koloa with eastern Poipu and the Hyatt Regency Hotel. Turn left off Maluhia Road at the center of Koloa, then take the first right onto Weli-weli, and follow the signs to Poipu.

While driving your rental car on Kauai, keep this in mind: speed limits are strictly enforced, especially in residential and business areas. It's illegal to make a U-turn in a "business district," even if it doesn't look like much of a business district. There's not much crime on this island, so you can guess how the police occupy their time!

The best places to explore on Kauai are accessible by either paved roads or established dirt roads in the cane fields which are maintained as 'rights of way' to the beaches. In our book, we have arranged the beach descriptions to follow the route you would travel if you were driving north along the eastern shore from Lihue to Kilauea to Princeville, Hanalei and Ha'ena, ending at spectacular Ke'e Beach. Then we explore the south shore, traveling west from Lihue towards Poipu, Hanapepe, Kekaha, and finally to Polihale, the magnificent beach at the end of the road on the westside.

So pack a picnic lunch and some beach mats, and explore the island's most beautiful hidden beaches!

Beach Adventures

Moorish idol

Eastern Shore
Beach Adventures

favorite sands

* Our favorite swimming beach is **Kalapaki Beach**, wonderful for swimming, skim boarding, and when the surf is right, boogie boarding. The sand is perfect for playing ball or frisbee, running, or simply sunning.

* **Lydgate Park** in Wailua is perfect for families — an enormous lava rock-rimmed pool offers wonderful swimming and snorkeling, and a smaller rock-rimmed pool is just right for toddlers. Beyond the pools, the beach is great for long walks. Lydgate also offers the best playground on Kauai, the Kamalani playground for the climbing and swinging set, and it's a great spot to watch glorious golden sunrises.

* For water activities, try **Wailua Bay**. The beach is popular with local surfers, and at the Wailua River, you can water ski, or rent a kayak and explore upstream towards the Fern Grotto.

* Bodyboarders will love **Kealia Beach**, where wonderful, even rollers can give great boogie board rides when conditions are right.

* For picnics and beach walks, visit beautiful **Anahola Bay**.

Kalapaki Beach

Kalapaki Bay is unforgettably beautiful. Almost enclosed by craggy green hillsides, this natural harbor has a wide sugar sand beach with some of the best swimming on the island. The waves roll to shore in long, even swells and break in shining white crests which are usually great for swimming and rafting. If the surf is too rough, you can stretch out on the warm, golden sand. Sometimes brilliant red and yellow windsurfers or catamarans skim gracefully across the blue water. The horizon is fascinating. On one side, the green ridges of the mountains have the contours of a giant animal sleeping in the sun, while on the opposite side, houses on stilts perch so precariously on the side of a sheer cliff that you wonder what combination of faith and hope keeps them standing.

Fronting this beach is the spectacular Marriott at Kauai Lagoons, a headline-maker from the time it first opened as a Westin because of its lavish design and elaborate collections of far eastern art and tropical birds and animals. Here you'll find Kauai's largest swimming pool, its tallest high-rise, and its only two-story escalator. You can also tour the man-made lagoons in an elegant launch and view exotic animals who live on the islands in a kind of waterway zoo.

Kalapaki Beach is a favorite spot with our family. The sand is firm, perfect for games and hard running, and the waves can break perfectly for boogie boards when the surf is right. Be sure to heed any high surf warnings, however, for at certain times, particularly in winter months, the waves can break straight down with enormous force, and every so often a really big wave seems to come up out of nowhere to smash unwary swimmers.

Directions: Take Rice St. through Lihue, and turn left into the main entrance of the Kauai Marriott. Pass the main lobby, and turn right at the first street, follow it down the hill to the parking lot. Map: 1

Ninini Beach

The drive to this tiny beach, "Running Waters," is more interesting than the destination. You wind along a cane road right next to the airport runway, so close, actually, that the jets taking off and landing almost make you want to duck. It's great fun having such a close–up view! Turn off Ahukini Road about a half mile after the fence at the end of the airport. The sugar cane road will be on your right, winding through brush and rustling grasses along the rocky coastline towards the lighthouse at Ninini Point. Driving the two and a half miles to the lighthouse requires maneuvering around the ruts and gullies for about 15 minutes. Walk to the lighthouse for a gorgeous view of the coast (Be careful of the footing on the rocks). You can try your luck getting permission to go up the winding stairs if an attendant is on the premises. Surf crashes on the rocks, and the beach is not safe for swimming; sharks have also been seen. Come instead for the view and the seclusion! Map: 1

Hanama'ulu Beach

A perfect crescent of soft shining sand, the beach at Hanama'ulu Bay is perfect for building sandcastles and hunting sunrise shells. In summer, the waves are gentle enough for children to enjoy. Rolling to shore in long, even swells only about a foot or two high, they break into miniature crests which turn to layers of white foam flecked with sandy gold, like the lacy borders of a lovely shawl. Even the occasional "wipe-outs" were not serious because the sandy bottom slopes very gradually.

Children can chase lots of tiny sandcrabs, and there is plenty of shade for babies beneath the tall, graceful ironwood trees which fringe the sand. Behind the beach, the Hanama'ulu Stream forms shallow pools as it winds toward the bay. Children can hunt for tiny crayfish and other river creatures to capture with nets.

This spot behind the beach is quite beautiful. The deep gold of the river is shaded by trees so tall and dense you can hardly see the sky, and the dark green leaves trail into the water behind stalks of lavender water hyacinths, their petals streaked with the colors of peacock feathers. A picnic pavilion faces the river, and other tables look out over the beautiful curve of the bay. Everything is uncrowded, even the playground, as this beach is frequented by few tourists. Unfortunately, it is also in the path sometimes used by helicopters returning to the airport at the end of their scenic tours, and so you may hear choppers. Try to ignore them, and plan your visit for the morning as the mosquitoes get hungry about 4 pm!

Directions: Turn off Rt. 56 towards the sea at Hanama'ulu, between the 7-Eleven and the school. Bear right at the fork which has a sign to the Beach Park. The road ends at the park. Map: 1

Lydgate Beach Park

Lydgate Park just south of the Wailua River is a favorite spot for families because it has something for everyone. A rock-rimmed pool provides safe swimming for babies and toddlers, even in winter months.

Adjacent is an enormous rock-rimmed pool which breaks the surf into rolling swells excellent for swimming, rafting, and floats of all kinds. The pool is one of the best year–round snorkeling spots on the island, for families of brightly colored fish feed along the rocky perimeter, so tame they almost swim into your hands. The rocky wall protects snorkelers and swimmers from surf and

Hawaiian petroglyph

dangerous currents. You can also fly a kite, play frisbee on the wide, sandy beach, collect shells and driftwood. There are showers for rinsing off sand and salt before going home, and a lifeguard.

Kids will love the Kamalani Playground, 16,000 square feet of funland, with mirror mazes, a suspension bridge, lava tubes and circular slide. The beach south of the lava rock pools is ideal for long walks, very beautiful and almost deserted. Continue past the rocky point in front of Kaha Lani condominiums, and you can walk all the way to the Kauai Outrigger, built along the section of beachfront called Nukoli'i. You'll have spectacular views of the coastline, particularly when sunrise or sunset paints the sky with gold and orange, and deepens the blues of the ocean, bright with shining foam. The patterns of foam crossing the sand are the most lovely we have ever seen. You'll probably find only one or two people, probably fishermen checking their lines. Swim with caution, however, for the surf is rough and currents powerful; Lydgate's pools are much safer.

Directions: If you are driving north on Rt. 56, turn right onto Leho Rd. just past the Wailua Golf Course. The right turnoff to the park is clearly marked. Follow this road to the Park and the rock pools. If you are driving south on Rt. 56, you must turn left onto the Leho Road just across the bridge over the Wailua River, at the Kauai Resort Hotel. Map: 1

Wailua Bay

You'll see Wailua Bay even before you come to it — a long, curve of golden sand perfect for walking, split by the Wailua River. Sometimes the river mouth is shallow enough to ford, but at other times it can be deep and treacherous. Swimming in the brackish, calm water of the river can be fun, although parents of young children should not let them stray from the edges because the water can become deep very quickly. Swimming where the river empties into the bay is not recommended because currents can be dangerous and unpredictable. South of the river, local kids come to one of the best spots for surfing and boogie boards on Kauai, particularly in summer! A lifeguard is usually on duty.

The Wailua River offers lots of activities. You can water ski, take a kayak upstream, or tour Fern Grotto with Smith's Boat Tours (822-4111).

Directions: On Rt. 56, just north of the bridge over the Wailua River.

Kapa'a Beaches

A white sandy beach, which runs almost the length of Kapa'a town, offers relatively safe swimming and fun for families with small children. An offshore reef breaks the surf and wind chop, creating a quiet lagoon, except in winter months when an eastern swell can make a strong current flow out of the channel. Usually, however, the water is calm, filled with children splashing while babies play in the shaded sand.

Directions: Take Rt. 56 through Kapa'a. Turn towards the water at Niu St. by Kapa'a ballpark. Map: 1

Kealia Beach

North of Kapa'a on Rt. 56 and   just past a scenic overlook turnout, you will see spectacular Kealia Beach, a long, wide curve of golden sand ending in a rocky point. When the surf is up, lots of surfers ride the long, even rollers. At low tide during summer months, the waves can be quite gentle at the far end of the beach where lava rocks extending into the sea create a cove where the water is quieter.  Kealia has been one of Jeremy's and Mikey's favorite beaches for boogie boarding! The sandy bottom slopes so gradually that you can walk out to catch some wonderful long rides, though at times the waves can be too powerful for children (even adults). Exercise caution, particularly in winter. Surf near the boogie boarders, and not the hard board surfers who are looking for the bigger thrill. Watch out for the small, blue 'men o' war' jellyfish, which wash into shore after high surf. If you see them on the sand, they are probably also floating in the water! They pack a nasty sting, so go to another beach for the day! Firm, level sand makes this a perfect walking beach, and children will enjoy playing in shallow pools behind the beach where a stream flows into the ocean. Strong rip currents near the river mouth, however, make ocean swimming hazardous.

Directions: Drive north of Kapaʻa on Rt. 56. Between mile markers 10 and 11, turn off to the right where you see all the cars parked. Map: 1

Donkey Beach

Ringed by rolling pasture crisscrossed by wire fences, Donkey Beach takes its name from its gentle, four-footed neighbors. This is a lovely and peaceful spot, a long curve of sand which ends in piles of rock on both sides. Surf and currents are strong, even in summer, and surfing is for experts. Waves rise slowly; curl in long, even swells; crest with gleaming foam, and break straight down with thunderous explosions of spray. The rhythm is hypnotic—you could watch them form and crash for hours. We saw no one in the water, though—our first hint that Donkey Beach was for sun-worshipers rather than swimmers. We soon discovered that this beach is unique—the only one we've seen on Kauai where nudity is the rule. Those on the beach were not tourists, judging from their dark allover tans. Some were more covered up than others, so you won't feel out of place if you hang onto your suit. Otherwise bring along some sunblock for parts not normally exposed! Or you may regret your frolic in the altogether when you try to sit down later on!

Directions: You can no longer drive to Donkey Beach because the cane roads are gated and locked. However, about 3/4 mile north of the mile 11 marker on Rt. 56, you will see cars parked on the shoulder, next to a well-worn path leading across the cane field to the beach. (The walk would take less than ten minutes). You can request a formal permit to cross private property to gain access to the beach (all beaches on Kauai are public) by stopping off during business hours at the Lihue Plantation office at 2970 Kele St. in Lihue and filling out a short information form.

Anahola Bay

The beach at Anahola Bay is so long that to walk from one end to the other may take you nearly an hour. The colors are magnificent, particularly as the sun is rising or in late afternoon as it moves to the west over the dark green mountains, deepening the blue of the water and the gold of the sand while brightening the tall white puff clouds until they seem to glow with light.

While the walking is spectacular, swimming can be risky, for the surf can be strong and currents powerful most of the year. At the southern end of the bay, which is more sheltered, camp shelters pretty much monopolize the shoreline, so check that area out first before you bring the family. You can also park at the northern end, where the Anahola stream flows into the sea. Children will love playing in the large shallow pools formed by the stream as it winds toward the bay, which is sometimes filled with tadpoles just slow enough to be netted by the younger set. The tiny river fish were harder to catch but fun in the trying, as were the small shrimp we discovered hiding by the grasses near the bank. The children also enjoyed making voyages of discovery on their boogie boards where the stream is deeper.

Anahola Bay is a favorite place for the whole family, and a good choice on weekends when other, more well known beaches become crowded. Watch out for the small, blue 'men o' war' jellyfish which are sometimes washed ashore after a storm. If you see them on the sand, go to another beach for the day, for the sting can be very painful.

A short drive (or long walk) north of the river will take you to Aliomanu Beach, popular with local families because its extensive offshore reef is terrific for fishing and seaweed harvesting. Snorkeling is for experts only, who should venture out if tradewinds are light and the current from the river is not strong. It's a great spot for a picnic, especially if you stop beforehand at Duane's Ono Burger next to the Anahola Store. Though expensive, the burgers are imaginative creations, featuring various combinations of avocado, sprouts, vegetables, teriyaki, and various kinds of cheeses. If possible, phone your order in ahead, for the staff runs low on manners during rush hour, and the waiting area is best described as charmless.

Directions: Turn off Rt. 56 at the Aliomanu Road just north of Duane's Ono Burger and the Anahola Store and follow it to the mouth of the stream. To get to the other end of Anahola Beach, take Anahola Road just south of Ono Burger. Map: 1

Hanalei Bay

North Shore
Beach Adventures

* Spectacular **Hanalei Bay**, an unforgettable image of Kauai to spark rainy evenings back home! Great for swimming and surfing, when surf conditions are right, and for running and walking at any time. Try breakfast first at *Cafe Hanalei* in the Princeville Hotel. The view is incredible!

* Our favorite family beach is **Kalihiwai**, which combines spectacular beauty with wonderful summertime swimming, as well as firm sand perfect for running. In winter, surf is up, to the delight of our boys, and even spectators can have fun watching the surfers catch spectacular rides. Kids will love the brackish pools behind the beach for fishing, swimming, and playing with a rope swing.

* **Anini Beach** is also fun for children, and a popular spot for snorkeling and windsurfing.

* For long, quiet beachwalks, try **Larsen's Beach** or **Moloa'a Bay**.

* At the end of a ten minute hike down a steep cliff, **Secret Beach** is secluded and spectacular, with magnificent views of the northern coast.

* The best snorkeling, when surf is calm, is at **Tunnels Beach** and **Ke'e Beach.**

* From Ke'e Beach, hikers can take the cliffside trail through the Na Pali wilderness to **Hanakapiai Beach**, which is magnificent, though too dangerous for swimming. Climb the first quarter mile to a spectacular overlook of Ke'e Beach and reefs.

* For sunset watching, don't miss the view from the *Princeville Hotel*, or, if you prefer to watch from the sand, visit **Tunnels Beach, Ke'e Beach** or **Anini Beach**.

* In Kilauea, try *Roadrunner Cafe & Bakery* or *Pau Hana Pizza* for a great lunch or snack.

Moloa'a Bay

At the end of a well-graded, semi-paved road which winds for several miles through the lush green countryside, Moloa'a Bay's lovely curve of sandy beach is discovered by few tourists. As you follow the road through this quiet, rural landscape, you can hear wonderful sounds emerge from the stillness—the breeze rustling in the leaves, the chirping of insects, the snorting of horses grazing in tree-shaded meadows. At road's end, you will find a gate attached to an unfriendly looking barbed-wire fence intended to discourage parking along the shoulder of the road. Walk through the gate and cross a winding, shallow stream, where our children discovered tadpoles apparently not informed that frog's eggs had hatched a month earlier everywhere else.

At this point the bay, hidden by the half dozen homes which ring the beach, suddenly comes into view—an almost dazzling half-moon of shining golden sand and turquoise water. The long, wide beach ends in grassy hills and piles of lava rocks on the left and a sheer cliff on the right. To the left, the rocks are fun to climb and search for shells and trapped fish, although this windward side of the bay is usually too rough for swimming, and the bottom is very rocky. To the right of the stream, the bay is more sheltered, the water gentler and the bottom more sandy. In summer, snorkelers can swim out through the sandy corridor to the rockier part of the bay, or float in the shallow water close to shore and dig in the sandy bottom for beautiful shells. In times of heavy surf, however, this bay, like all windward beaches, can have dangerous currents. During these times, Moloa'a Bay is a beautiful place for walking. The peaceful solitude is filled with the sound of waves. The crystal blue water, traced with the shadowy patterns of the rocks below, stretches out to the distant horizon where pale clouds fade into a limitless sky. At 5 pm you might see a dozen horses, wandering home after another difficult day of grazing, stop at the stream for a drink or a roll in the shallows—a spectacular sight with the setting sun glistening on the water and the horses darkening slowly to silhouettes.

Directions: Take Rt. 56 to Kuamoʻo Road, a half-mile north of the mile 16 marker. Turn right at Moloaʻa Road and follow it to the end. Moloaʻa is about 16 miles north of Lihue; 30 miles from Poipu; 6 miles from Kapaʻa. Map: 2

Larsen's Beach

Getting to Larsen's Beach is half the fun. A right-of-way-to-beach road wanders through pasture-land, where horses grazing peacefully seem sketched into a landscape portrait of silvery green meadows with waving dark green grasses, trees and mountains, and masses of white, shining clouds. At the end of the well-graded, sandy road is a small parking area and a gate leading to the top of the cliff, where the beach below seems a slender ribbon of white against the dark blue water. Although a second, smaller gate seems to direct you to the right, walking through it takes you to a steep path ending in rocks.

Instead, walk down the hillside to the left on a well worn path with a gentle slope. Even our youngest had little difficulty managing the descent or the climb back up. In fact, she accepted the job of trailblazer and earned a "pathfinder" badge for leading us back up to the car again! A five-minute walk down the slope brings you to a long, lovely beach curving along the coastline and disappearing around a distant bend— perfect for lazy afternoons of beachcombing and exploring. Although a rocky reef extending about 70 yards offshore seems to invite snorkeling, Larsen's Beach is one of the most dangerous on the island.

Before you begin the hike down, observe the ocean carefully and locate the channel through the reef, just to the left of the rocky point where you are standing. The churning water caused by the swift current makes the channel easiest to see from this height, and once noted, it can be recognized at sea level. Once you see this channel, you can also pick out the smaller channels which cut through the reef at several other points. Swimmers and snorkelers should avoid going near any of these channels, particularly the large one, because currents can be dangerously strong and even turn into a whirlpool when the tide is going out. Remember, Larsen's Beach has no lifeguard, and help is not close by. Currents can be exceptionally treacherous at *any* time, but particularly in winter months, and four years ago two experienced local fishermen drowned here. The watchword is caution: swim in pairs, never go out beyond the reef, try to stay within easy distance of the shore, and examine the surface of the water carefully to avoid swimming near a channel. If you snorkel, stay where you can stand up at will, and don't get so absorbed in looking at the fish that you lose track of where you are. Have the judgment not to go out at all if surf conditions don't seem right to you.

A trip to Larsen's Beach does not require swimming or snorkeling. If you bring reef-walking sneakers to protect your feet, you can walk around in the shallow water and watch colorful fish who don't seem afraid of people. Or walk for miles along the magnificent coastline of this picture-perfect beach. Hunt for shells, or simply lose yourself in the spectacle of nature's beauty. You will probably encounter only another person or two. The drive back is wonderful, with spectacular views of the rolling hills, lined by fences and stands of trees, and beyond them the dark and majestic mountains reaching to touch the clouds.

Directions: From Kapa'a, turn right off Rt. 56 onto Kuamo'o Road just 1/2 mile past the mile 16 marker (If you pass the dairy farm, you've missed the turn). Bear left at the Moloa'a Road turnoff, go about 1.1 miles and look for a dirt road on the right. The right turn marked 'beach access' will be very sharp and angled up an incline. Then another beach access sign will mark the left turn onto the long, straight road to the beach. From Hanalei, turn left off Rt. 56 at the mile 20 marker, and look for the beach access road on your left. Drive to the end of the beach access road, park, lock up, walk towards the cliff, and take the trail downhill on the left. Larsen's is about 7 miles east of Princeville; 20 miles north of Lihue; 10 miles north of Kapa'a. Map 2.

Kilauea Bay

If you've ever had the fantasy of searching through the jungle to find a remote and hidden paradise, Kahili Beach at Kilauea Bay should be your destination. The road to this unspoiled beach tests the mettle of both car and driver with new challenges at practically every turn. Deeply rutted, even gouged in places by ditches and holes, it can turn into a quagmire in rain, but in dry weather, it can be navigated without too much difficulty by a careful driver even in a rented subcompact. Pick a dry day, and the road will add the zest of adventure and heighten the excitement of discovering, just beyond the last ditch and bunches of trailing vegetation, a bay shaped like a perfect half-moon, the deep blue water sparkling with light and the golden sand outstretched between two rocky bluffs like a tawny cat sleeping in the sun.

At the northern end is the Kilauea stream. One year it may be shallow enough for small children at low tide, the next, too deep. The width can vary from a few yards to fifty. To the left of the stream, the beach ends abruptly in an old rock quarry, the original purpose for the road and now a great spot for pole fishing. To the right of the stream, the sandy beach extends a long way before ending in piles of lava rocks which children will enjoy climbing and exploring for tidal pools. Chances are you'll encounter only another person or two and can watch in solitude as the waves roll towards the beach in long, even swells, break into dazzling white crests, and rush to shore in layers of gold and white foam.

Although the surf can be dangerously strong and the currents treacherous at certain times, particularly in winter when the beach may almost disappear beneath the crashing waves, we found the swimming safe enough in summer for our seven and ten-year-olds to surf on their boogie boards in the shallow water, although even close to shore the pull of the undertow made us watch them closely. The tiny blue Portuguese 'men o' war' are sometimes washed ashore here after a storm, so if you see any on the sand, go to another beach, for these small jellyfish pack a giant sting!

Behind the beach, the stream forms brackish pools where children can swim safely, except near the stream's entrance into the bay where the current can be swift, particularly at high tide. One August, the pools were wider than we had ever seen, like a shallow lagoon, and our family had a great time netting tadpoles. Our children preferred this beach to almost any other because of the variety of things they could do and the challenge of ripping the leaves off the branches that scraped the sides of the car as we maneuvered around the gullies on the way down and back. We loved the beach because we had it, almost, all to ourselves.

Directions: Just south of Kilauea, turn towards the ocean at Wailapa Road (between mile markers 21 and 22) and after .4 of a mile, turn left onto a dirt road and follow it (only in dry weather) for about a mile until you reach the beach. Kilauea is about 25 miles north of Lihue; 39 miles from Poipu; 15 miles from Kapa'a. Map: 2

Secret Beach

Secret Beach is one of those rare and special places where the world can be forgotten, where you can feel, for a few hours, as if you were alone at the beginning of time. The colors are brilliant, the breeze fresh and tangy with salt. The ocean reaches out to touch the sky at an endless horizon, and the crashing of waves is all you can hear. As you walk, you may leave the only footprints on warm, golden sand shining in the sun.

Nestled at the base of a sheer cliff just north of Kilauea, Secret Beach is well off the beaten track for good reason. You must hike down (and back up!) a rocky trail which zigzags through trees, gullies, and brush. You can drive only to the trail's beginning at the top of the cliff. From here, you can hear the waves crashing below—apparently not very far away—which is reassuring as you look down on a trail which seems to disappear into a tangle of jungle. The path is steep in places — sneakers are a good idea — but branches, roots, and vines offer plenty of hand-holds, and if you're out of shape, you can always resort to the seat of your pants!

The walk down will take about seven minutes, and it is pretty much straight down. As the path makes the last sharp plunge before leveling off to the sand, you can see, at last, through a screen of trees and hanging vines, a magnificent stretch of golden sand and a shining turquoise sea. In rainy times, this enormous triangle of sand may be partly covered by a lagoon fed by a stream winding down behind the beach. Towards the left, you can climb a rocky outcropping and find a small beach ending in a steep cliff. Towards the right, you can see the Kilauea lighthouse and walk a long way across the sand.

Secret Beach is not a place to come alone, for the obvious reason of its isolation. Swimming is not a good idea. The surf is rough, and the current strong and unpredictable; you'd never find a lifeguard if you were caught in a current. In fact, during the winter, this beach, enormous as it is, can disappear almost entirely under huge, crashing waves. Instead of swimming, walk along the water, hunt for shells, and forget everything but the feel of wet sand between your toes. Since the hurricane, some who cannot afford rent have taken up semi-permanent residence in tents, and so you might find your solitude shared by someone wanting to live close to nature.

The walk back up the cliff will give you time to adjust to the world you left behind—just about 10 minutes of mild exertion, with the air cool under the trees and the leaves speckled with sunlight. This would not be a pleasant hike in the mud, though, so plan your adventure with an eye to the weather and don't go after a soaking rain. By the time you reach your car and remember that you have to stop at the store for chocolate milk, the peaceful solitude you left behind will be as hard to recapture as a wave rippling on the sand. But for a few moments, you were lost forever to your working-day world. This may be the secret of Secret Beach, and it is a secret worth keeping!

Directions: Drive north of Kilauea on Rt. 56 about a half mile. Turn right onto Kalihiwai Road. Just a few feet beyond the first bend, turn right onto a dirt road which looks like a broad red gash in the landscape. Follow towards the water till it ends. Park, lock up and walk down the trail. The rest is up to you! Note: One reader discovered another secret about this beach, when she and her family reached the bottom of the trail and ran into "a long-haired young man wearing nothing but a guitar!" So be prepared for strange music! Secret Beach is about 25 miles north of Lihue; 39 miles from Poipu; 15 miles from Kapa'a. Map: 2

humu humu nuku nuku apu a'a

Kalihiwai Bay

You'll catch your first glimpse of Kalihiwai Bay as you drive down the narrow road carved into the side of the sheer cliff which encloses it on one side. From this angle, the bay is a perfect semicircle of blue, rimmed with shining white sand and nestled between two lava cliffs. Ironwood trees ring the beach, just about completely regrown after being sheared of their branches by Iniki's winds. A clear, freshwater stream flows into the bay near the far end, so shallow and gentle at low tide that small children can splash around safely. It becomes deep enough behind the beach for kayak adventuring up-river, although swimming in the river itself, beyond the brackish water near the ocean, is not recommended.

One of our favorite family beaches, Kalihiwai Bay offers wonderful summertime fun for people of all ages. Little ones will love the shallow pools behind the beach where they can fish or float on rafts. Ocean swimming is terrific too! The waves rise very slowly and break in long, even crests over a sloping sandy bottom, perfect for wave jumping and boogie boarding. One summer day we watched a dozen children celebrate a birthday with a surfing party. In winter, the surf and currents in the bay can become formidable. Even experienced surfers may have difficulty managing the currents which can be particularly strong when a swell is running. Even if the surf is too rough, Kalihiwai is a lovely beach for walking, with firm sand and magnificent views of the cliffs.

Directions: A yellow siren atop a pole just south of the beach is a reminder of the *tsunami* or tidal wave of 1957 which washed away the

bridge originally linking the two roads leading from Rt. 56 to the bay.
Both are still marked Kalihiwai Road at their separate intersections with
Rt. 56. Either one will take you to the bay, although, if you choose the
Kalihiwai Road just north of the long bridge on Rt. 56, you'll have to
wade across the stream's mouth in order to reach the beach. The Kalihiwai Road south of the bridge and just northwest of Kilauea is the preferable route. It winds through the countryside before curving down the
steep cliff on the southern edge of the bay. Kalihiwai is about 25 miles
north of Lihue; 39 miles from Poipu; 15 miles from Kapa'a. Map: 2

Anini Beach

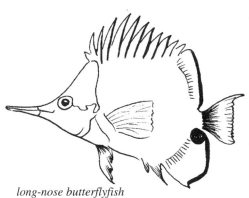

long-nose butterflyfish

At the edge of Anini
Road, you will find miles of
white sandy beach protected
by a reef. At some places the
beach road is so close to the
water that you could almost
jump in! A beach park offers
restrooms and picnic facilities,
although you can turn off the
road at almost any spot, park
between the stately iron-
woods, and find your private paradise. The reef creates a quiet lagoon,
and summertime snorkeling can be very good, though swimmers should
be cautious in the shallow areas. During periods of high surf, particularly
in winter, the current which runs parallel to the beach can become strong
enough to pull an unwary swimmer out through the channel in the reef at
the west end of the park. Swim inside the reef at all times.

Across the street from the Beach Park, the Kauai Polo Club hosts
polo matches on summer Sunday afternoons. Continue along Anini road
through a quiet residential area all the way to its western end, where a
sandbar extending quite far out invites wading and fishing. Children love
the quiet water and the tiny shells along the waterline. The scene is so
peaceful that you can hear an amazing combination of sounds— the roar
of the surf breaking on the reef far offshore, and near your feet, the gentle
rippling of the sea upon the sand.

If you begin your sunset drive to Hanalei too late to reach there
before dark, you can watch the sun set into the ocean at Anini Beach, a
glorious sight which can be yours in perfect solitude. The tall ironwood
trees darken to feathery silhouettes against a pale gray and orange sky,

filled with lines of puff clouds. The water shimmers gold as the sun's dying fire fades slowly to a pearl and smoky gray, to the songs of crickets and the lapping of gentle waves.

Directions: Drive north on Rt. 56, pass Kilauea, and turn towards the ocean at Kalihiwai Road (the northern one, between mile markers 25 and 26). The road passes the park and continues to the base of the cliffs at Princeville. Anini is about 1 mile east of Princeville. Map: 2

Pu'u Poa Beach, Princeville

Tucked beneath the Sheraton Princeville Hotel's ocean bluff perch is a sandy beach set inside a reef. When you look down from the hotel, you can see the rocky bottom that makes swimming less than perfect. This same reef can make for good snorkeling in calm summer seas, but you must negotiate your way carefully through one of the small sandy channels into the deeper water. In winter, waves crash against the reef, making it one of the most challenging surfing spots on the island.

Public access is available though a cement path leading from the left of the gatehouse entry to the Hotel. Be forewarned: on the way down the cliff, you'll have to descend nearly 200 steps (and then come back *up* those same steps later on)! You can explore the beach more easily if you visit the hotel for breakfast or lunch, both wonderful meals in a spectacular setting anyway. Simply take the hotel elevator down to the beach level, where lovely gardens frame the sand. Bring your camera! Map: 1

Directions: Drive Rt. 56 north, enter Princeville at the main entrance (pick up a free map) and stay on Ka Haku Road until the end. Park in the hotel visitor's lot if you're going to the hotel for lunch. If not, a small public lot is located just in front and to the right of the hotel entry gate.

Pali Ke Kua or 'Hideaways' Beach

At the base of the cliff near the Pali Ke Kua Condominiums in Princeville is a lovely sandy beach set inside a reef, where you can watch the sun sparkle on the waves in near solitude. It is a peaceful spot, secluded and beautiful, actually two beaches connected by a rocky point. Swimming is not the best because of the coral bottom and the offshore rocks, but snorkeling can be very good in calm summer seas. Be cautious. As on all north shore beaches, snorkeling can be risky and is advisable only in a calm ocean; when the surf is up, currents can become dangerous. In winter, waves can cover the beach entirely.

This beach is called Hideaways for good reason. It's hard to get to, popular primarily with surfers or with people staying at Pali Ke Kua who can use the condominium's improved concrete pathway down the cliff. The public right-of-way is much more difficult, half of it made up of steep steps with a railing, and the rest dwindling to dirt path. It can be slippery, even treacherous, when wet. The trek down will take about ten minutes, and the way up, as you can imagine, somewhat longer!

Directions: Enter Princeville, drive to the hotel and park in the lot. (The hotel usually doesn't mind if you take one of the back spaces nearest the cliff, where you'll see the path down to the beach.) Map: 2

Hanalei Bay

A long half-moon of sandy beach carved into the base of a sheer cliff on one side and narrowing into a rocky point on the other, Hanalei Bay has a spectacular beauty which even Hurricane Iniki could not diminish. In fact, the hurricane winds cleared the underbrush and opened up many new views of the bay, even as far away as the entrance to Princeville. Any road off Rt. 560 towards the water will take you to the Bay. If you turn right off Rt. 560 onto Weke Road, then right onto Aku Road, you will find the Hanalei Pavilion, with showers and re-strooms; at the far end of Weke is the Hanalei pier. Several Trans-Pacific Cup Races from California to Hawaii end in this natural harbor, and during summer months, gaily colored boats rock gently at anchor on the eastern side where the Hanalei stream flows into the bay (below). The boats are moved out of the bay, however, by mid-October, and by

winter, twenty-foot waves are not uncommon. Keep that in mind as you consider a zodiac adventure!

Looking for surf? You'll find the biggest breakers near the center of the curving coast-line, where surfers come to hunt the perfect ride. During winter months, when the surf can become dangerous, Hanalei Bay is still wonderful—the wide sandy beach firm and level for hard running. Our favorite parking spot, "Second Parking Lot" is at the end of Ama'ama Road, towards the western end of Weke Road.

West of the little town of Hanalei on Route 560 are several beautiful places, and you can explore almost any road turning off towards the water. At the western-most curve of the bay, near the mile 4 marker, you'll find a calm, protected beach where the water is relatively quiet even when most of the north shore is too rough for safe swimming.

Directions: Drive Rt. 560 north, pass Princeville, and enter the town of Hanalei (mile 3 marker). Aku Road (or any other right turn) will take you to Weke Road, which runs along the bay from east to west. If you turn right on Weke, the road passes public facilities and showers at Hanalei Pavilion before it ends at Hanalei River. If you turn left onto Weke, you can turn right onto several 'right of way to beach' streets leading to the Bay. Showers, restrooms available at Ama'ama Rd. Hanalei is 33 miles from Lihue, 47 miles from Poipu; 23 miles from Kapa'a. Map: 2.

Lumahai Beach

The setting for the Bali Hai scenes in the movie *South Pacific*, Lumahai Beach is stunningly beautiful, a curve of white sand nestled at the base of a dark lava cliff, with a giant lava rock jutting out of the turquoise sea just offshore. Getting there may require a trek down from the roadside through slippery mud (showers are frequent on the Hanalei side of the island), and the trip back up is even worse, especially if you have to carry a tired child. If there are toddlers in you family, you might consider hiring a babysitter or buying a postcard!

Swimming at Lumahai Beach is dangerous, particularly during winter months. There is no reef to offer protection from the unpredictable currents and rip tides which make Lumahai Beach one of the most treacherous on the island. Beware also of climbing that spectacular offshore rock for a photograph, as a sudden powerful wave can easily knock you off!

At the western end of Lumahai, about a mile further, is a beach with some of the biggest breakers we found; a sign warns against swimming in winter because of high surf and strong currents. The stream which flows into the sea here is ice cold from mountain rainwater, a refreshing way to rinse off sand and salt. After the waves break and the foam washes over the sandy spit at the stream's mouth, miniature waves form and roll across the shallows for children to enjoy in summer months.

The stream meets the ocean at a huge rocky bluff, a spectacular place to sit quietly and watch the waves crash against the rocks, sending dazzling spray into the air. It is also a beautiful beach for walking, although the coarse sand is hard-going near the waterline, and you must cross a vast expanse of hot sand to get from the parking area to the sea. Bring sandals! You can hunt for striped scallop shells shining in the sun, or wander all the way to the other rocky bluff that separates this part of Lumahai Beach from the part pictured in all the postcards. Trying to cross the rocks would be hazardous, however, even at low tide, due to the occasional "killer wave" which can come up suddenly out of nowhere and smash you into the rocks. A small cave etched into the base of the cliff with a floor of powder soft, cool sand is a perfect spot for daydreaming and wave-watching, preferably with someone special.

Directions: Drive past Hanalei on Rt. 560 and look for the mile 4 marker. You'll see a lot of cars parked on a shoulder just past a 25 m.p.h. speed zone sign. Park on the right, opposite a No Passing Zone sign, lock up, and begin the hike down. To get to the western end of Lumahai, drive to the mile 5 marker, look for an emergency telephone by the road. Across the street is the entrance to a sandy parking area under the trees and beside the stream. Lumahai is about 34 miles from Lihue; 49 miles from Poipu; and 24 miles from Kapa'a. Map: 2

Tunnels Beach

You'll see lessons in snorkeling and scuba diving at Makua Beach, popularly known as Tunnels Beach. This large, protected lagoon can be perfect for swimming because it is protected by two reefs, the outer reef favored by surfers for perfect arcs, and the inner reef filled with cavities and crevices for snorkelers to explore for fish and sea life. Tunnels is about the only beach on the north shore that is usually calm enough for beginners, although even here you may find rough surf and treacherous currents during winter months.

Listen to the surf reports, and plan any winter visits for times when surf is flat on the north shore, and preferably at low tide! In summertime, bring the kids and let them paddle about on boogie boards while the older ones try their luck with mask and snorkel. Bring a plastic baggy of fish food, or even a green leaf, swish it in the water and you'll be surrounded by fish! Swimming through the coral formations of the reef, which is almost like a maze of tunnels, can be great fun when the water is quiet. Enter the reef through one of the small sandy channels or the large one on the right, and dozens of fish in rainbow colors will swim right up to your mask. If the showers which frequent the north shore rain on your parade, you can take shelter under the ironwood trees—or under your boogie board!

Tunnels can get crowded, particularly in summer. The beach is the departure point for Captain Zodiac boat tours, and both swimmers and the boats have to share the large sandy channel through the reef. Zodiac staff may try to motion you out of the channel to make way for the boats, but don't be intimidated! People—not boats—have the right of way. On the other hand, keep a lookout for the boats and be ready to get out of the way if you have to. If you see a monk seal lying on the beach, give it a wide berth. It's probably exhausted, resting before heading out to sea! Seals don't trust humans and need privacy to recuperate.

Even when the area between the two reefs may look calm enough for safe swimming, watch out for these danger signs: high surf on the outer reef or fast moving ripples in the channel between the reefs. These indicate powerful, swift currents that could sweep you out through the channel into open ocean. Instead of swimming, hunt for shells on the beach, or walk around the rocks to the east, where you may find sunbathers with very dark tans in all the best places!

Directions: Drive west of Princeville on Rt. 560, and go 1.1 miles west of the entrance to Charo's at the Hanalei Colony Resort. You will pass the mile 8 marker and the turnoff to the YMCA camp. Parking is difficult if not occasionally impossible. The area close to the beach is fenced off. Just look for all the cars on the shoulder, get as close as you can, and walk in. No public facilities. Tunnels is about 38 miles from Lihue; 53 miles from Poipu; 28 miles from Kapa'a.

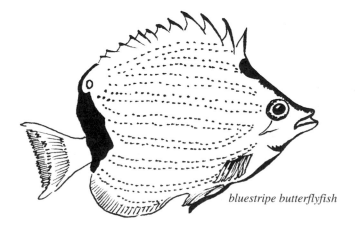

bluestripe butterflyfish

Ha'ena Beach Park

An icy stream winds across this lovely golden sand beach curving along the coastline. The water is a dazzling blue. Reefs bordering both sides of the beach, named 'Maniniholo' after the large schools of striped convict fish feeding on the coral, provide summertime snorkeling, when the waves are gentle enough for swimming and rafting. During winter months, however, large waves can break right onto the beach, making swimming, even standing, a hazardous activity! Restrooms, showers, picnic and barbecue facilities are available, as well as camping by permit. You might even find a sandwich truck if you forget to bring lunch! You can walk a long way in both directions, with spectacular views of the towering cliffs and shimmering sea.

Directions: From Princeville, follow Rt. 560 west and pass the mile 8 marker. Ha'ena Beach Park will be on your right, about 40 miles from Lihue; 54 miles from Poipu; 30 miles from Kapa'a; 8 miles from Princeville. Map: 2

Ke'e Beach

When you can drive no further on the main road along Kauai's north shore, you will discover a beach so beautiful you won't quite believe it to be real. The Na Pali cliffs rise like dark green towers behind the golden sand, and a reef extending out from shore creates a peaceful lagoon ideal for summertime swimming. As you walk along the shining sand, new cliffs come into view until the horizon is filled with their astonishing shapes and you begin to imagine captive princesses in enchanted castles.

Like all windward beaches on the north shore, the surf at Ke'e Beach varies with the seasons. Winter surf can reach 20 feet, and then the ocean roars with crashing waves and churning foam with undercurrents far too strong for safe swimming. In summer, however, the turquoise water can be perfectly still and so clear that bubbles on the surface cast shadows on the sandy bottom.

Snorkeling can be spectacular alongside the reef, where the water, though warmed by the sun, will feel ice cold along the surface from rainwater. If the tide is not too low, you can snorkel on top of the reef itself. Be careful: The coral reef may look shallow enough to walk on, but you won't want to take a chance on coral cuts. Be careful too of unpredictable currents in the channel to the left of the reef, as they can be strong enough to pull a swimmer out of this sheltered area into the open sea. A lifeguard is usually on duty to keep swimmers out of the channel.

Large trees at the beach provide shade for babies and protection from the occasional rainshowers which cool the air and make the coastline sparkle. Small children can play and swim safely in the shallow water or climb over the rocks at low tide. Bring nets and pails for small fishermen! They will also love collecting limpet shells or the tops of spiral shells.

Because of an unusual combination of low tide and calm summer sea, we were able to walk west across the rocks and around the point for the first time in more than six years. From this vantage point, the Na Pali cliffs are truly magnificent —jutting into the cobalt blue ocean in vivid green ridges, the surf crashing in thundering sprays of foam. This walk can be dangerous in any but the calmest sea, and you must watch the direction of the tide carefully so that your return trip does not involve crossing slippery rocks through crashing waves. Keʻe Beach, lovely as it looks, can have treacherous currents and unpredictable surf, and so extra caution is a must. For a spectacular, bird's eye view of Keʻe Lagoon, consider climbing the first quarter-mile of the hiking trail to Hanakapiai Beach. If possible come early and come midweek, for parking at this lovely and popular spot is hard to come by, especially in summer.

Directions: Follow Rt. 56 north to Princeville and then continue (The road becomes Rt. 560) to the very end. Park alongside the road, as close to the beach as you can get. Or turn right at the dirt road by the showers and restrooms, and look for a space (if you are lucky) under the trees. About 40 miles from Lihue; 54 miles from Poipu; 30 miles from Kapaʻa. Map: 2

About halfway around Hanalei Bay, you'll find Waioli Stream, where the water is cool and the skim boarding fantastic!

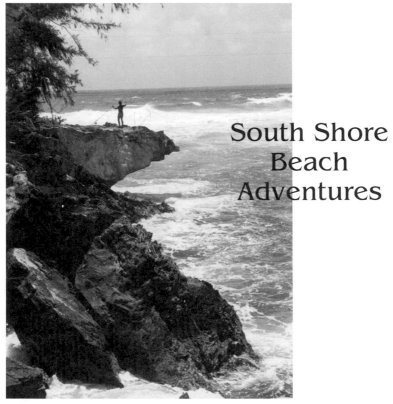
Maha'ulepu

South Shore Beach Adventures

favorite sands

When it's raining up north, you may want to travel south (even west) to find the sun! In the island's lee, south shore beaches offer relatively calm swimming conditions all year, except during a south shore 'swell.'

* **Poipu Beach Park** is perfect for families, the rock rimmed pool a safe place for kids and the snorkeling adjacent wonderful for their parents!

* Our favorite hidden beach (though increasingly popular), is **Maha'ulepu Beach** east of Poipu, in the midst of sugar cane fields. Wild and beautiful!

* When you get hungry for lunch, try the salad & sandwich bar at *Poipu Bay Grill & Bar*, next to the Hyatt, or enjoy lunch with a slice of ocean at *Brennecke's Beach Broiler*. A short drive away in Kalaheo, you'll find great lunches at *Camp House Grill* and *Brick Oven Pizza*.

* Enjoy great sunsets at **Poipu Beach Park**, or watch the colors change while sipping a Mai Tai at *Brennecke's Beach Broiler* across the street. *The Beach House* is another favorite spot for sunset watching.

Kipu Kai

You can't get to Kipu Kai except by boat, for the private road crossing the gap in the mountains between Rt. 50 and the south shore is deeply rutted and gouged, suitable only for the sturdiest of 4 wheel drive vehicles. It's best to go by boat, and some boat cruise companies offer trips to this lovely section of Kauai's coastline.

Kipu Kai is actually three beaches which share a rocky peninsula shaped like an alligator. Long Beach is, as you would expect from the name, stretches out in a long line of fine sand in the shape of a half moon, nearly enclosed by outcroppings of rocks at each end. Set at the base of the rocky mountains behind Kipu Kai, Long Beach is special among south shore beaches, combining the favorable weather of the south with a strikingly rugged beauty more characteristic of the north shore. As if this weren't enough, the ocean is relatively gentle due to the rocky points which embrace the beach, breaking the surf and creating a protected lagoon.

A wonderful old rambling ranch house sits atop Turtle Beach, so named for its shape. The house was built in stages by the Waterhouse family using orders of wood and supplies floated ashore from cargo ships. From the veranda overlooking the bay, Jack Waterhouse used to communicate with the "rest of the world" by signals. According to the terms of the will, the Waterhouse family descendents retain use of the land until the end of the next generation, when Kipu Kai Ranch is destined to become a state park.

Maha'ulepu

At the end of a dusty drive through winding sugar cane roads, you will find a beautiful sandy beach carved into a rocky point. This part of the south shore is very dry and very hot — and you'll soon find a thin red film on every surface inside your car, including you! But it's worth the dust to reach a beach astonishing in its wild beauty, the surf crashing against the rocks and sand, the churning turquoise water almost glowing with sunlight. Beautiful it is, but often not safe enough for swimming. Except for times when surf on the whole south shore is flat, you'll find the waves crashing with enough force to knock you down, and currents powerful enough to make even local people wary.

Maha'ulepu is a lovely beach for walking and exploring. On the eastern end, a lovely half-moon of golden sand nestles at the base of a rocky cliff. A long walk to the west takes you past a rocky reef which at low tide juts out of the sand in fascinating formations. As you reach the end of the curve, the tip turns out to be a point, and on the other side, you'll find another, even longer stretch of beach. Here the water ripples in toward shore, protected by an offshore reef where the waves roll in long, even swells. You might see a fisherman casting his line or even a swimmer snorkeling among the rocks if the sea is calm. When the tradewinds are strong, windsurfers splash color on the sparkling sea. At the western-most end, at Gillin's Beach, you will find a new house built on the spot where plantation manager Gillin once lived. Sunwarmed tidal pools are shallow and still. Kids can bring nets to catch the tiny fish!

At the far eastern end of Maha'ulepu is a rocky bluff, great for exploring. After a moderate uphill climb, you will come to a promontory with spectacular views of the coastline. Rock formations are astonishing, and a tiny beach set into the cliffside shelters interesting pools of tiny sea life. Be careful near the rocks, as a sudden wave could knock you off! Remember: this is a beautiful—but isolated place. Use caution.

Directions: Take Rt. 50 to Rt. 520 (the Koloa Road). Follow signs to Poipu. Take Poipu Road past the Hyatt Regency. Pass the turnoff to Shipwreck Beach and continue east, past the golf course and the quarry. When you come to a stop sign, turn right and head toward the water. This

is sugar company land, and you'll have to stop at a gatehouse and sign a release form to gain entry. At the end of the road, you can turn right or left, either east or west along the beach. Map: 3

Shipwreck Beach

Shipwreck Beach along Keoniloa Bay was never much of a beach—until the hurricane blasted the south shore of Kauai and created a new coastline. What was once a thin curve of sand is now enormous, a long, golden crescent divided by lava rocks. To the right of the rocks, the waves roll across a long, shallow reef ending in a rocky point. To the left, the wide, gleaming sand stretches to the base of a low cliff flanked by sand dunes.

This place is called Shipwreck Beach with good reason. The surf is powerful, breaking in long, shining arcs which crest slowly, one at a time, with deceptive smoothness, and then crash in thunderous explosions of spray not far from shore. Local people warn that beyond the break point are dangerous currents and large rocks. A better place for family swimming would be Poipu Beach Park, and novice surfers would be better off at Wailua Beach, where rocks and wind are not a problem and a lifeguard is on duty. Be particularly careful, during summer months, of high surf.

Instead of swimming, you can climb the cliff to explore strange caves and rock formations. The colors are breathtaking—the deep blue of the water and the gold of the cliffs dazzle the eye, and the view down is a dizzying spectacle of surf crashing against the rocks. Be careful, though. Avoid going close to the cliff's edge, as the footing is slippery with loose sand. It's great for photographers but not for children.

Directions: Take Poipu Road past the main entrance to the Hyatt Hotel. Turn toward the water on Ainako Road. Park in the lot. Public access restrooms and showers by the parking lot. Shipwreck is 14 miles from Lihue; 24 miles from Kapa'a; 44 miles from Princeville. Map: 3

Brennecke's Beach

Legendary for years as the best beach for body surfing, Brennecke's Beach is today only a memory. Hurricane Iniki hurled giant boulders into the water, destroyed the sea wall, and washed away most of the sand. Even worse, the currents which created those wonderful long rolling waves of the past have changed. Today, the big rollers break too close to shore for riding, and it will take years for the sand to shift back and the currents to return to their old pattern. The Army Corps of Engineers is redesigning a sea wall to accelerate the restoration. It took nearly ten years to bring the waves back after Hurricane I'wa, so perhaps by our twentieth anniversary edition. . . .

Directions: Take Poipu Beach Road past Kiahuna, turn right on Ho'owili Road then left at Ho'one Road and park in the lot next to Brennecke's Beach Broiler. Walk east. From Lihue, 14 miles; from Kapa'a 24 miles; from Princeville 44 miles. Map: 3

Poipu Beach Park

You could not imagine a more perfect beach for children than this lovely curve of soft golden sand sloping down to a gentle, friendly sea. The waves, with changing shades of turquoise sparkling with sunlight and dazzling white foam, break gently over a protective reef across the entrance to this small cove. For babies and toddlers, a ring of black lava rocks creates a sheltered pool where the water is shallow and still. For older children, waves beyond the pool roll to shore in graceful swells perfect for rafting, under the watchful eye of a county lifeguard. Children also love to explore the long rocky point at the far end of the beach and look for tiny fish trapped in the tidal pools. Bring nets and pails for the hunt! Restrooms, outdoor showers, barbecues, and picnic tables are available. Pavilions offer shade for babies. "Mama's Beach," as it is called by many local people, is perfect for families, and a great place for a sunset picnic, barbecue, or occasionally, on weekend afternoons, listening to a free concert.

Beyond the rocky point you can explore several crescent shaped, lovely sandy beaches. Just across the point in another sheltered cove fronting the Waiohai Hotel, is some of the best snorkeling on the island. Hundreds of fish in rainbow colors feed on the coral, so tame they almost swim into your hands. Carry stale bread or crackers in a plastic bag, or the snorkeling fish food available in dive shops, and they'll come right to you! Be careful not to follow the fish out too far. Stay inside the reef for safety. Further west, the beaches in front of the Kiahuna Plantation, the Poipu Beach Hotel, and the Sheraton have stronger surf.

Although the number of hotel rooms and apartments sharing the Poipu beaches has quadrupled in the last ten years, Hurricane Iniki has temporarily depressed the south shore tourist count, particularly at Poipu Beach Park, long a favorite of both tourists and local residents.

Directions: Take Poipu Beach Road past the Waiohai, turn right on Ho'owili Road then left at Ho'one Road and park in the lot next to Brennecke's Beach Broiler, or turn right onto Ho'one Road and park in the lot behind the beach. From Lihue, 14 miles; from Kapa'a 24 miles; from Princeville 44 miles. Map: 3

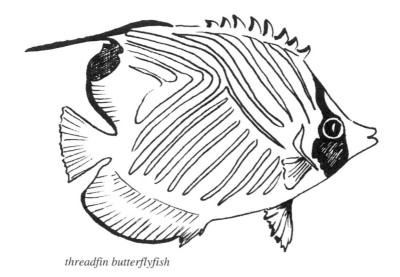

threadfin butterflyfish

Westside Beach Adventures

favorite sands

* **Salt Pond Beach Park** offers great swimming, protected by a reef, as well as warmer temperatures. Kids love exploring the tidal pools.

* At **Kekaha**, you'll find firm sand and miles of beach perfect for beachwalking and running.

* Drive all the way to the end of the road to magnificent **Polihale Beach**, the western-most part of the island, perfect for sunsets.

* On your trips west, stop off at *Wrangler's Restaurant* in Waimea for great hamburgers and salads, or Hanapepe's *Green Garden* for inexpensive island style food and salad bar — and lilikoi chiffon pie!

Salt Pond Beach Park

What is most astonishing about Salt Pond Beach Park is the intensity of the colors—the brilliant blues of the water and sky, the bright gold of the sand, the vivid greens of sugar cane fields extending in squares and rectangles up the slopes of nearby mountains—all bathed in sunshine that makes everything sparkle. The beach is a perfect semicircle, where the sand slopes downward with the lovely grace of a golden bowl to hold the sea. A reef near the mouth of this sheltered cove breaks the surf into slow, rolling swells that break again gently near the shore so that children can raft and swim safely inside this natural lagoon most of the year. Rock formations at both ends of the beach create large pools which are calm enough at low tide for babies and toddlers. Older children can try their luck at catching the tiny, swift fish with nets.

Walk along the beach and explore tidal pools and the ancient salt ponds where local people still harvest sea salt. The park is spectacular, especially when brightly colored windsurfers race out across the reef, and particularly favored in terms of weather. Even when clouds and rain prevail elsewhere, this little point of land seems to escape them, and in winter, the water seems a few degrees warmer and more friendly.

Showers, rest rooms, picnic tables, and barbecues make Salt Pond a popular spot for local families and increasingly for tourists, particularly on weekends, although the beach never seems crowded. Be careful in periods of high surf, however, when unpredictable currents can create hazardous swimming, and stay inside the lagoon. On the way home, stop at the Green Garden for fabulous coconut cream or lilikoi chiffon pies.

Directions: Take Rt. 50 west to Hanapepe and pass through the town. Turn left at Lele St., and take the first right onto Lokokai Rd. Continue until you see the parking area. Salt Pond Beach Park is 18 miles from Lihue; 28 miles from Kapa'a; 58 miles from Princeville. Map: 4

rainbow butterflyfish

Pakala's Beach or 'Infinities'

On this lovely, curving beach, the sand and sea are deep gold, as if sprinkled with cinnamon, because the A'akukui stream carries red sugar cane soil to the sea. As you walk from the road across private pastureland, you can hear the crash of the waves before you can see the beach, and by the time you pass through the trees which ring the sand, you'll feel you're on a desert island.

It is a lovely spot. The waves rise gracefully in long, even lines crested with gold. Each wave breaks and rushes onto the sand in shining foam, and then it rolls back out again to meet the wave coming in. In a fascinating ballet, the waves sometimes meet like dancers in perfect rhythm, and shining spray bursts into the air as they join. Sometimes the waves clash or collide, but there's a beauty even in this more dissonant rhythm. You could watch the waves for hours and never see two waves embrace in exactly the same way.

The bay is divided by a rocky point where local fishermen try for pompano. If you cross the stream and climb the rocky ledge, you come to a sandy beach dotted with shells, sea glass, and coral. Beyond the reef is a surfing spot famous for long, perfectly formed waves that surfers can ride on to "infinity." Paddling out over the shallow reef takes a long time, but the ride, according to our son Jeremy, is well worth it! Be careful at low tide, when shallow water over the reef which can expose an unwary surfer to spiny sea urchins.

To the right of the rocky point, the beach stretches a long way before disappearing around a bend. The firm golden sand is perfect for walking, and the waves can be quite gentle. This western spot is a good place to try when other parts of the island are in rain.

Directions: Drive west of Hanapepe on Rt. 50 past the mile 21 marker. Look for a low concrete bridge and a level area on the shoulder of the road for parking. Next to the bridge over the A'akukui Stream, an overgrown path leads through pasture to the beach. Wear sturdy sandals and stay away from the thorny kiawe which grows near the beach. About 1 mile further on Rt. 50 you'll find public restrooms, and just across the Waimea River, public showers. Map: 4

Lucy Wright Beach Park, Waimea

Just off the main street of Waimea town is a long beach, and unusual on Kauai, this one is dark sand. The beach looks eerie, as if dusted with coal, and the water is dusky. A recreational fishing pier extends out into the ocean, and along the beach, restored plantation cottages afford a glimpse of what life was like when sugar was king. In this quiet spot, you can wander along the beach and invent stories — perhaps an angry goddess, jealous of the sun mirrored so brightly on the surface of the sea, tried to darken the water and sand with ash from her volcano.

Directions: Between the mile 22 and 23 markers on Rt. 50 in Waimea, turn towards the ocean until you find Lau Road. Follow to the end. Map: 4

Kekaha Beaches

Stretching for miles along Kauai's western coast, the Kekaha beaches combine swimming, surfing, and walking with the predominantly dry weather of the island's leeward side. As Rt. 50 curves toward the sea at the small town of Kekaha, the beach is narrow, but a mile or two north, it widens and becomes more golden, with long, rolling waves breaking evenly in brilliant white crests. At times, the waves can break perfectly for boogie boards, although, as everywhere on Kauai, surf and currents can be dangerous and unpredictable, and you may find high surf and rip currents. Watch where local people are swimming and follow their lead – especially if they are not going into the water!

Even if swimming is not advisable, the sand is firm and flat, one of the finest beaches on Kauai—or anywhere—for walking or running, or playing frisbee or football. At several places along the road, stands of trees provide shade for babies. We recommend driving the full length of this stretch of beach so that you can select the most favorable spot and then double back to park. Despite its clear, sunny weather, the western side of the island has not yet been developed as a tourist area, and so these beaches are frequented primarily by local residents and are not very crowded. You can walk for miles along the sand, with beautiful views of Ni'ihau, purple on the horizon. Or drive north towards Barking Sands and Polihale Beach, winding through sugar cane fields where silvery grasses wave in the breezes against the deep red-gold of cleared fields and the vivid blues of the sea and the enormous sky.

Directions: Drive northwest of Waimea on Rt. 50 until the road curves towards the water near the mile 25 marker. Map: 4

Barking Sands

The sandy beach from Kekaha to Polihale extends for about 15 miles, and the section off the Pacific Missile Range Facility is often available for public use. Call 335-4111 in advance to be sure that the area has not been closed for maneuvers! After signing in at the main gate, you can drive to a long stretch of sandy beach along Major's Bay. Like Polihale Beach, the surf here can be extremely strong, often too powerful for safe swimming. While the waves break magnificently in long, shining tunnels that look like a surfer's dream, unpredictable currents as well as a sudden drop-off make for particularly hazardous swimming conditions. You have to look carefully for channels through the coral reef fronting the beach to find sandy bottom, or you can go to the northernmost point of Major's Bay where the reef ends. The wide, sandy beach is both hot and difficult to walk on, and shade is almost nonexistent. It is a spectacular place for a picnic, though, and you can see Niʻihau, purple on the horizon, just past the golden, shining sand and glistening turquoise sea.

Directions: Drive northwest of Kekaha on Rt. 50 until you see the gate-house entrance. Map: 4

Polihale Beach Park

From the time you leave paved road behind to jolt north through a maze of sugar cane fields, you know you're in for something special. Gradually, beyond the tall sugar cane rustling in the breeze, a dark ridge of jagged peaks appears on the right. As you get closer, these giant cliffs reveal splendid colors— trees and bush in vivid greens against the black rock slashed with the deep red of the volcanic soil. When you can drive no further, the beach at Polihale emerges from the base of the cliffs—an enormous stretch of brilliant white sand more immense, it seems, than the cliffs which tower above and the band of deep blue sea beyond. Only the sky seems the equal of this vast expanse of glaring sand, so wide that to walk from your car to the ocean on a sunny day will burn your feet, and so long that no single vantage point allows the eye to see its full extent. "Beautiful" is too small a word for this awesome place. Polihale—home of spirits—is more appropriate, not only because the majestic cliffs and beach dwarf anything human to insignificance, but also because here man's access to the western coast really ends. Beyond lies the Na Pali wilderness, unreachable except by boat or helicopter, or by the handful of hikers who dare to climb the narrow and dangerous trails. Polihale is the threshold between the known and the unknown, the tamed and the untamed, the familiar and the wild.

Swimming is treacherous; the rolling, pounding surf even at its most gentle is only for strong, experienced swimmers. No reefs offer protection from the powerful ocean currents. Come instead for the spectacle, to picnic and walk, to gaze at the grandeur of the cliffs above the endless sea and sand, to listen to the silence broken only by the crashing surf, to appreciate in solitude the splendor of nature's power. A feeling of awe lingers even after you return to paved road and a world of smaller proportions.

Directions: Just before Rt. 50 ends, a State Park sign will mark the left turn onto the dirt cane road. Follow signs for about 5 miles. Restrooms, showers, picnic tables. Be careful about getting your car stuck in muddy roads, or in the sandy dunes. Map: 4

Beach Safety

We describe the beaches in their summer mood, when the surf and currents can be at their most gentle. From mid-October to mid-April, however, swimmers must be particularly cautious on the windward beaches to the north and northeast where the surf and currents are more unpredictable and dangerous. On the south shore, surf is "up" in summer months, and the ocean more calm during winter. Plan your beach adventures according to surf conditions (Call 245-6001 for a report on the size of the swell and the times of high and low tides).

A few simple suggestions: Don't swim alone or too far out at a beach where the currents are unfamiliar, and avoid swimming where a river flows into the sea. Never turn your back on the ocean; keep your eye on the waves. Before you swim, observe the water carefully. Look out for the fast moving water running laterally which indicates a rip current. Should you ever find yourself caught in a strong undertow or current, and if your efforts to free yourself are not successful, remember this: don't panic, conserve your energy and drift with the current until it weakens. These currents usually weaken beyond the point where the waves break, and many are shaped like horseshoes, so that at some point you will probably be able to swim back in.

Be particularly careful when you are snorkeling, when you can easily get distracted by the fish and lose your sense of direction. Stay close enough to shore that you can swim (or walk!) in at any time, and remember that unfamiliar beaches will have unknown currents. You'll find the safest snorkeling in the rock-enclosed pool at Lydgate Park on the eastern shore, or at sheltered Poipu Beach to the south. Beware of walking or even standing close to the edge of cliffs or rocks to photograph the pounding surf, as waves vary in size and strength and a huge one may come up suddenly and wash your camera away—perhaps you along with it! These sudden large waves can be treacherous because they are unexpected as well as powerful, particularly on the northern and western beaches without reefs to protect against strong ocean currents.

When surfing, watch where the local surfers ride the waves. They know where to avoid strong currents, rocks, and dangerous wave breaks.

They are also experienced, however, and seek a bigger thrill! Keep an eye out for that occasional oversize wave. Rather than trying to ride it (or worse, run from it!), you may want to dive through or drop down under it. These big ones often come in threes, so be ready!

The Portuguese 'man o' war', a tiny blue jellyfish, packs a walloping sting in its long, trailing tentacle. They sometimes dot the waterline after being washed ashore by heavy surf. Don't step on them or pick them up. If you are stung while swimming, pull the jellyfish off carefully, trying not to touch the stinger any more than you have to, or use some sand to scrape the stinger off. Vinegar is sometimes used as a poultice to help break down the poison. The best medicine, however, is prevention. If you see them on the sand, pack up and head out for another beach! An even smaller critter, the bacterium leptospirosis has been found in Kauai's rivers and streams, so avoid freshwater swimming far from the ocean's edge if you have open cuts or sores. Instead, swim in the ocean or the brackish water where a stream flows into the sea.

You may see a monk seal lying on the beach. Give it a wide berth; it's probably exhausted, resting before heading back out to sea! Seals don't trust humans and need privacy to recuperate.

Your beachbag should contain some antibiotic ointment and bandaids for coral cuts, and, if possible, some vinegar in case you meet a man o' war. Keep a spare sun tan lotion in the glove compartment of the car.

On Kauai, as anywhere, follow normal rules of self-protection: Lock your car against theft as you would at home, and avoid walking alone at night in unlit, deserted areas—including those romantic beaches.

Monk seal on 'Hawaiian time.'

Beware the Hawaiian Sun

If you lie out in the sun between 11:30 am and 2:30 pm you will fry like a pancake, even in a half hour, because Hawaii lies close to the equator and the sun is exceedingly strong. You'll need a good sunscreen, even on cloudy days, for ultraviolet rays can cause a burn. Sunscreens which contain PABA may give some people a rash. New 'PABA- free' sunscreens are available and are highly effective. Read the labels carefully. The best lotions protect against both UV and UA rays. Choose 'waterproof' rather than 'water-resistant' lotions, though don't put too much faith in manufacturer's claims! Even waterproof sunscreens wash off in salt water and should be reapplied periodically, as we do every two hours in summer. We've had good luck with lotions which form a skin-like coating, like Sundown, and sticky gels like 'Bullfrog.'

Children need special care and effective lotions. Dermatologists currently recommend a lotion rated SPF 15. For spots which kids rub often, like right under the eyes, you can try sticky gels like 'Bullfrog' or a lotion in chapstick form. It's a good idea to make a firm rule that kids get 'greased up' in the room or parking lot before heading for the beach as they hate to stand still once the sand is in sight! Bring T–shirts (the most reliable sun-protection) for after-swimming sandcastle projects. It's a good plan to schedule family beach visits for the early morning or late afternoon, and plan meals, naps, or drives for the noonday sun hours. Sunburns are often not visible until it is too late, but you can check your child's skin by pressing it with your finger. If it blanches dramatically, get the child a shirt of consider calling it a day. Keep a spare lotion in the car, for without lotion, beaches can be hazardous to your health!

Babies need a complete sunblock and a hat to protect the scalp; use lotion even on feet. Babies should stay in the shade as much as possible, so an umbrella would be a wise purchase for the beach.

Activities

Snorkeling

One of our favorite family activities! Lauren (age 13) loves Poipu Beach Park, and the best spot is on the right as you enter the park, west of the rocky point dividing the park from the Waiohai Hotel. Here you can find brilliant yellow tang, striped manini fish, butterflyfish, parrot fish, and silvery needle fish, all feeding on the coral. More than once, we have met a spotted box fish (Lauren has nick- named him 'Fred') who seems curious enough to swim right up to our masks. For Jeremy (age 19), the best snorkeling spot is Tunnels, on the north shore. He likes to swim through the intricate pathways of

Fred

"tunnels" to the edge of the reef where the water seems to plunge to unfathomable depths. We also like Ke'e Beach, where we can chase the *humu humu nuku nuku apua'a*, and Lydgate Park, where large blue fish with yellow fins swim in friendly families along the sandy bottom of the lava rimmed pool.

Safety should be your top priority. Plan your snorkeling with an eye to the tides, the weather, and the season. The north shore is best in summer, when the ocean is calmer and you can even find it pancake flat. In winter months, when surf is up on the north, Poipu Beach Park and Lydgate Park will probably have calmer water. Always snorkel where others are snorkel- ing, so you can get help if you need it (the main reason why we never snorkel at deserted beaches). Don't lose track of where you are when you are admiring all the fish, and don't snorkel at all if the surf looks too rough, or a rippling pattern in the waves indicates strong currents.

Feeding the fish can be lots of fun. If you use the snorkel fish food available in all the stores, you may have a problem when the plastic film casing begins to disintegrate in the water, bringing lots of fish, perhaps too many fish for your taste! This plastic film casing is made to be biodegrad- able, not like the tougher plastics which are dangerous to sea life. When we snorkel, we usually carry our fish food inside a plastic zip-lock bag so that we can release it more slowly.

It almost doesn't matter what you put inside the bag as long as it stimulates the fish's curiosity. (Just don't use frozen peas, which are hard for the fish to digest.) We have learned that using a green leaf or piece of seaweed inside the plastic bag may work even better than food because it attracts the curious, rather than the ravenous, fish. Tuck your plastic bag securely into your suit, then once you are in the ocean, let the water fill it and float your 'visual display' around. Swirl the bag gently and you'll be amazed at how much interest it creates! Be sure to take your bag back out of the water with you.

Coral cuts can be dreadful. Keep bandaids and antibiotic ointment in your beach bag and avoid touching the coral with any body part! Don't walk on it or try to pick it up. Your fins won't completely protect your feet.

Snorkeling can be a drag when your mask leaks! You might consider buying a mask that fits correctly before you leave home. To test the fit, place the mask on your face (without using the straps) and breathe in; a well-fit mask will stay on by itself. Anti-fog drops will enhance vision.

Snorkel and scuba lessons & tours are available from *SeaFun Kauai* (245-6400, Lihue), *Ocean Odyssey* (245-8681, Lihue), *Aquatic Adventures* (822-1434, Kapa'a), *Sunrise Diving* (822-REEF, Kapa'a), *Dive Kauai Scuba Center* (822-0452, Kapa'a) *Bay Island Water Sports* (826-7509, Princeville Hotel), *SeaSport Divers* (742-9303, Poipu), and *Fathom Five Divers* (742-6991, Poipu).

Surfing & Skim Boarding

As our children have grown older, surf has become a consideration when we decide where to go! When they were small, they loved to take their boogie boards to Poipu Beach Park. As they grew older, they wanted bigger waves. Kalihiwai is our favorite family beach because summer surf can be suitable for surfers at all levels. Hanalei, Kalapaki and Kealia are other good summertime choices, depending, of course, on surf conditions.

In winter months, north shore surf becomes unpredictable and currents can be dangerous. Hanalei can be gentle enough for you one day and a crashing, thundering caldron too tough even for experienced surfers the next. The same is true for Kalihiwai, and eastern shore beaches like Kealia, Kalapaki, and Wailua, where you may not be able to paddle out with your board to where the waves are breaking, even with fins, because of strong currents. As in all water sports, caution is a must! The wave pattern varies along the beach, and some spots are safer than others, so watch where the local kids are surfing and follow their lead. Don't go out alone, and don't take a boogie board to an area where you see only hard board surfers.

When surf is too flat (or too rough) for boogie boards, our kids like to use their skim boards to catch long, exciting rides across the shallows, or in an inch of foam along the shorebreak. They love Kalihiwai, where the

Catching a wave at Hanalei

stream flows into the ocean, Hanalei, Anahola, and Kalapaki.

For serious surfing, *Margo Oberg*, a seven time world surfing champion, offers lessons at all skill levels, in Poipu, in front of the Kiahuna (742-1750). She can advise you about the best surfing spots for your level of expertise. Arrange surf board rentals at *Progressive Expressions*, in Koloa. For surfing lessons on the north shore, call *Celeste Harvel, Windsurf Kauai* (828-6838).

Windsurfing & Water Skiing

Sheltered Anini Beach is an ideal spot for windsurfing, and two companies offer lessons, both private and for groups. At *Windsurf Kauai*, Celeste Harvel (828-6838) can teach anyone, even youngsters, the basics, and also offers a complete certification course. *Anini Beach Windsurfing* (826-9463) also uses the latest in equipment. Questions? Stop in at *Hanalei Surf Company* for advice and information.

Water skiing is available on the Wailua River on the eastern shore. Call *Kauai Water Ski & Kauai Surf Company* (822-3574). For $85/hour you can get a driver, equipment, lessons, and the boat!

Ocean Sports Equipment Rentals

Water sports equipment can be rented at all over the island. Expect to pay about $5/day or $15/week for mask, fins, snorkel) and about $5/day for a boogie board. In Wailua, *Chris the Fun Lady* (822-7447) will offer you free coffee and cookies, as well as advice. *Kauai Surf Co.* (822-3574) in Kinipopo Shopping Village, and *Aquatic Adventures (822-1434)* have excellent selections. In Hanalei, *Pedal & Paddle* rents just about everything and is a good place to get advice on surf conditions. *Hanalei Surf Company (826-9000)* has equipment for sale as well as rent, and knowledgeable personnel. On the south shore, you'll find a great selection at *Brennecke's Beach Center (742-7505),* including chairs! *Snorkel Bob's* (245-9433 Lihue & 742-8322, Poipu) offers a multi-island rate.

Hiking

Hiking can be a spectacular way to see Kauai, for more than half of the island's 551,000 square miles is forestland, and many of its most beautiful regions are inaccessible by car. However, hiking Kauai is not without risks. Many trails can become dangerous from washouts and mudslides, and in the Na Pali coastal region, where trails are often etched into the sides of sheer cliffs, hikers must be wary of waves crashing over the rocks without warning, as well as vegetation which masks the edge of a sheer drop. A good friend, for example, broke his ankle one summer when plants gave way under his feet near the edge of a ravine. Since Iniki, many trails have been repaired and are now in even better condition than before.

Careful planning is a must. Before your trip, write the *Division of Forestry*, Kauai District, PO Box 1671, Lihue HI 96766 for a free information packet with maps and descriptions of trails in the forest preserves. For a similar free packet on the Na Pali region, write to the *Division of State Parks* at the same address (808-241-3444).

Kathy Morey's *Kauai Trails: Walks Strolls and Treks on the Garden Island* is a clear, thorough, easy-to-use resource, particularly for the trails in Koke'e or behind Kapa'a where you can explore Sleeping Giant Mountain and discover panoramic views of the coastline. Bob Smith's *Hiking Kauai* describes a variety of hikes, and his company also organizes hikes: Hawaiian Outdoor Adventures (714-960-0389). Request a catalog of books and maps for hiking and camping on Kauai and other Hawaiian islands available from *Hawaii Geographic Society*, PO Box 1698, Honolulu HI 96806.

When you arrive on Kauai, call the *Division of Forestry* in Lihue (808-241-3433) for a report on current trail conditions. You can also call the *Kauai Visitor's Bureau* in Lihue (808-245-3971) for advice and help in arranging hiking trips, and finding local guides.

The most famous trail, the *Kalalau trail*, is a spectacular but strenuous 11 mile hike through the Na Pali cliff region. If your body is reasonably sound, you will enjoy the first few miles. This subsection, the Hanakapiai trail, has breathtaking views of the coast along switchbacks which take you into forest and back out to the ocean. About a quarter-mile of uphill walking brings you to a magnificent view of Ke'e Beach and the Ha'ena reefs. Two miles of rigorous up and down hiking will bring you to Hanakapiai Beach, nestled like a brilliant jewel in a picturesque, terraced valley (Hiking beyond this point requires a day-use permit from the Division of State Parks). Unfortunately, this beach has currents far too dangerous for swimming, and the rip currents can be so powerful that more than one unwary hiker standing in the surf at knee level has been caught up in a sudden, large wave, pulled out to sea and drowned. The Kalalau trail begins where the paved road ends on the north shore, at Ke'e Beach. Remember, here you will find the last source of safe drinking water.

Important safety information: When it rains, this narrow trail gets muddy – and dangerously slippery, a fact we appreciated first hand when we saw a woman slip over the steep edge and disappear down into the slick vegetation. Fortunately, her quick-thinking companion had managed to grab her hand and so we could pull her back up! In many places, the trail is actually a stream bed, and fills with water after heavy rains. Essential items: shoes with good traction for slippery rocks and mud (instead of jogging shoes or flip flops), sunscreen, strong insect repellent, a hat, perhaps a nylon poncho, and even a walking stick! Plan on carrying your own drinking water because the bacterium leptospirosis is found in almost all of Kauai's rivers and streams. You can get the most recent update about trails and conditions in Na Pali from *Pedal 'n Paddle* (826-9069) in Hanalei, the *Division of State Parks* (241-3446), or *Kayak Kauai Outfitters* (826-9844), which offers guided hikes of the Kalalau Trail, as well as combination camping and ocean kayak excursions along the Na Pali.

The *Koke'e forest* region and Alakai Swamp are beautiful in a different way. Within this 4,345 acre wilderness preserve are 45 miles of trails, from pleasant walks to rugged hikes, as well as fresh water fishing streams, and most have been repaired after Iniki. From the Koke'e Lodge, day hikers can choose from three trails which explore the plateau and Waimea Canyon rim, ranging from the half-mile Black Pipe Trail to the 1.5 mile Canyon Trail along the north rim of Waimea Canyon, past upper Wa'ipo'o Falls to the Kumuwela Overlook. From this perch you can see the canyon's 3,600-foot depth and 10 mile stretch to the sea. For longer hikes, you can arrange for guides, as well as hunting and fishing licenses, at the Koke'e Lodge.

The *Sierra Club* sponsors 3 or 4 day hikes on Kauai each month. The most popular destinations: Kalalau Trail to Hanakapiai on the north shore; the trails across Sleeping Giant mountain on the eastern shore; Shipwreck Beach to Maha'ulepu on the south shore; and on the west, the first few miles beyond Polihale along the rocky coast. Call 823-6000.

Camping

Several state and county parks allow camping, for example Anahola, Ha'ena, Anini, Salt Pond, and Polihale Beach Parks, as well as specified areas of the Na Pali region and other wilderness preserves. Camping is limited to five nights in a 30 day period per campground, and less on some stopovers on the Kalalau Trail. For information, permits, and reservations well before you arrive, write the *Department of Land and Natural Resources*, Division of State Parks, P.O. Box 1671, Lihue, HI 96766 or call 808-241-3444. Photocopies of identification are required for campers over 18. For information about hiking in the Alakai Swamp, or hiking and camping in Waimea Canyon, contact the Division of Forestry at the same address. Call 808-241-3433.

For those who want to be close to nature — and to a shower and refrigerator at the same time, *Koke'e Lodge*'s cabins might be just the answer. Cabins include stove, refrigerator, hot showers, cooking and eating utensils, linens, bedding, and wood burning stoves and cost only $35-$45/ night (maximum stay of 5 nights during a 30 day period). For information and reservations, write Koke'e Lodge, Box 819, Waimea HI 96796. (808-335-6061). The Lodge serves breakfast and light lunch (9 am - 3:30 pm). Bring warm clothes for cold nights, and remember, on Kauai as elsewhere, to lock your gear in the trunk of your car before you head out. Map: 4

You don't have to travel far to escape the rush! Conveniently located just outside of Koloa, *Kahili Mountain Park* offers reasonably priced, rustic cabins ($44 for two) and even more rustic one room 'cabinettes' ($33 for two). Newer cabins for 4 persons are $55. The setting is beautiful and serene, a meadow backed by mountains with a view of the sea, and you can't beat the prices; extra persons cost only $4 a night. Contact Kahili Mountain Park, Box 298, Koloa HI 96756; (808-742-9921). Map: 3.

After Iniki's winds, tufted new grown on Norfolk pines.

Near road's end on the north shore, *YMCA Camp Naue* in spectacular Ha'ena offers beachfront camping in bunk houses (or your own tent). It's popular with local clubs and families, but individual tourists are also welcome to stay in the bunkhouse for $12 each per night (children half price!), or if you bring your own tent, it's only $10. For information and reservations, contact YMCA of Kauai, Box 1786, Lihue HI 96766; (808-246-9090 or 742-1200). Map: 2

To rent camping equipment, try *Pedal & Paddle* in Hanalei (808-826-9069), a good place to ask about current trail conditions, or *Kayak Kauai Outfitters* in Hanalei (808-826-9844) and in Kapa'a (808-822-9179). In Poipu, check out *Outfitters Kauai* (808-742-9667). You can buy camping equipment in *Long's Drug Store*, *K-Mart* in Kukui Grove, the new *Wal-Mart* in Lihue, as well the small variety stores like *Waipouli Variety* (Wailua), *Village Variety* (Hanalei) or *Discount Variety* (Koloa).

Horseback Riding

The guided trail rides in Hanalei are a unique way to explore Kauai's beautiful north shore.

Princeville Ranch Stables (formerly Po'oku Ranch) offers an hour's ride across the ranch lands; a two–hour ride takes you back towards the mountains for views. The four–hour ride includes a hike to a waterfall for a picnic lunch and swim (808-826-6777). Groups of 6-8 are taught horsemanship, a unique feature of this program, and then proceed at a walk so that inexperienced riders will have no difficulty with their means of transportation. A morning ride avoids the heat of the day. Wear sun-glasses, and perhaps a hat which won't blow off; once you're on board, it's hard to climb down and chase it! Closed Sundays. Map: 2

On the south shore *CJM Stables* offers a variety of tours for one to two hours along the coast and mountains near Maha'ulepu Beach (808-742-6096). Some include breakfast. Tour guides are very friendly and provide historical information, as well as photo-opportunities. Closed Sundays. Map : 3. On the westside, near Waimea, *Garden Island Ranch* offers tours of the ranch land along the ocean and along the lower western rim of the Waimea Canyon (limit 2 riders). 808-338-0052. Map: 4

Community Calendar	
Kauai Concert Association	245-7464
Kauai Community Players	245-3408
Kauai Society of Artists	245-6931

Eastern Shore

Kalapaki Beach, a family favorite for swimming & playing — and exploring the Marriott Hotel afterwards. Page 23.

North Shore

Moloaʻa Bay, perfect for solitary beach strolls. Page 30.

Beach fun at Kilauea. Surf or sand, both are great! Page 32.

Kilauea Lighthouse has a bird's eye view of Secret Beach, a great beach for walking. Page 33.

Sunset Drive to Hanalei

If your accommodations are on the eastern shore, consider dinner in Hanalei, for the drive north as the sun begins to set is an experience not to be missed! Check the paper for the exact time of sunset, which may be earlier than you expect because the state of Hawaii never changes to daylight savings time. Plan to reach Hanalei about ten minutes before sunset so that you have time to park and ready your camera and are assured a spectacular drive north.

As you begin the drive, hundreds of clouds, already tinged with peach and gold, float in an azure sky above a shimmering sea. Rt. 56 winds through the countryside and along the coast, with fields of sugar cane turning silver, and the colors of land and sky changing almost mile by mile as the declining sun deepens the greens and blues and touches everything with shades of pink and gold. At Kilauea, where the road curves to the west, a line of tall, graceful Norfolk pines stands starkly silhouetted against the blazing sky. Even the grasses, their feathery tops waving gently in the evening breeze, are touched with pink, and the cattle grazing in the field seem positioned

Sunset in the rain, a spectacular view from Bali Hai Restaurant. Page 148.

by an artist's hand. Near Princeville, the clouds, luminous with reflected golds and pinks, seem enormous, dwarfing the cliffs, whose great jagged peaks have turned an astonishing purple.

We never tire of this drive, as each sunset is different—the gleaming expanse of ocean, the sharply angled mountains, the masses of clouds are blended each night by the sun's magic into a composition of colors that will never occur again in exactly the same way. One night the sun's descent may be screened by great masses of clouds rimmed with gold and glowing tangerine against the deep purple mountains and the shimmering blue gray sea. Another time the sun may almost blind you with its blazing, fiery gold, suffusing nearby clouds with impossible shades of orange and pink and brushing distant clouds with peach. Or, one evening the clouds may be so thick that the setting sun is apparent only in delicate touches of apricot on the clouds hovering over the sea, muted purples on the mountains, and the silver sheen on the surface of the sea. As the seasons change, so does the angle of the sun, gilding the landscape with new patterns of light and color.

In fact, as we discovered one summer, a sunset in the rain is the most astonishing of all, for it excites the imagination with impossible combinations. The tops of the mountains are shrouded with gray, yet above the sea, the sky is brilliant with color, with sunny clouds stretching along the horizon, their shapes rimmed with pink light from the setting sun. As dark showers move across the horizon like 'legs of the rain,' blurring the line between ocean and sky, the sun's vivid orange is turning the water purple and the clouds violet. The sun descends into stormy clouds moving slowly toward it, and, as the last light fades, dark clouds hovering above the cliffs slowly creep across the mountains, and the world turns slowly still and dark.

If the clouds are not too thick, there are several places at Hanalei to enjoy the dramatic moment when the shining disk of sun slips silently into the sea. Less than a mile past the entrance to Princeville, you can park at a scenic overlook on Rt. 56 and see most of Hanalei Bay's western side. But you have to contend with the distractions of traffic and car radios as well as the conversations of other sunset seekers ("Ralph! I *told* you we were going to miss it! We should have left earlier!") For a more panoramic view with greater privacy, enter Princeville and follow the signs to Pali Ke Kua, park in the lot, and enjoy the view discreetly from the lawn between buildings.

The drive home after dinner is another sensuous experience of cool evening breezes you can almost taste as well as feel. As you drive south almost alone on the road, you can hear wonderful sounds—the chirping of crickets, the leaves rustling in the breeze—and see the different shades of darkness in the landscape, lit by the moon against an enormous star–filled sky and the shimmering waves of the wide ocean beyond.

Sunset Watching

Watch spectacular sunsets from the 'Living Room' at the *Princeville Hotel*, with cocktails and music, or at the *Beach House* on the south shore. Or go to the beach! Bring a blanket (and possibly beach chairs, CD player with headphones, a good book, a small ice chest with drinks and snacks). Try *Poipu Beach Park* on the south shore, or if you are really ambitious, drive to *Polihale Beach*, at the farthest end of the road on the westside. On the north shore, try *Anini Beach*, Princeville's ocean bluff (at Pali Ke Kua condos), *Hanalei Bay*, or further west, *Tunnels* or *Ke'e Beach* .

Golf

The Princeville Makai Course in Hanalei, designed by Robert Trent Jones, Jr., is a 27 hole, world-class championship course with 3 challenging nines: Lake, Woods, and Ocean, famous for spectacular views and the dramatic 141-yard seventh hole, where the ocean, foaming like a cauldron, separates tee and green. Ranked 5th in the state, and one of *Golf Digest's* top 25 resort courses for 16 years. Fees, including carts, are $110 ($75/ Princeville Hotel guests; $95/Princeville Resort guests). (808-826-3580 or 800-826-4400). Enter Princeville from Rt.. 56, stop at the gate house and get directions and a free map. Map: 2

The Prince Course, is Hawaii's number one rated course according to Golf *Digest*. The 18 hole, 6521-yard course, designed by Robert Trent Jones, Jr., is spectacular, set in 390 acres of pastureland, with rolling hills, deep ravines, tropical jungle with streams and waterfalls. Fees, including carts, are $145 ($115/Princeville Hotel guests; $90/Princeville resort guests). (808-826-5000 or 800-826-4400). Enter from Rt. 56 at the Clubhouse, just east of Princeville. Map: 2

Kiahuna Golf Course, Poipu, designed by Robert Trent Jones, Jr. is an 18 hole, par 70, links-style course, predominantly flat, with smooth, fast greens and tradewind challenges. At 6,353 yards from the tips, this course is geared more for the recreational golfer. Daily fees: $53/18 holes or $27/9 holes, including shared cart. 742-9595. Enter from Poipu Beach Road at the Poipu Shopping Village. Ask about twilight discounts. Map 3

Poipu Bay Resort Golf Course, Poipu, designed by Robert Trent Jones, Jr. is a par 72 Scottish links-style course, 6845 yards from the blue tees, set in 210 acres of sugar plantation land along the ocean adjacent to the Hyatt Regency. Views are spectacular! With cart, $135 ($85/Hyatt guests). Discounts for guests at some island hotels. The Clubhouse is adjacent to the Hyatt's main parking lot. 742-8711 or 800-858-6300. Map 3

Wailua Municipal Golf Course, Wailua (245-8092). Ranked in top 25 U.S. municipal courses by *Golf Digest,* this popular 18 hole, 6658 yard, par 72 course is built along the ocean on rolling terrain amid ironwood trees and coconut palms. Fairways are narrow, greens smallish, and grass on the tough side. Fees are unbeatable: $20 on weekends (it gets crowded!) or $18 on weekdays. Carts cost $11.50/18 holes or $6.75/9 holes, and pullcarts are available. On the ocean side of Rt. 56 just south of Wailua. Map 1

Kukuiolono Golf Course, Kalaheo. 9 holes, par 35 with spectacular views and a lovely Japanese garden. Bring your camera for the beautiful plumeria grove! Honor system: $5/green fees and $6/cart. A local favorite, a secret most don't want to share! 322-9151. Turn south off Rt. 50 in Kalaheo at Papalina Rd. (the stoplight) drive .8 mile, and enter the gate on your right. Map 3

Kauai Lagoons Golf & Racquet Club, in the Kauai Lagoons Resort, Lihue, overlooks beautiful Kalapaki Bay. Designed by Jack Nicklaus, the 262 acre *Kiele course* is designed for golfers with a 20-handicap or better and was named on of the Top 100 courses in America by *Golf Digest..* The front nine is long and rugged with many mounds and swales. The back nine runs out to the ocean, with spectacular views of waves crashing against the rocks, and prevailing tradewinds of up to 15 m.p.h. on the southeast corner. Fees, including cart, are $145 ($100/Marriott guests). An extra-long course (7070 yards) with 4 tees, the *Kauai Lagoons course*, ranked by *Golf Magazine* in the top ten of "America's most playable courses," is a shotmaker's course with many bunkers and more undulating greens. 6,942 yards from the tips. Fees, including cart, are $140 ($60/Marriott guests). 241-6000 or 800-634-6400. Discounts for guests at some hotels.

Beachwalking & Running

If you can't get through your day without a run, you'll love Kauai's beaches! Our favorite running beaches, with firm sand and just the right slope, are Hanalei Bay and Kalihiwai Bay in the north, Kalapaki Bay on the east, Maha'ulepu on the south shore and Kekaha to the west. For long meandering walks, we like Moloa'a Bay, Larsen's Beach, Maha'ulepu, and Lydgate Park south of the rock pools, along the Wailua Golf Course, especially at sunrise or sunset.

For details about races on Kauai, call *Hawaii Visitors Bureau* (800-262-1400). For a free schedule of races, triathalons and fun-runs statewide, send a SASE to *Dept. of Parks and Recreation*, City and County of Honolulu, 650 King St., Honolulu HI 96813, or call *Running Room* (808-737-2422). Remember the sun! Fluids, sunscreen, even a hat are a must!

Kauai Specialties

For something truly special, visit Angeline Locey in Anahola for an unforgettable, authentic Hawaiian *lomi lomi massage*. Angeline is a kahuna, an 'elder' with especially gifted and gentle hands. The massage, which takes place in a special steam room of her own design, begins with a salt scrub with sea salt to cleanse your skin in preparation for the indescribable lomi lomi, fragrant with oil of coconut and lavender. Angeline calls this place Muʻolaulani, and considers it sacred to the Hawaiian tradition of healing. This extraordinary, wonderfully relaxing two-hour experience costs a reasonable $100. Since the steamer may be shared by others, specify if you prefer being with your own sex. Reservations 822-3235.

Look for special island creations at the unique *Kauai Products Store* in Kukui Grove Center, as well as at *Hilo Hattie's* in Lihue, *Kong Lung* in Kilauea, *Hula Moon* in Koloa, and *Kiʻi Hale* in Coconut Plantation Marketplace, Wailua. Soaps made by *Island Soap Co.* in Kilauea are especially gentle and fragrant. Try coconut, pikake or plumeria! You'll also find beautiful note cards with one-of-a kind photographs of Kauai. Look for *Lois Coleman's* striking Kauai images, and for *Barbara Foxcroft's* cards featuring vintage Hawaiian black & white photographs.

Mark White and *Nancy Smith* of Koloa craft lovely bowls, platters, and cups, glazed to capture the beautiful colors and contours of Kauai's mountains, sea, and sky. Oriental doll patchwork quilts created by long time Kauai resident *Sally Akazawa* at *Kapaia Stitchery* make a great baby gift. New teenage driver in your family? How about a 'Hawaiian Helmet,' a miniature warrior's head with feather headdress to hang (for good luck, of course!) on the mirror. Call *Del Seager* (826-7109) for custom designs.

Hawaiian Luaus & Other Fun

For centuries, Hawaiians have celebrated birthdays, weddings, anniversaries, any festive occasion, with a luau feast, with a whole pig roasted in an 'imu' or underground oven and served with a sumptuous array of colorful dishes, including sweet potatoes, poi, fresh island fish, chicken cooked in coconut and taro, tropical fruits and salads. The most popular are the luaus at the Coconut Beach Hotel in Wailua (822-3455), which showcases Hawaiian hula traditions, and the all-Polynesian extravaganza at Smith's Tropical Paradise (822-4654). Both offer children's discounts, and at Smith's you can buy a ticket to the show, which is presented in a natural ampitheater, without buying the family-style buffet beforehand. The Coconut Beach Hotel has a kid's special rate on Saturdays (Map 1). Some excellent shows are free! Monday, Wednesday, Friday and Saturday at 4:30 pm, come to the Coconut Plantation Marketplace in Wailua for an excellent production by *halau Na Hule O Kaohikukapulani*! Call Kiahuna Shopping Village (742-2831) or Kiahuna (742-6411) for south shore showtimes.

At the Princeville Hotel (Map 2), John Akana and Mauliola Cook enchant audiences with stories & legends of old Hawaii performed in dance and chants, in the spectacular 'Living Room.' Bring the kids, and while they have fun, you can enjoy a glass of wine and the incomparable sunset view (T, Th, Sun at 6:30 pm). Later, listen to haunting Hawaiian melodies, sung by Manulele, with Kimo Garner, pianist (Wed, Sat, Sun 7-11 pm).

In summer months, O'Bon dances celebrate the ancestors of the congregations of island Buddhist temples. Old and young dance together in large circles under colorful, lighted lanterns. Write Waimea Shingon Mission, 3770 Pule Rd., Waimea HI 96796 for a schedule.

Hawaiian Music

Pop these tapes into the stereo of your rental car, or play them at home on cold winter evenings! For the classics, listen to the Brothers Cazimero (*Hawaiian Paradise* and *'The Best'*), or The Makaha Sons of Ni'ihau (*Ke Alaula* or *Ho'oluana),* or Hui Ohana. For a more contemporary sound, try Israel Kamakawiwo'ole's albums *E Ale E* and *Facing Forward.* Keali'i Reichel's unforgettable *Kawaipunahele* has become one of the bestselling albums of Hawaiian music, of all time! A remarkable achievement for a remarkable album launched with the proceeds of a giant bake sale of 40,000 shortbread cookies baked by Keali'i's friends and supporters! One of them, Kekuhi Kanahele, has a great new album, *Hahani Mai—* her voice and variety are amazing. 'Slack Key' guitar music brings you haunting melodies without words, and Keola Beamer is a master. At *Borders Books & Music* in Lihue, you can listen to a wide selection before you buy.

Weddings on Kauai

Getting married on Kauai? You must apply in person for a license ($16), valid for 30 days. For a brochure and list of marriage license agents contact the *Department of Health* (808-241-3495). The bride needs a rubella screening test certificate from a physician, but there are no residency/citizenship requirements. Contact the *Division of State Parks* for a list of scenic wedding sites (808-274-3444). For a descriptive list professional wedding companies on Kauai, call the *Kauai Visitor's Bureau* (800-262-1400). Reserve a private tea room at *Hanama'ulu Restaurant & Tea House* for a reception; try *Kauai Tropicals* (p. 74) for wonderful flowers.

Farmers' Markets

Farmers' Markets happen almost each day of the week. Some are "official," some informal, and all are a great place to catch the flavor of the island, talk to local people, and enjoy a kaleidoscope of tastes and colors!

Come early for the best selection! From truck beds, tiny stands, or the trunks of cars, local farmers will sell their fruits, vegetables, and flowers at prices more reasonable than the supermarkets. Manoa lettuce, as low as $1.00 for a half-dozen small heads, will be fresh from the garden and taste of Kauai's sunny skies and salt air. You'll never want iceberg again! You may find avocados at 2 for $1; fresh basil, oregano, marjoram, or chives; a shiny dark purple eggplant with just the right sound when you thump it, and bananas of all kinds—Williams, and Bluefield, and Kauai's special apple-bananas. Don't be put off by the short, fat, drab-skinned exterior, for inside the fruit looks like golden sand at sunset and tastes like bananas laced with apples!

The starting time is important to know! At the Kapa'a market, you'll see a rope tied across the parking lot which looks—and serves—as a starting line, complete with a shrill whistle, to ensure an equal chance for buyers and sellers. It drops at five minutes to 3 pm, so don't be late! Sellers quickly become friends. One may offer you a slice of star fruit, or

Monday	noon	Koloa, Ball Park on Rt. 520 next to the fire house. Map: 3
Tuesday	2 pm	Hanalei, west of town on Rt. 560. Map: 2
Tuesday	4:30	Kalaheo Neighborhood Center, Papalina at Rt. 50. Map: 3
Wednesday	3 pm	Kapa'a behind the armory. Map: 1
Thursday	2 pm	Hanapepe, on Hanapepe Road. Map: 4
Thursday	4:30	Kilauea, Kilauea Neighborhood Center
Friday	3 pm	Lihue, Vidhina football stadium parking lot, near airport. Map: 1
Saturday	9 am	Kekaha Neighborhood Center, Elepaio off Rt. 50. Map: 4
Saturday	9 am	Kilauea, Christ Memorial Church. Map: 2

section of honey sweet orange with deceptively green skin, or a slice of juicy pineapple topped with passion fruit. Papayas will be giants, the Sunrise variety if you're lucky, for their red-orange center rivals the color of the sun. Try fresh lime juice, or Jeremy's favorite, the juice from a passion fruit, to spark the papaya's mellow sweet flavor with tartness. Even if you aren't cooking, you'll be tempted by stringbeans as long as shoelaces, squash with squeaky skins, tomatoes still warm and fragrant, all kinds of Oriental vegetables with odd shapes, even fresh coconuts. You may even

find leis of pakalana or plumeria for $2 a strand! Take home tropical flowers—bird of paradise, parrot colored heliconia blossoms, stalks of fragrant white or yellow ginger. Be ready to bargain if you are buying in quantity from one seller, and take their advice about venturing into new tastes. Most sellers price in $1 pack-ages, so bring plenty of singles!

The largest markets are in Kapa'a and Lihue, and both are a little tricky to find. On Fridays, the market is in the parking lot behind the Vidhina football stadium just south of the airport in Lihue. You can enter off on Kapule Highway (Rt. 51) at the northern corner of the stadium, or turn off Rice St. at Holoko Road. The Wednesday Kapa'a market is in the parking lot opposite the armory. In Kapa'a, take Kukui Road off Rt. 56 and turn right at the end; then make the next right onto Kahau Road and park on your left. Or take the new bypass road from Wailua to Kapa'a; it comes out just at the end of Kahau Road. Map 1

Island Tastes

Fresh fruits can be bought all over the island, sometimes from a truck parked by the side of the road! In Kilauea, on the road to the lighthouse, the *Martin Farm* roadside stand sells papayas on the honor system. You choose your fruits and leave your money in a box! (Closed Sundays). To taste Kauai's special sunrise papayas back home on a cold winter morning, call *John Akana* in Kalihiwai (800-572-7292), and he will ship 10 pounds of sunrise papayas by federal express for $32.68. Order before 7 am on Wednesday, and the fruits will arrive on the mainland by Friday afternoon.

While you're on the island, call John for a free fruit taste (828-1746).

Fresh tropical fruit 'smoothies' are a special taste treat! Try *Banana Joe's* just north of Kilauea on Rt. 56. Joe also makes a fantastic frozen treat, a whipped 'frostie' of fresh papaya, banana, or pineapple. Sample Joe's pineapples, coconuts, and fresh red 'Cuban' bananas.

At nearby *Mango Mama's* you can enjoy exotic smoothies made from combinations of fruit you'll find nowhere else! Near Lihue, stop in at the *People's Market* in Puhi, opposite Kauai Community College.

Kauai has its own ice cream factory, founded by Walter Lappert who wanted to retire in paradise and ended up in business! *Lappert's* ice cream is rich and made with the finest flavorings. 'Kauai pie' is a family favorite. Kids may find sightings of Mr. Lappert himself pretty exciting. Shave Ice is a special island treat. Stop in at the *Wishing Well* in Hanalei (in the silver trailer by Kayak Kauai) for some of the best flavors and textures.

Macadamia nut cookies taste like Kauai even if you're back home. Try several island bakeries: *Kauai Kookie Kompany*, sold in Big Save Markets or at the factory store in Hanapepe. In the Waipouli Complex, *Po Po's* mixes these heavenly nuts with chocolate chips or coconut into a confection Mrs. Fields would envy! *Kauai Tropical Fudge* comes in wonderful island flavors, including banana, macadamia nut, Kona coffee, even pina colada! Look for it in many island stores, including *Nutcracker Sweet* in Coconut Marketplace, Wailua, and the *Kauai Products Store* in Kukui Grove, Lihue.

Be sure to sample *Kauai Coffee*, grown near Kalaheo and Koloa, near the location of the first coffee plantation in the state, which opened in 1836. Coffee grown on this 4,000 acre estate is free of insecticides. Try it with lilikoi chiffon pie, a light confection of passion fruit. Great pies can be found at *Hamura's Saimin* in Lihue, The *Green Garden Restaurant* in Hanapepe, and at *Omoide Bakery* on Kaumualii Highway in Hanapepe, where according to local legend the island's best pies have been baked by secret family recipe since 1956. Pies are sold frozen (order in advance 335-5291) and so will keep for several hours in the car (best in a cooler). Other locally produced specialties include *Anahola Granola* (Try it with apple bananas), for the perfect breakfast. Papaya seed salad dressing, brewed in Kalaheo, will give lettuce a whole new dimension, and 'Thai Vinegar,' blended in Kilauea by *The Secret Ingredient*, is spectacular with fresh tomatoes! Look for them at Kauai Products Store in Kukui Grove.

Kukui jams and syrups are the best! Be sure to sample some coconut syrup on your pancakes and guava-strawberry jam on your PBJs. Stop in at the factory in Kalaheo and make up your own gift boxes (four 6 oz. jars cost about $6). Pack them in your suitcases, or have them shipped. Call the office (332-9333) to be sure it's open. Take Rt. 50 west, pass the junction with Rt. 530, drive .8 mile and turn into a driveway on your right. There's a new sign, and you'll soon see the light blue building ahead. Don't pass up a Kukui specialty: macadamia nuts dusted with chocolate!

For the freshest local fish, try *Fish Express* at 3343 Kuhio Hwy. (Rt. 56) just north of Lihue for filets of whatever has just been hooked—shibiko (baby yellow fin tuna), ono, ulua, and snappers of all hues—pink, grey, red. Prices vary with the weather, the season, the tides, even the moon, and are generally higher in winter, when fishing boats face rougher seas. The adventurous can try opihi (limpets) raw in the shell with seaweed, or smoked marlin. Your fresh fish selections can be vacuum sealed for shipping (245-9918). In Hanama'ulu stop in at *Ara's* for homemade ahi poke and sushi platters. In Kapa'a, stop in at the inexpensive Kuhio Market on Rt. 56, one block south of the park. There's good news in Hanalei! *Hanalei Dolphin* has opened a fish market right behind the restaurant, so you can buy the same high quality fish to grill at home.

Tropical Flowers & Leis

Tropical flowers! The exotic shapes and colors of heliconia — 'lobster claw,' sexy pink,' 'caribea' —the geometric precision of awapuhi, the fragrance of pikaki or plumeria! At farmers' markets, you can buy armfuls of spectacular flowers for a few dollars. And for those friends back home

Hibiscus

taking care of your dog, what better way to say thank you than a bouquet? From Judy and Roger Peckenpaugh at *Kauai Tropicals*, you can order a lovely assortment of flowers for a modest price ($39.95) carefully boxed and shipped via Federal Express, arriving fresh and gorgeous in any mainland city! Some blooms last nearly two weeks, and it makes a very special mother's day or birthday present! The Peckenpaughs, members of the Kauai Tropical Growers Association, will also include an informative color brochure about tropical flowers upon request (800- 303-4385). Flower lovers should visit the Kauai Marriott, to see spectacular tropical flower arrangements by *Irma Lee Pomeroy*, a gifted artist in floral design.

Flower leis! The fragrance of pikake or white ginger; the cool, silky touch of petals; the delicate yet rich colors of orchids and plumeria—even in words, flower leis conjure up moonlit nights and ocean breezes. No vacation is complete without one, especially on your last night. Many stores offer ready-made leis in a refrigerated case, but these strings of imported carnations cannot compare with a local lei which reflects the traditions of the island as well as the individual artistry of the lei maker. Order your lei a day in advance and pick it up on your way out to dinner!

The *Mauna Loa lei* ($18), is a wide woven band of small purple orchids; very handsome, it is often given to boys at graduation. Another favorite is the lei of *white ginger*, a spectacular creation of white buds so fragrant that heads will turn as you walk by. The tightly threaded ginger blossoms look almost like white feathers. If the blossoms are in season, try a beautiful *Ilima lei* made of papery orange-colored blossoms, very rare and difficult to string. Or try the slender strand of fragrant green *pakalana* ($8/ strand of 100 flowers). The small, white *stephanotis*, similar in shape to a lilac blossom and even more fragrant, can be threaded in single strands ($8) or in a thick round "triple" lei of 300 flowers, striking to look at though heavy to wear. *Pikake*, a tiny and delicate white flower, is the Hawaiian lei for weddings and has a wonderful, spicy scent ($8/strand). *Plumeria* leis are the most common. Usually white or yellow and sometimes pink or deep red, the large blossoms have a wonderful perfume.

The best place to buy a lei is at the farmers' markets, where you can find them for $2 to $5. *The People's Market* in Puhi, opposite the Kauai Community College, offers leis made fresh each morning by Gladys; you can ususally find plumeria leis, and depending on the season, sometimes even pikake, pakalana, or ilima. In Anahola, you can buy plumeria leis in yellow or mixed colors; just turn off the main road at the sign and follow the arrows to 3805 Makio. Lei making is becoming a cottage industry on Kauai. You may see leis for sale hanging in a tree in someone's front yard!

Your lei will look wonderful for only one wearing, but the fragrance lingers even when the petals turn brown. Store your lei in a plastic bag in the refrigerator overnight and wear it, even though wilted, as you get ready for breakfast the next morning! Hang it to dry for a Hawaiian potpourri.

Surprisingly, you will have no trouble wearing a lei through agricultural inspection and onto the plane home, though the flowers quickly turn brown in air conditioning. Many shops will package leis for your return trip, so they stay fresh to cheer your first cup of morning coffee back home!

Contact *Hawaii Tropical Flower & Foliage Association* for a free color brochure of Kauai's exotic flowers. PO Box 1067, Lawai HI 96765.

Photographing Kauai

* **Shoot in early morning or late afternoon.** Strong sunlight can wash out colors and shadow your subjects' faces! Choose early morning (before 10:00) or late afternoon (after 4:00), when the light is low. Light is best if it comes from the side rather than over the photographer's shoulder.

* **Vary your composition.** For a 3-D effect, combine something in the foreground, like a palm tree, with the middle-ground and background. Try vertical shots, great for people and flowers; a vertical composition of sky, ocean, surf and sand can look like a "slice of Kauai."

* **Watch out for horizons!** They should be level, not tilting. The sea will look like it is "dumping water" to the right or left, if it's not straight! Placing the horizon across the middle of the picture cuts it in half. A higher horizon emphasizes the foreground; a lower one is a better "sky shot" for great sunsets or cloud scenes. Experiment starting with the horizon down in the lower third; then in the upper third.

* **Use ISO 200 film.** The improved faster films will allow you faster shutter speeds and sharper images. For action shots, consider ISO 400 film. A polarizing filter can enhance color and really improve the appearance of clouds, the ocean, and the surf break. Make sure you have a cap or

at least a filter on your lens, as well as a zipper case, when you are travel to the beach. Sand and salt can be disastrous!

* **Move in close for people pictures.** Fill the frame with your subject. If you are trying to show your companion as well as the location, place the person to one side, the location to the other. Watch out for palm trees that may appear to be growing out of the subject's head, and avoid noonday sun.

* **Great spots for great shots:** sunsets & rainbows from the terrace at Princeville Hotel, Na Pali cliffs from Ke'e Beach (or first mile of Kalalau trail), Maha'ulepu Beach, windsurfers at Anini Beach, plumeria grove at Kukuiolono Park, surfers at Shipwreck Beach.

Shopping

NORTH SHORE. In KILAUEA, *Kong Lung* offers a striking collection of works by local artists, as well as antiques, souvenirs, beautiful gourmet cookware and tableware, and Hawaiian style shirts and dresses, including a special section of toys for children. The owners have faithfully restored the old plantation store building, constructed of lava rock, and filled it with marvelous giftware, including Hawaiian jewelry. Browsing is a treat!

In HANALEI village, you'll find a collection of wonderful shops in the growing "downtown." Don't miss the *Evolve Love Gallery* in Ching Young Village for a wonderful collection of jewelry, clothes, and Hawaiian artifacts, as well as exhibits of works by the best of Kauai's artists. Across the street in the Hanalei Center, visit *Yellowfish Trading Company* for a fanciful collection of Hawaiian antiques, jewelry and decorative items, and original art. *Rainbow Ducks* has an outstanding array of clothes and toys for the short set.

EASTERN SHORE.

At KILOHANA about a mile west of Kukui Grove on Rt. 50, you can visit a historic sugar plantation homestead and browse shops from the elegant to the cute. At *Kahn Galleries*, you'll find works by the most respected Hawaiian artists. *The Country Store* and *Hawaiian Collection Room* feature wonderful collections of island crafts and jewelry. *Sea Reflections* showcases beautiful glass, marine and nautical gifts, while *Dolls & Furrie Little Critters* will amuse the child in everyone.

In LIHUE, *Kukui Grove*, Kauai's most modern shopping center, includes major department stores like *Liberty House* and *Sears,* as well as a host of specialty shops including the *Kauai Products Store, Indo-Pacific Trading Company* and *Longie's Crack Seed* snack shop, where you'll find close to one hundred jars of sweet and sour treats, like shredded mango, dried plum, or Mike's favorite "Honey Lemon." Adjacent is an enormous *K-Mart. Borders Books & Music* is a sumptuous place to browse Kauai's largest selection of books, tapes and CD's, and now has an Espresso cafe offering excellent 'food for the body'—as well as the mind!

Anchor Cove in Nawiliwili, near the Marriott, has a *Wyland Gallery*; collectibles in *Amber Door*, as well as *Crazy Shirts* and *Sophisticated You.*

The once sleepy town of KAPA'A has grown into a trendy shopping area. *Tin Can Mailman* has a wide selection of books, botanical prints, as well as one of the largest collections of oceanographic works. *Earth Beads* offers an eclectic collection of jewelry from the inexpensive production centers of the world. *Island Hemp & Cotton* has wonderful clothes.

Near KAPA'A stop at the *Coconut Plantation Marketplace*, where you can find a shop specializing in Russian Treasures, the lacquer boxes and the dolls-within-dolls called Matryushkas. At *Gecko Store,* geckos appear in shirts, jewelry, pens and pencils, stickers, glasses, cups, even hats! At *Kauai Magic* you can select magic tricks for magicians of any level, and for kites, stop in at *Kyle Vision Kites.* *Ye Olde Ship's Store* displays scrimshaw, and the *Indo European Trading Company* has a wonderful collection of clothes, furniture, scents, chimes, and boxes. *Plantation Stitchery* will solve all your crafts and fabric needs. *Nutcracker Sweet* and *Island Surf Shop* have wonderful souvenir selections and friendly service!

Kauai Village in WAILUA has a variety of clothing and souvenir shops, a large aquarium at *Wyland Galleries.* *Waldenbooks* is a friendly spot for browsing. Ask about the frequent reader card!

SOUTH & WEST SIDE.

HANAPEPE, Kauai's 'biggest little town' has developed a cluster of specialty shops. *Kauai Fine Arts Gallery* offers a wonderful collection of antique maps and prints, with a particularly fine selection of nautical and Pacific themes. Next door, the *Hanapepe Bookstore & Espresso Cafe* is a great place for a mid-afternoon pick-me-up on a rainy day. For a snack, try *Taro Ka* chips factory. You can watch them being made and taste a sample (or two, or three...) At *Annie's Antiques*, we found an authentic set of vintage jacks, better balanced than the new stuff! Next door, at *AM Monty's*, browse the marvelous collection of art, crafts, beautiful glassware and jewelry. Down the street *Uncle Eddie's Angels* is a must stop for angellovers!— or for anyone who appreciates the celestial in crafts. His 'aloha angels' are handcrafted in Hanapepe and sell as fast as they fly in! (800-538-6514. Stop in at *Mariko's*, an island style 'department store' with clothing, jewelry and gifts at reasonable prices. Visit *Lawai General Store* in Lawai for a glimpse of convenience shopping before Seven-Eleven! *Poipu Shopping Village* near Kiahuna has galleries, including *Ships Store Gallery*, clothing stores, collectibles, as well as Whaler'*s General Store*.

Jewelry

Līhue. Stop in at *Kauai Products Store* in Kukui Grove for original jewelry by Kauai artists, and also *Zales Jewelers*, one of the oldest jewelers on Kauai. *Roberts* on Kress Street advertises the largest selection of Hawaiian heirloom jewelry on the island. *East West Imports Wholesale Jewelry and Hobby Beads* near the junction of Rt. 56 and Rt. 50 in Lihue sells inexpensive souvenir type shell jewelry as well as findings. *Sea Reflections* in Kilohana has jewelry in all price ranges.

Kapa'a. *The Goldsmith's Gallery* in the Kinipopo Shopping Village is a must stop! You'll find original designs crafted of gold, silver, and precious gems by award-winning artists. Ask Eric Vogt or the other designers to show you photographs of their designs, or to devise something special just for you, like a gold charm in the shape of a petroglyph or one of those cute butterfly fish you saw on the reef while snorkeling. Jock's seashell designs are also lovely, and prices are reasonable. On Rt. 56 in Kapa'a, *Jim Saylor* specializes in jewelry designs with precious stones. Lovely rings, necklaces, and bracelets are on display, although Jim will also be happy to create something unique according to your specifications. For ready made jewelry, *The Jewelry Box* in Kilohana as well as the Coconut Plantation Marketplace, features many one-of-a-kind designs in gold, silver, and pearls, including black pearls from Tahiti. Find less expensive prices at *Kauai Pearls* and *Kauai Gold* in the Coconut Plantation Marketplace.

South shore. Stop in at *Hula Moon* in Koloa for jewelry and other crafts by Kauai artists, and in Hanapepe, try *Mariko's*. Cheapest prices (and quality) can be found at the daily outdoor souvenir market at Spouting Horn, or at the *Hawaiian Trading Post* at the junction of Rt. 50 and Rt. 530 near Koloa. And of course, there's always WalMart and K-Mart. . .

Apparel

Lihue. Be sure to stop at *The Kapaia Stitchery* just north of Lihue on Rt. 56 (Don't take the bypass road, or you'll miss it!). Julie Yukimura has collected a tasteful array of women's clothes at very reasonable prices. Many items are handcrafted by island seamstresses who still make quilts and dresses with the same care their own grandmothers did. Beautiful vests, shawls, and dresses are priced well below what work of this quality sells for on the mainland. One woman in her '80's designs and stitches patchwork quilts, one featuring Japanese doll figures in different costumes, a great gift for a new baby. Men's 'Aloha shirts' made by Julie's seamstresses sell for less than mass-produced shirts in many stores, or you can custom order one from Julie's selection of 100% cotton fabrics in Hawaiian designs. *Hilo Hattie*, at the corner of Kuhio Highway and Ahukini Road in Lihue, is a great spot to stop for aloha wear, souvenirs, and hats at factory-direct prices with the friendliest of service.

KAPA'A. *Crazy Shirts*, Coconut Plantation Marketplace (also in Koloa and Anchor Cove) has great designs which resist fading and shrinking. Wash them inside out. One of our favorite family stops is *M. Miura Store* in Kapa'a, an old-time local business where you can pick out souvenir T-

shirts from a huge assortment at affordable prices, plus shorts, beachwear, mu mus and aloha shirts, and even boogie boards! Service is very friendly and the store uncrowded. At *Tropical Tantrum* in Kapa'a, you'll find an attractive assortment of colorful and comfortable women's clothes imported from all the islands, as well as interesting jewelry and artwork. *Bleu Papaya* displays original handpainted clothing designs, as does an interesting little shop with the unusual name, *Bo Ku Ma Rue*. A hardworking Kauai family has built the *Happy Kauaian Shops* from one store to more than a dozen branches in island hotels as well as the Coconut Plantation Marketplace, with reason-able prices for Hawaiian-style clothing and gifts, and particularly nice children's clothes.

HANALEI. *Tropical Tantrum* (also in Kapa'a) showcases island-style clothing, some featuring the Kauaian batik designs of artist Trish Stein-hauer; in *Hanalei Surf Company* you'll find wonderful beachwear.

PRINCEVILLE. Be sure to stop in at *Sandudes* for beachwear and at *Pretty Woman* for sophisticated clothes and jewelry.

WESTSIDE. *High Tide T-shirt Factory* in Port Allen, near Hanapepe has unique designs, and *Mariko's* has an enormous selection. *Barbie & Ken's Hawaiian Wear* factory warehouse store in Kekaha (823-6053) has a large selection of 100 % cotton apparel for everyone in the family. Free tailor-ing. The newest tourist craze, *Red Dirt Shirts* by Paradise Clothing has a factory outlet in Kalaheo, with the promo that the red dirt confers good fortune and good health! Just be sure you get the real red dirt and not some muddy imitation !

Galleries

In KILAUEA, *Kong Lung* is a *must* stop for beautifully displayed works by island artists. In Hanalei, at *Ola's* Doug and Sharon Britt present an eclectic collection of handcrafted puzzles, glass, jewelry, wooden bowls, baskets, and furniture, each piece almost a collage of extraordinary and interesting bits and pieces. In Hanalei, island artists exhibit at *Evolve Love Gallery* and *Yellowfish Tuna Company*. *Mark Daniels* will talk with you about his work in his studio-store.

At KILOHANA, the *Kilohana Galleries* features work by Hawaiian artisans working in wood, glass, ceramics, and papers, as well as work by Kauai's artists— beautiful batiks, porcelains, jewelry, handpainted silk scarves, needlework, original oils, watercolors, and drawings. Look for fabric art, beautiful collages, and interpretations of Hawaiian quilt designs by Jule Patten. Browse *The Hawaiian Collection Room* for Ni'ihau shell leis, Hawaiian coins scrimshaw, and artifacts. In Lihue, the *Kauai Museum* has a wonderful shop for books, maps, as well as some crafts and memorabilia, including Ron Kent's fine, almost translucent wood bowls. You won't have to pay the museum entrance fee to visit the gift shop. In Koloa's *Kauai Fine Arts*, (also in Hanapepe), you'll find maps, engravings, and books, with particular focus on the exploration of Hawaii by French, Russian, English and American explorers.

In KAPA'A, *Far-Fetched Designs* and *Treasures of Kuan Yin* feature works by Kauai's artists. *Kela's Gallery* displays beautiful contemporary glass art by more than 35 Hawaiian and international artists. In Coconut Plantation Marketplace and Poipu Shopping Village, browse through *Ship Store Gallery* for a superb collection of art and antiques, including sea life paintings by Robert Lyn Nelson, works of maritime history by Ray Massey, and striking baskets woven by Kauai artist Stephanie Campos Arthur. A favorite with our children, *Wyland Galleries* in Kauai Village has friendly staff and a fascinating collection of marine life paintings. Kids love watching the tropical fish and spotted eel in the 2,300 gallon aquarium. *Kahn Galleries* at the Kauai Village and Coconut Plantation Marketplace, as well as Kilohana and Koloa, features paintings by noted island and mainland artists, including Roy Tabora's dramatic seascapes, George Sumner's environmental paintings, as well as Barbara Murdoch's luminous paintings of Kauai. In Kapa'a's Hee Fat Building, *Montage Galleries* presents original art by Kauai artists.

Further west, in HANAPEPE, *Giorgio's Gallery* is marked by the vintage car painted in flaming colors, and *AM Monty* exhibits her paintings in a gallery cum souvenir shop with espresso bar in front. *Andy Lopez* captures Kauai's disappearing rural buildings and scenes.

Artists' Open Studios

Please phone for appointment.

Carol Bennett & Wayne Zebda
742-9415, Lawai
painting, commissions
iron works, sculpture

Sharon & Doug Britt
828-1289
PO 175, Hanalei 96714
furniture, photos, painting
American self taught & outsider art

A. Kimberlin Blackburn
822-9304
PO 181, Kapa'a HI 96746
paintings, mixed media sculpture
Ocean, mountains, spirits,
bright colors & patterns

John Davison
PO 959, Kapa'a 96746
island inspired landscape painting,
graphics, T-shirts

Lillian de Mello
823-8962
PO 1679, Kapa'a 96746
nature & fine arts photography

Margaret Ezekiel
742-7933
PO Box 2290, Puhi, HI 96766
painting, pastel
evocative days, enigmatic nights

Sally French
822-5489
PO Box 1347, Kapa'a HI 96746
painting, cards, prints

Robert Hamada
822-3229, Wailua
Hawaiian woods, bowls

Jean K. Inaba
332-8285
Po 697, Kalaheo HI 96741
painting, prints

Paul Kosberg
823-8508, Kapa'a
glass, sculpture, jewelry,
art workshops

Kenne Brittain Mahoney
822-9399, Kapahi
mixed media works

Kathy McClelland-Cowan
822-5760
PO 627, Kapa'a HI 96746
glass & jewelry

Barbara Murdoch
828-6665
PO Box 686, Kilauea HI 96754
oils on canvas, visions of Kauai

Ray Nitta
337-1875
PO 875, Waimea HI 96796
wood, furniture, jewelry boxes

Kathleen Rimko
822-0251
PO 1645, Kapa'a HI 96746
photography, prints, cards

Gary Slatter
337-9337
PO 400 Kekaha, HI 96752
watercolors, pastels
realistic & interpretive

Family Fun

Our favorite family beaches, with something for everyone, are Kalihiwai (page 35) and Anini Beach (page 36) on the north shore, and Poipu Beach Park (page 48) and Salt Pond Beach Park (page 49) on the south shore. On the eastern shore, the best family beaches are Kalapaki Beach (page 23) and Lydgate Park (page 25) where you can snorkel safely and see whole families of very tame, colorful fish who live in Lydgate's unique, man-made ocean pool enclosed with lava rocks. At Lydgate Park you'll also find the best playground on Kauai—*Kamalina Park*—16,000 square feet of funland with a volcano theme, with mirror mazes, a suspension bridge, lava tubes and circular slide.

Other fun spots: *Fernandez Fun Factory* (in Wailua next to Foodland) is video game heaven. In Kukui Grove, *Wally World* offers miniature golf, a video arcade, and "splash & bash," a motorized bumperboat ride (245-5252). For rainy days, rent a VCR and some movies!

Kids will love the free hula shows sponsored at the major shopping centers. Coconut Plantation Marketplace (4: 30 pm M,W,F, Sat). Check times with Poipu Shopping Village (742-2831) and Kiahuna (742-6411).

With a plastic pail and an inexpensive net ($6 for an 8" net at Long's), children can also have lots of fun trying to catch fish trapped in tidal pools. Net fishing is fun at the rivers behind the beaches at Anahola, Kalihiwai, and Moloa'a, and at the tidal pools at Salt Pond Beach Park and Poipu

Beach Park. If children collect shells and sand during visits to the beach, they can have fun with art projects on rainy days back home. Sand can be sprinkled over glue in all sorts of designs for "sand paintings." Kids will also enjoy gluing small shells to small boxes, large shells or pieces of driftwood to give as gifts.

Kids will also like to try Hawaiian treats, like Mike's favorite, 'Honey Lemon' which he buys at *Longie's* in Kukui Grove. Try the *Wishing Well* in Hanalei, with the smoothest shave ice and lots of flavors (including root beer!). *Mustard's Last Stand* in Lawai offers hot dogs garnished with miniature golf!

Kauai Children's Discovery Museum offers changing exhibits that can be great fun on a rainy day. Call 823-8222 for information.

Great children's books: *Hawaii is a Rainbow* (beautiful photographs); *Peter Panini and the Search for the Menehune; Pua Pua Lena Lena*; Keiki's First Books board books. Look for them at *Borders*, where kids can enjoy *Keiki Story Time* on Saturday mornings at 11 am and on first and third Tuesdays (246-0862).

For cribs and other child equipment rentals, call *Baby's Away* (800-571-0077). To arrange family tours and activities, call *Family Vacation Helpers* (808-246-0745) or *Chris the Fun Lady* (808-822-7447).

The major resort hotels (Hyatt Regency, Marriott, Princeville Hotel, Kiahuna) all offer daycamps for children of guests (about $40 per day).

Special Mornings with Daddy

During our summer vacations, each of our four children plans a "Special Morning with Daddy," a wonderfully private adventure including dining, shopping, beaching and swimming. When they were small, they chose the same destination— the old Kauai Surf Hotel, which had ducks and a fish pond and a wonderful meandering swimming pool. Then the Surf closed. And while the new hotel was being built in its place, the children were growing older and beginning to look for wider horizons beckoning different interests. At first, this independence was risky business: what if one child could claim to have had a morning more special than anyone else's? Now they enjoy leading Daddy in different directions.

Jeremy still likes breakfast at Kountry Kitchen in Kapa'a, where he can feast on 'Cheesy Eggs'– poached eggs with bacon on toasted english muffins, topped with lots of melted cheese sauce. There's a nod to tradition here: he's loved this dish since he was 4! After breakfast, it's off to shop at the M. Muira store in Kapa'a. Afterwards, they head for Kalihiwai, where, if the surf is right, the wonderful, long rollers give spectacular boogie board rides. Dad sits in his chair and reads his book while Jeremy glides along the waves with local kids. Lauren at 13 still prefers Poipu. That's fortunate, for Daddy has always liked the south shore, and he particularly likes the luxurious Hyatt Regency. The long line for Ilima Terrace sends them to the golf club restaurant, Poipu Bay Grill & Bar, for excellent food without crowds. After breakfast, it's off to Poipu Beach Park. Thank heavens Lauren still knows how wonderful it is to jump the waves with Daddy!

At 16, Mike prefers the breakfast buffet at the spectacular Princeville Hotel, and then he and Daddy head for Hanalei Bay, where they can enjoy a catch and a long walk around the bay. Our oldest, Mirah , likes vegetarian meals, and so she prefers lunch or even better, dinner! Her favorite– the vegetable stir fry that Jean Marie can create upon request at A Pacific Cafe.

Special Mornings With Daddy. When we first conceived the idea, we thought of how important they would be for each child in a crowded family. Now we're wiser– we know who the mornings are *really* for!

Some Useful Hawaiian Words

aloha – *(a LOW ha) hello, good-bye, love, kindness, friendship*
hale – *(HAH lee) house*
haole – *(HOW lee) foreigner white man*
heiau – *(HEY ow) ancient Hawaiian temple*
hui– *(HOO' ee) club or group*
kahuna– *(ka HOO na) an elder, wise person*
kalua– *(ka LOO a) to roast underground*
kai – *the sea*
kama'aina – *(ka ma EYE na) a native*
kane – *(KA neh) man*
kapu – *(KA poo) forbidden, keep out*
keiki – *(KAY kee) child*
kona– *(KOH na) leeward side of the island*

lani – *(LAH nee) heavens, sky*
lomilomi – *(low me low me) massage*
mahalo – *(ma HA lo) thank you*
makai – *(ma KAI) ocean side*
mauka– *(MOW ka) towards the mountains*
menehune– *Kauai's legendary little people'' & builders*
nani – *(NA nee) beautiful*
ohana – *(o HA na) family*
'ono– *delicious*
pali – *(PA lee) cliff, precipice*
paniolo – *(pa nee O lo) cowboy*
pau– *(pow) finished, done*
puka – *(POO ka) hole*
wahine – *(wa HEE neh) woman, wife*
wikiwiki – *hurry up*

Adventures

Helicoptering Kauai

Many of the most beautiful places on Kauai are inaccessible by car. For this reason, a helicopter tour is an unforgettable way to see this spectacular island. Kauai is breathtakingly beautiful from the air, almost like an America in miniature, with rolling hills and valleys on the eastern shore and majestic mountains on the west. The island has a flat, dry southland as well as a forested wilderness to the north, and, on the west coast, wide sandy beaches where the setting sun paints the sky with gold before slipping silently into the enormous sea. There is even a "Grand Canyon" on a small scale, where pink and purple cliffs, etched by centuries of wind and rain into giant towers, seem like remnants of a lost civilization. So much variety is amazing on an island only 30 miles in diameter!

And what you'll see is beyond your fantasies—a mountain goat poised for an instant in a ravine, a white bird gliding against the dark green cliffs, a sudden rainbow in the mist, incredible, tower-like mountains of pink and brown in the Waimea "Grand Canyon," a glistening waterfall hanging like a slender silver ribbon through trees and rocks, a curve of pure white sand at the base of the purple and gold Na Pali cliffs, a spray of shining white foam bursting upon the rocky coast. Then, like the unveiling of the island's final mystery, the entrance into the very center of Mt. Waialeale's crater, where in the dimly lit mists of the rainiest place on the earth, waterfalls are born from ever falling showers. You have journeyed to the very heart of the island, the place of its own birth from the volcano's eruption centuries ago. From your hotel room, you would never have believed that all this splendor existed, and your only regret will be that you didn't take more film!

It's so special, you yearn to go up again. Even the second time, the tour is exhilarating. In fact, with a better sense of the island's geography, you are more sensitive to details too easily missed when you are overcome by the majesty of the scene

A 'whirly-birds' eye view of the Na Pali coast

for the first time. You may see some of the amazing irrigation canals and tunnels carved into the mountains a century ago to bring water to the sugar cane fields below. Or, on some remote and sheer escarpment along the Na Pali coast, a terrace where taro was once cultivated by the ancient Hawaiians. When gilded by the sun, these knife-like green ridges look like 'the skirts of Pele,' Hawaiian goddess of the volcano's fire.

Of the many companies offering tours, Jack Harter Helicopters stands out as special. Jack Harter is the most experienced pilot around, having offered the first air tour on Kauai more than 30 years ago. A local legend, he is often called upon for help in emergencies, and he himself has had an accident-free record on Kauai since 1962. His flights are about an hour and a half, the best value for your money, and his pace is slow enough to offer a good look at the island's remote terrain. As he pilots his Bell Jet Ranger with skill and finesse, as smoothly as a dandelion seed in almost any weather, he makes sure that each passenger with a camera has a chance at the 'great shots' which can happen at almost every moment.

Jack's enormous knowledge is enough to make his tour memorable. Throughout the flight, he talks non-stop about the island he clearly loves, telling its legends and history, describing its plants and animals, reflecting on its politics and problems, and arguing the need for conservation and planned development. Helicopters seem to be more than just a business to him, and several Division of Forestry botanists doing research in a remote rainforest, or telephone workers repairing cables on an isolated mountain top, have told stories of receiving a miraculous "drop" of pizza, pot roast, and beer from a helicopter appearing out of nowhere!

Because of the expense of the tour, we worried about picking the "perfect day." We began on what seemed in Lihue to be only a partly sunny day, but once in the air, we realized that the clouds would be above us rather than in our way and even enhanced the island's beauty with changing patterns of light. If the weather is too poor for a satisfying flight, Jack's policy is to cancel the trip. Even if you have already set out and he decides it is wiser to return, he will refund your money.

In choosing your tour operator, we recommend interviewing several companies by asking specific questions (see 'Helicopter Tours & Safety' below). Over the years, Jack Harter Helicopters (808-245-3774) and Will Squyres Helicopters (808-245-7541) have earned wide respect for their owners' good judgment and meticulous maintenance. Jack Harter or Will Squyres may not be available at the time you want to fly, but their companies offer daily scheduled scenic flights with pilots they directly supervise, with Jack's company featuring the 1.5 hour tour he originated as well the standard hour-long flight. If you want to fly with Jack Harter himself, you might inquire about arranging a special four-person charter.

Looking at our slides and videos back home almost brings back the magic of that hour, when we seemed suspended in a horizon so vast as to seem limitless, and any effort to confine it within camera range was impossible. It is always the best day of the trip!

Helicopter Tours & Safety

Helicopter tours are big business, with intense competition for tourist dollars. Many people on Kauai feel that there is a wide variation in quality and safety, however. We have heard disquieting reports: some companies speed up tours in order to cut costs and squeeze as many tours into the day as possible. Some are plagued with high turnover in pilots who may have sufficient flying hours to be licensed but limited experience over Kauai's unique wilderness terrain. With pilots from a dozen companies crowding the skies, safety is becoming an increasingly important issue. In 1994, two accidents involving fatalities occurred on Kauai, and the companies involved in these incidents, Papillon Hawaiian Helicopters and Inter-Island Helicopters, no longer offer air tours on Kauai. The Papillon accident involved the ASTAR 350, a larger capacity touring helicopter seating six passengers and a pilot. In 1994, two other accidents in Hawaii involving the ASTAR helicopter resulted in fatalities.

As a result of these and other helicopter accidents, in which 24 persons were killed in the state of Hawaii between 1991 and 1994, the Federal Aviation Administration (FAA) issued sweeping new 'Special Federal Aviation Regulations' (SFARs) in October, 1994. These include protocols for extensive and detailed safety briefings for passengers, and a requirement for single-engine helicopters to carry emergency flotation devices. The most controversial rule is the 'standoff requirement' prohibiting flights closer than 1,500 feet to the ground or water, except during takeoff and landing. This means that helicopters must fly higher and farther away from the cliffs, craters and valleys that passengers most want to see.

This rule has caused enormous controversy. To many pilots, this rule prevents them from showing passengers the special wonders of Hawaii, whose unique mountainous terrain, trade winds, and special cloud layer conditions often make it impossible to fly 1500 feet above the cliffs and valleys, and at the same time observe the FAA required safe distance (500 feet) below the cloud layer. On certain days, these two requirements may force pilots to avoid the interior mountain wilderness—and its spectacular views—altogether, and fly out along the coastline instead. The increased noise in these residential coastal areas has angered many residents and caused local government officials to protest, and the National Transportation Safety Board has also asked the FAA to consider whether this standoff requirement will lead to increased air traffic congestion at certain altitudes.

The FAA has responded to the controversy by granting individual companies an exemption to the stand-off requirement, reducing it from 1500 feet to 500 feet. Be sure to inquire when you call a company for information, and also ask what the company's policy is on days when low hanging clouds make flying over the island's interior mountains impossible. If you're going to be limited to a flight around the island's perimeter, you might want to have the right to cancel your reservation.

These are some key questions to ask when you are interviewing companies. First, find out whether the company is operating under a certificate issued by the FAA under Part 135 of Federal Aviation Regulations. In order to maintain a certificate of this type, the company must follow a more rigorous (thus more expensive) maintenance program, and its pilots must pass annual flight tests not required of companies operating under Part 91 of Federal Aviation Regulations. This certificate must be displayed in the company's office. Ask to see it! To verify or ask questions, call the FAA in Honolulu at (808) 836-0615. The distinction between Part 91 and Part 135 operators can tell you about the standards a company operates under, although this information is no guarantee of performance!

Beware of the advertisements—they can be very misleading. An ad which hypes the number of flying hours logged by the company's owner tells you nothing about the flying experience of his pilot employees. Ask who *your* pilot will be. Not every pilot employee who qualifies for a helicopter license has had extensive experience with Kauai's wilderness terrain. You also have a right to know whether the company, or *your* pilot has been involved in any accidents during the past three years. Beware of companies which are reluctant to provide specific answers, or say they "can't be sure" who will be piloting your flight, and don't take at face value advertisements which claim that the owner is the "operator." Any owner can "operate" his company without being the pilot for every flight. That may be true of some flights—from one a day to one a month—but very possibly not true of your flight! You should also ask if the company's FAA certificate has ever been revoked or suspended, and whether it is currently under FAA investigation for accidents or maintenance deficiencies, as opposed to record-keeping, violations. Since each helicopter must display its individual 'certificate of airworthiness,' look for it or ask to see it.

Another important question to ask is the exact length of the tour. Actual in-flight time for the around-the-island tour should be no less than 60 minutes, or Kauai will appear to whiz past your window! Even a 60-minute tour limits your opportunities to explore the more remote terrain inside the island's perimeter, or to take satisfying photographs. Doublecheck by asking for the daily flight schedule, subtract 5 minutes for landing and changing passengers, and draw your own conclusions! This is one area, in our opinion, where economy is not always the best policy. Given the high operating cost of the air tour business, cheaper tours will almost certainly be short, possibly too short, and the extra dollars you spend for a longer tour will be well worthwhile.

Also consider the type of aircraft you will be flying. We prefer the Bell Jet-Ranger, which seats one passenger in front and three in back. In some Bells, the rear windows can be opened for fresh air, which prevents fogging and helps photographing. Most fun is the co-pilot's seat, where you can look down as well as out the window. The Hughes 500-D helicopter seats two passengers in the rear and two in front next to the pilot. Like a large glass bubble, however, it has no windows to open. The ASTAR helicopter is like a tour bus seating 6 passengers—2 next to the pilot in front and 4 in the rear. For passengers in the center rear seats, the view is obstructed by the passengers seated next to the windows as well as those in front. If you are assigned those center rear seats, you will have a harder time seeing or taking photographs, so ask before you commit! Ask about the cancellation

policy in case of bad weather. Even in a rainstorm, we often see the choppers flying! Find out whether you can get your money back if you're not very comfortable — or if you can't see very much — once you're in the air!

We consider helicopter tours a unique and special way to see Kauai. We wouldn't go ourselves, or let our children fly, if we thought they were unsafe. But we make careful decisions about the pilots we fly with. We think you should do your homework carefully and have all pertinent information when making your choices as well!

Na Pali's amazing jagged escarpments.

Boat Tours

The spectacular cliffs of the Na Pali coast are off limits to most visitors—unless they dare to hike on narrow and slippery trails or explore these steep and jagged ridges from a helicopter. Coastal boat tours are an increasingly popular way to see at least some of these amazing cliffs up close. In fact, on a clear summer's day, Hanalei Bay is busy with an assortment of large and small launches, catamarans, and inflatable 'zodiacs' loaded with tourists either on their way out or coming back in!

At about half the price of a helicopter tour, boat tours are a more affordable alternative and, to some people, a lot more fun. Boats offer rough and ready adventure, particularly the zodiacs originally made popular for white water river rafting. In a calm ocean, the zodiacs can carry passengers right up to touching distance of the incredible cliffs, so close you can see water from mountain springs trickle through the rocky ridges and drop in shining ribbons to the sea. You can trace the patterns made over centuries by mineral deposits, or chronicle the island's history in lines of lava. You can explore caves etched into the cliffs, watch waterfalls sparkle in the sunshine, and marvel at how tenaciously plants and trees can cling to inhospitable rock. Dolphins may leap in arcs around you, so friendly they seem to be seeking companions in these strange looking black boats decked with brightly colored tourists.

Spectacular and romantic, boat tours are also big business. About a dozen companies are licensed on Kauai, offering half and full-day tours costing upwards of $65 per person. Because these companies compete so aggressively, many people on Kauai worry about safety: some companies run tours in marginal weather; others cram their boats to the maximum.

As a general rule, Na Pali coast tours are the safest from May until October when the ocean is usually flat off the Na Pali coast. But the weather becomes much more unpredictable after winter storms begin in late October. Because winter surf can reach twenty feet in Hanalei Bay, sailboats and small craft are actually moved out of Hanalei to more pro-tected Nawiliwili harbor on the island's southeastern leeward shore. At this time of year, companies offer 'whale watching' excursions from Nawiliwili, or visits to beautiful sosuth shore beaches like Kipu Kai or Lawai Kai.

Even after the small craft leave Hanalei for the winter, however, some companies still offer Na Pali coast boat tours. And although the companies will assure you that they run Na Pali tours only in safe weather, part of what makes the north shore so dangerous in winter is the unpredictability of the winds and the ocean swell. Winds can shift in twenty minutes, and so predicting surf conditions for up to six hours ahead can be risky business!

Even on the best of summer days, the trip out along the Na Pali coast is a lot smoother than the return trip, when you ride into the wind and the water is more choppy. If the captain tells you the trip will be "wet and wild," he means the boat will be rolling up and down the swells, smacking into them with bursts of spray, definitely not a good idea for someone with a bad back! The return trip has been described as "riding the bull," and some adventurers even choose to sit astride the boat's inflated sides, although dangling legs are fair game for any Portuguese men o' war who happen to be floating by.

Because winter weather can be so chancy, you should pay careful attention to the company's cancellation policy. Many companies will charge you between 20% and 50% of the tour price if you cancel less than 24 hours in advance, and the company can collect this cancellation charge because the reservationist will probably take your credit card imprint as a way of confirming your reservation when you make it. Be forewarned: this policy leaves you little option if you don't feel comfortable with the look of the sky or the ocean on the morning of your tour. You may end up being charged if the company decides to send out the boats, even if your own assessment of the weather has made you decide not to be on board!

Zodiac Tours

Captain Zodiac	826-7197	Na Pali Explorer	335-9909

Power Catamaran Tours

Hanalei Sport Fishing	826-6114	Whitey's Cruises	826-6853
Na Pali Eco-Adventures	826-6804	Hanalei Sea Tours	826-7254

Sailing Yacht Tours

Blue Water Sailing	822-0525	Captain Andy's	822-7833
Catamaran Kahanu	826-4596	Blue Dolphin	246-4482

Kayak Tours

Outfitters Kauai	742-9667	Pedal & Paddle	826-9609
Kayak Kauai Outfitters		826-9844	

Boat traffic is another safety problem. You can see the results at Tunnels Beach, for example, long a favorite spot for north shore snorkeling. Because it's also the departure point for Captain Zodiac boat tours, you have to watch out for the boats as well as the fish when you're in the water! Boats and people have to share the only sandy channel out into the reef, and sometimes boat personnel can be overzealous in trying to keep swimmers out of the channel when boats are coming in or going out. Just

Na Pali coast

remember: people, not boats, have the right of way!

Most Na Pali coast boat tours leave from Hanalei Bay, where a debate still rages concerning the environmental impact of the boat tour industry on the Hanalei River. Some tour operators now originate from the south shore or the westside, touring the Na Pali coast from the opposite direction.

The Na Pali coastline is spectacular from the sea. You and the porpoises share the same view of the craggy rock formations, the caves etched into sheer cliff, and the magnificent colors of sea and sky in the changing light of sun and shadow. If you ride into the caves, you plunge into a cold, wet world where the water sloshes eerily against the rocks, making you grateful to return to sunlight again. In one cave, the sunlight streams in through a giant hole in the ceiling, and a waterfall plunges in shining streams of sparkling drops.

You'll see an enormous change in the landscape, from the dark, rich green of Ke'e Beach, where rainfall measures nearly 125 inches a year, to the reds and browns of Polihale on the westernmost end of the cliffs, where it measures only 20 inches.

Most tours include a stop for snorkeling and snacking, usually at Nu'alolo Kai, a calm spot with a protective reef where you can see hundreds of colorful fish. If you don't enjoy snorkeling, however, or if the weather is not cooperative, this stop can seem like a waste of time. If it's sunny, beware of a burn! Bring plenty of sunscreen, and perhaps a hat and sunglasses to protect against the glare.

Different craft will give you a different ride and a different experience of the coast. The zodiacs offer the wildest rides, especially on the trip back to Hanalei, when the boats head into the wind and current. In this direction, the ride is much more choppy, and you might bring towels and dry clothes in a plastic bag. As the boat slaps head on into the waves, the salt spray can douse everything in the boat, including you and your camera! If you prefer comfort to adventure, power cruisers are a good choice. *Liko Kauai Cruises* (338-0333) tours the Na Pali coast from south to north, departing from Kekaha on the westside, so that the return trip, when you are tired, is smoother. The comfortable, 26-person cabin cruiser is fully equipped, even with a toilet, and stocked with a lunch of salads, cold cuts, and cold drinks.

Power boats are more comfortable than the rubber zodiacs, but they cannot hug the cliffs like the zodiacs, and the larger ones can't go into the caves. A compromise may be the small power catamarans, which are agile enough to go into the larger caves, and yet able to cut through the swell rather than riding up and over it. The larger catamarans, like the popular *Catamaran Kahanu* (826-4596), provide greater comfort but less agility.

Before you choose your tour, call several companies. Inquire about the expected weather and surf conditions—and the company's cancellation policy. Check the weather report (245-6001). Ask about the number of passengers the company usually takes on board, keeping in mind that the more crowded the boat, the less comfortable you may be. Inquire about your captain's experience; although every captain has to be coast guard licensed, some have more experience than others! Look carefully at discount coupons. One company, for example, offered a coupon for a $30 discount off a list price of $90. However, the same tour averaged about $65 at activity centers around the island, and almost no one ever paid full price! For an overview of the options, you might consult a knowledgable activities agent, like *Chris the Fun Lady* (822-7447).

Kayaking

Exploring Kauai's rivers by kayak can be lots of fun, and several companies offer tours as well as equipment rental. *Chris the Fun Lady* (822-7447) helped Mike (age 16) and his friends organize a kayak trip up the Wailua River past Fern Grotto to a rope swing over the water. They also took a 45 minute hike to a nearby waterfall. Chris rents kayaks ($25/day/single and $45/day/double) for self-guided tours on most rivers, and includes a tarp to use as a sail (If the wind is right, you can 'sail' upriver), flotation cushions, map and complete instructions, even a cooler! Also call *Water Ski & Surf Company* (822-3574).

For river tours of the Wailua River and the area to the southeast, including the Hule'ia Stream (scene of *Raiders of the Lost Ark)* and Menehune Fish Pond and nearby wildlife refuge, contact *Paradise River Rentals* (245-9580). For the Hule'ia Stream, call *Island Adventures* (245-9662); for tours of the Wailua River, call *Waialeale Boat Tours* (822-4908).

Hanalei River tours are offered by *Luana of Hawaii* (826-9195), or rent a kayak and tour on your own. *Pedal & Paddle* rents kayaks, camping and snorkel equipment, even mopeds. Go early for the best selection!

Kayak Kauai Outfitters (800-437-3507 or 826-9844) offers tours and also rents 2-person and 1-person kayaks for a 2-hour minimum. From its riverside location, you can travel upriver, or venture downriver to Hanalei Bay. In summer months, when Hanalei Bay is calm, you may be able to paddle among the boats at anchor in the bay, or along the bay's edge and pull up on the Princeville Hotel's sandy beach. The views are spectacular! Everything in the kayak is in danger of getting wet, so take your camera in a waterproof bag. You might bring some drinks and snacks, and perhaps snorkeling equipment so that you can explore the reef. A 2-hour trip may be all you need (and all your muscles may be able to take!) You can also load your kayak on top of the car and drive it to the nearby boat pier at Hanalei Bay, or to Anini beach or Kalihiwai Bay about 10 minutes away. In winter months, when ocean surf and currents become too strong, your best options will be the Hanalei River or the Kalihiwai River, which you can explore up to some waterfalls.

Between May and mid-September, guided ocean kayak tours of the north shore and Na Pali can be spectacular, but you must be ready for a strenuous workout. *Kayak Kauai Outfitters* (800-437-3507 or 808-826-9844) starts its daylong kayak excursions at Ke'e Beach in Ha'ena and ends at Polihale State Beach on the westside. Traversing the 16 miles of rugged coastline takes about six hours of paddling — hard work even for the athletically advantaged! Occasional squalls and choppy water often punctuate the ride, but in your kayak you can explore sea caves, play with dolphins, and visit with turtles ($125/pp). When Na Pali waters become too rough, between October and April, the company offers guided whale-watching tours along the south shore. *Outfitters Kauai*, based in Poipu (808) 742-9667, offers guided kayak trips as well as bike tours of the mountains.

Remember the sun! A hat, sunscreen, and drinking water are a must! Bring a towel and spare shirt for an emergency cover up! If you paddle up river, don't drink the river water, and if you have an open cut you must be particularly cautious. The bacterium *leptospirosis* has been detected in all of Kauai's rivers, and can cause serious, even fatal, flu-like symptoms.

Museums and Historical Tours

The story of Kauai is in many ways the story of the sugar plantations which shaped the island's multi-ethnic culture as much as its agriculture and economy, For this reason, a visit to the *Grove Farm Homestead* in Lihue offers a fascinating glimpse into the island's past. One of the earliest Hawaiian sugar plantations, Grove Farm was founded in 1864 by George Wilcox, the son of Protestant missionary teachers at Waioli Mission in Hanalei. Planting and harvesting Grove Farm's sugar crop, which grew from 80 acres to more than 1000, ultimately involved a workforce of several hundred Hawaiians, Chinese, Koreans, Germans, Portuguese, and Filipino laborers, who brought to Kauai a rich heritage of ethnic cultures. A two-hour tour takes you through Grove Farm's cluster of buildings nestled amid tropical gardens, orchards, and rolling lawns, but be warned: the tour is extremely popular and you'll need to reserve a place at least a week in advance. You'll see the gracious old Wilcox home, the large rooms cooled by breezes from shaded verandas, and elegantly furnished with oriental carpets, magnificent koa wood floors and wainscotting, and hand crafted furniture of native woods. You will also tour the "board and batten" cottage of the plantation housekeeper, who came to Kauai, like many Japanese women, as a "picture bride" for a laborer too poor to travel home to select his wife in person. All buildings are covered by traditional "beach sand paint" (literally sand thrown against wet paint) to protect them against both heat and damp for as long as 20 years. The leisurely, friendly tour includes a stop in the kitchen for cookies and mint ice tea. For students and scholars, the library's extensive collection of Hawaiiana and plantation records is available by appointment. Grove Farm Tours are conducted

Man in gourd mask by John Weber, artist on Captain Cook's third voyage

Monday, Wednesday, and Thursday at 10 am and 1 pm. Reserve in advance (808-245-3202) or write to PO Box 1631, Lihue HI 96766.

Like other Hawaiian sugar plantations, Grove Farm was established at a significant point in the economic history of the islands. In the 1850's, the monarchy first began to sell land, and Hawaii entered the age of private property. Before this time, land was never sold but given in trust to subjects in pie shaped slices from the interior mountains to the sea, so that each landhold would include precious fresh water as well as coastline.

The Wilcox family, particularly two Wilcox women, made significant contributions to the development of Kauai. Elsie Wilcox, a Kauai School Commissioner, was the first woman in the territory to be elected to the State Senate, and Mabel Wilcox, a public health nurse, was decorated by both France and Belgium for outstanding service during World War I. Elsie and Mabel restored *Waioli Mission House* in Hanalei (open T, Th, and Sat 9 am-3 pm), and Mabel planned the *Grove Farm Homestead* in 1971 at age 89.

If the Grove Farm tour doesn't fit into your schedule, you can visit the *Kauai Museum* on Rice St. in downtown Lihue Monday-Friday 9:30 am to 4:30 pm. The Rice Building exhibits the *Story of Kauai*—the volcanic eruptions which shaped the land, the Polynesians who voyaged to the island in canoes and left behind marvelous petroglyphs, or rock pictures; the missionaries who altered its culture; and the sugar planters who, like George Wilcox, defined much of its agricultural destiny. To complement this permanent display, the monthly exhibits in the adjacent Wilcox building feature the work of local artists as well as the contributions of Kauai's different ethnic cultures. For example, one summer we saw an exhibit of Japanese, Chinese, Hawaiian, and Filipino wedding dress and traditions. Another time, we explored a marvelous retrospective on Filipinos in Kauai, from their arrival in 1906 as poorly paid laborers to present day achievements in education and social work. The Folk Arts Exhibition includes quilt and tapa making, lei making, and Hawaiian games and sports. The museum shop has an extensive collection of books and maps on Kauai and Hawaii, and several times a year sponsors a craft fair, where you can find shell jewelry, feather headbands and hatbands, koa carvings, and other local art forms. To visit the museum costs $3 for adults (If you don't finish touring by the end of the day, you can get a free pass for the next!). Gift shop is free. For information about exhibits and lectures: 808-245-6931.

Armchair travelers should request a catalog of books on Hawaiian history & natural history (including *Petroglyphs of Hawaii* by L. R. McBride, whose drawings are on pages 25, 79, & 203), as well as reprints of hard-to-find titles by Hawaiian authors, maps, cards & stamps. Contact Petroglyph Press, 201 Kinoole, Hilo HI 96720 (800-903-6277).

Natural History Tours

Halfway between Kapa'a and Princeville, be sure to visit the *Kilauea Lighthouse*, built in 1913, which once warned mariners away from Kauai's rugged north coast until technology replaced light flashes with radio transmissions. Come for spectacular views of the coastline and Mukuaeae island, and if you're lucky, a glimpse of Spinner Dolphins or Humpback Whales on summer vacation in the waves. This is the northernmost point of Kauai, indeed of all the Hawaiian islands, and changes in weather are often first detected by the weather station here. Best of all, you will see a tiny part of the *Hawaiian Island National Wildlife Refuge*, which shelters more than 10 million seabirds in a chain of islands scattered over 1200 miles of ocean–like the Red-footed Booby. You will hear the amazing story of how seamen carried 4 tons of French prisms up a sheer cliff to build the giant clam shaped light. Call 808-828-1413 for the latest schedule of hours. Closed weekends, federal holidays. Above the lighthouse, *Crater Hill* offers a panoramic view of the north shore, a great spot for a picnic! Sometimes the new road (You'll see the security gate on the right as you drive along Kilauea Rd. towards the lighthouse) is locked. For information about hiking tours of Crater Hill and advance reservations, call 828-1520. Map: 2

More of Kauai's rare birds and plants can be seen at the *Koke'e Natural History Museum* in Koke'e State Park. If you are interested in exploring the island's natural history, visit the museum daily between 10 am and 4 pm (808-335-9975). Donations welcome! You can also arrange bird watching tours in the Alakai Swamp near Koke'e with Terran Tours (808-335-3313). Map: 4. Curious about those bison you've seen grazing near the Hanalei River? Hanalei Institute for Environmental Agriculture sponsors 'pasture' tours by haywagon as a fundraiser. 826-9028. Map: 2

Botanical Tours

The guided tour of *National Tropical Botanical Gardens* in Lawai is a unique opportunity to explore a 186 acre preserve of tropical fruits, spices, trees, rare plants, and flowers of astonishing variety and beauty. You can find 50 different kinds of banana and 500 species of palm. Instead of a formal garden, the plant collections are part of the natural landscape of the Lawai Valley. Park and join your group at Spouting Horn and climb aboard a vintage 1941 Dodge touring bus which takes you into Lawai Kai, the Allerton family's spectacular private gardens, a rustic paradise irrigated by an ingenious water system of fountains, streams, waterways, and rocky pools. Stroll at a leisurely pace among the shaded pathways, under spread-ing, giant trees, to pavilions where a statue reflects a graceful image in a

pool speckled with fallen leaves. The "cutting garden" is filled with brilliantly colored heliconia, some reaching high above your head! As Iniki damage is repaired, more of the gardens are reopening. Call NTBG at 808-742-2623 or write to PO Box 340, Lawai HI 96765. Reserve in advance as the 2 hour, 2 mile walking tour ($25/pp) is usually fully booked. Don't forget your camera! Map: 3

On the north shore in Ha'ena, walking tours of NTBG's *Limahuli Gardens* lead you uphill through 17 acres of lush rain forest and gardens filled with native plants to an ocean lookout. You'll love spectacular Limahuli falls, which plunge more than 800 feet, as well as the ancient terrace constructed for growing taro nearly a thousand years ago by the earliest Hawaiians. Choose between formal tours ($15/pp) and self-guided strolls ($10/pp) on T, W, Th, and Sundays. Reservations: 808-826-1053. On Rt. 560, 1/2 mile past the nine mile marker. Map: 2. At *Guava Kai Plantation* near Kilauea, learn about the propogation of this wonderful tropical fruit. Free tastes!

Southside, stop in at *Olu Pua Gardens*, one mile west of Kalaheo on Rt. 50. Originally designed in the 1930's as the Alexander family residence, this 12 acre plantation and botanical preserve showcases spectacular tropical flowers in manicured gardens, a glimpse into the charm and elegance of Kauai's past. Information about guided tours call 808-332-8182. For spectacular photographs of flowers, visit the *Kukuiolono Golf Course* and take your camera to the plumeria grove — a rainbow of colors! Turn south on Papalina (at the traffic light), drive up the hill for .8 miles, and turn into the entrance on the right. Map: 3

Above Kapa'a, the *Keahua Arboretum* is a 30-acre preserve of grassy meadows, trees, streams. Bring your camera and picnic treats. Map: 1

Restaurants

Cafe Hanalei, page 157

Eastern Shore Restaurants

Lihue

			page		meals
Barbecue Inn	245-2921	Oriental	107	$$	LD
Portofino Cafe	245-2521	Italian	110	$$$	LD
Dani's	245-4991	Island-style	111	$	BL
Duke's Canoe Club	246-9599	Seafood/steak	113	$$$	D
Fisherman's Galley	246-4700	Fresh fish	114	$$	LD
Gaylord's	245-9593	Continental	116	$$$$	LD
Hamura's Saimin	245-3271	Saimin	118	$	D
JJ's Broiler	246-4422	Steak/seafood	122	$$$	D
Kalapaki Beach Hut	246-3464	Burgers/sand	123	$	BLD
Kauai Chop Suey	245-8790	Chinese	124	$$	LD
Kiibo	245-2560	Japanese	125	$$	LD
Ma's Family Inc.	245-3142	Island-style	130	$	B
OK Bento & Saimin	245-6554	Island-style	133	$	LD
Si Sisco's	246-1563	Mexican	142	$$	LD
Sumo	246-0113	Japanese	144	$$	BLD
Tip Top	245-2333	Amer/oriental	145	$	BL
Tokyo Lobby	245-8989	Japanese	145	$$	LD

Kapa'a

Hanaya	822-3878	Japanese	121	$$	D
Kapa'a Fish&Chowder	822-7488	Seafood/steak	122	$$$	D
Kountry Kitchen	822-3511	American	129	$$	BLD
Norberto's El Cafe	822-3362	Mexican	132	$$	D
Ono Family	822-1710	American	135	$$	BLD

Wailua

A Pacific Cafe	822-0013	Pacific Rim	136	$$$$	D
Al & Don's	822-4221	American	106	$$	BLD
Aloha Kauai Pizza	822-4511	Pizza/veget	151	$	LD
BeachBoy	822-7163	Buffet	108	$$	BLD
Bull Shed	822-3791	Steak/PRibs	109	$$$	D
Dragon Inn	822-3788	Chinese	111	$$	LD
Eggbert's	822-3738	American	116	$$	BL
Flying Lobster	822-3455	American	115	$$$	D
King & I	822-1642	Thai	126	$$	D

$ See Restaurant Reviews for specific prices.
BLD Breakfast, Lunch, Dinner

			page		meals
Kintaro	822-3341	Japanese	127	$$$	D
Margarita's	822-1808	Mexican	129	$$	D
Mema's	823-0899	Thai/Chinese	131	$$	LD
Nanea	821-0040	Island-style	132	$	LD
Papaya's	823-0190	Vegetarian	139	$	BLD
Panda Garden	822-0092	Chinese	139	$$	D
Rocco's	822-4422	Italian	141	$$	D
Sizzler	822-7404	American	142	$$	BLD
Sukothai	821-1224	Thai/etc.	144	$$	D
Violet's Place	822-2456	Everything	146	$	BLD
Wailua Marina	822-4311	Everything	148	$$	LD
Waipouli Deli	822-9311	Island-style	149	$	BLD
Wild Palms Bistro	822-1533	American	150	$$$	D

Hanama'ulu

Tea House	245-2511	Chin/Japanese	118	$$	D
JR's Plantation	245-1606	American	140	$$$	D

North Shore Restaurants

Kilauea

Casa di Amici	828-1555	Italian	160	$$$	LD
Pau Hana Pizza	828-2020	Pizza	165	$	LD
Roadrunner Cafe	828-TACO	Mexican	168	$	LD

Princeville

Bali Hai	826-6522	Pacific Rim	155	$$$$	LD
Cafe Hanalei	826-9644	Pacific Rim	158	$$$$	BLD
Chuck's Steakhouse	826-6422	Steak/seafood	162	$$$	LD
Hale O'Java	826-7255	Pizza/sandw	153	$	LD
La Cascata	826-9644	Italian	168	$$$$$	D
The Prince	826-5050	American	168	$$	BL

Hanalei & Ha'ena

Cafe Luna	826-1177	Italian/pizza	159	$$	LD
Charo's	828-1388	Mexican	161	$$	LD
Hanalei Dolphin	826-6211	fresh fish	163	$$$	LD
Hanalei Gourmet	826-6113	Sandwiches	164	$$	BLD

			page		meals
Tahiti Nui	826-6277	Steak/seafood	169	$$$	BLD
Wind of Beamreach	826-6143	Steak/seafood	170	$$$	D
Zelo's Beach House	826-9700	American	171	$$	BLD

South Shore & Westside Restaurants

Koloa

Koloa Broiler	742-9122	Steaks	185	$$	LD
Taisho	742-1838	Japanese	191	$$	D
Tomkats Grill	742-8887	American	194	$$	LD

Poipu

Beach House	742-1424	Pacific Rim	173	$$$$	D
Brennecke's	742-7588	Seafood/steak	174	$$$	LD
Dondero's	742-6260	Italian	178	$$$$$	D
House of Seafood	742-6433	fish/steak	180	$$$$	D
Keoki's Paradise	742-7543	Steak/seafood	183	$$$	D
Piatti	742-2216	Steak/seafood	186	$$$	D
Poipu Bay Grill	742-8888	American	187	$$$	BLD
Roy's Poipu Grill	742-5000	Pacific Rim	189	$$$$	D
Taqueria Nortenos	742-7222	Mexican	192	$	LD
Tidepools	742-6260	Seafood/steak	193	$$$$$	D

Kalaheo

Brick Oven Pizza	332-8561	Pizza	176	$$	LD
Camp House Grill	332-9755	Burgers/chicken	177	$$	LD
Kalaheo Steakhouse	332-9780	Steak/PRibs	182	$$$	D
Pomodoro	332-9780	Italian	188	$$$	D

Hanapepe & Eleele

Green Garden	335-5422	Everything	196	$$	LD
Hanapepe Espresso	335-5011	Vegetarian	197	$$	LD
Sinaloa	335-0006	Mexican	199	$$	LD
Toi's Thai Kitchen	335-3111	Thai	200	$$	LD

Waimea

The Grove	338-2300	Weekend buffet	196	$$$	D
Wrangler's	338-1218	Steaks/sandw	201	$$	LD

READERS' CHOICE . . .

FOR OCEAN VIEW
Eastern Shore
    Bull Shed 109
    Duke's Canoe Club 113
North Shore
    Bali Hai 155
    Cafe Hanalei 157
    La Cascata 166
South Shore
    Beach House 173
    Brennecke's 174

FOR FRESH ISLAND FISH
Eastern Shore
    A Pacific Cafe 136
    Duke's Canoe Club 113
    Fisherman's Galley 114
North Shore
    Cafe Hanalei 157
    Hanalei Dolphin 163
South Shore
    Beach House 173
    Brennecke's 174
    Piatti 186
    Roy's Poipu Grill 189

FOR STEAKS & PRIME RIB
Eastern Shore
    Duke's Canoe Club 113
    Bull Shed 109
North Shore
    Chuck's Steakhouse 162
South Shore
    Keoki's 183
    Kalaheo Steakhouse 182

FOR SAIMIN
Eastern Shore
    OK Bento & Saimin 133
    Hamura's Saimin 119
    Kalika's Noodles 152
    Violet's Place 146

FOR ORIENTAL FOOD
Eastern Shore
    Hanama'ulu Tea House 118
    King & I 126
    Kintaro 127
    Mema's Thai Cuisine 131
South Shore
    Pattaya (owned by Mema's)
    Toi's Thai Kitchen 200

FOR FAMILY—FRIENDLY DINING
Eastern Shore
    Barbecue Inn 107
    Bull Shed 109
    Dragon Inn 111
    Duke's Canoe Club 113
    Fisherman's Galley 114
    Hanama'ulu Tea House 118
    Kountry Kitchen 129
    Nanea 132
    Norberto's El Cafe 132
    Ono Family Restaurant 135
    Violet's Place 146
North Shore
    Cafe Hanalei 157
    Tahiti Nui 169
South Shore
    Camp House Grill 177
    Brennecke's 174
    Brick Oven Pizza 176

FOR PASTA
Eastern Shore
    Cafe Portofino 110
North Shore
    Casa di Amici 160
    La Cascata 166
South Shore
    Piatti 186
    Pomodoro 188
    Dondero's 178

Eastern Shore Restaurants

'favor...eats'

The eastern shore's potpourri of dining reflects Kauai's rich multicultural heritage. **Hanama'ulu Restaurant and Tea House** combines reasonable prices and friendly service with excellent Japanese and Chinese cuisine. In LIHUE, **Hamura's Saimin** is a local legend for steaming bowls of saimin and tender brochettes of chicken or beef. **Barbecue Inn's** bargain-priced lunches and dinners include soup, a beverage, fresh-baked bread, entree, even dessert! You'll have to pay cash, but in this family-friendly restaurant, you'll find some of the tastiest food and best values on the island! For the freshest island fish, **Fisherman's Galley** is operated by the owners of Gent Lee Charter Fishing Company, who cook what has just been hooked that day! Don't miss fresh island 'fish & chips!'

Gaylord's at Kilohana provides a romantic garden setting for lunch and dinner in an elegantly restored sugar plantation estate house. At the Kauai Marriott, **Duke's Canoe Club** offers a beautiful beachfront setting, as well as excellent food, reasonable prices, and the most sumptuous salad bar on the island. **Cafe Portofino** nearby features excellent Italian cuisine at reasonable prices. Vegetable lasagna is terrific! At **Kalapaki Beach Hut**, the fresh island ono sandwich is one of the best fish dishes on Kauai, and costs less than $6! Steve also grills first-rate hamburgers!

Ten minutes north of Lihue, WAILUA is fast becoming the dining center of Kauai, with a wide range of cuisines and prices. **Mema Thai & Chinese Cuisine** and **King &I** offer truly memorable Thai food at a great price. **Kintaro** prepares excellent Japanese dinners, sushi and sashimi. For the most imaginative in Pacific Rim cuisine, particularly fresh fish, Jean Marie Josselin's **A Pacific Cafe** has earned well-deserved fame as one of the outstanding restaurants in Hawaii. Don't miss the **Bull Shed** for the biggest, tastiest prime rib on the island as well as steaks, chicken, and fresh fish at affordable prices with an ocean view.

On a budget? Mexican cuisine at **Margarita's** or **Norberto's El Cafe** is excellent. **Wah Kung** in Wailua is a great spot for tasty Chinese take-out food, and **Violet's Place** serves wonderful sandwiches and stir fry, as well terrific saimin, at unbelievably reasonable prices. **BeachBoy Hotel** offers buffet-style all-you-can-eat breakfasts, lunches, dinners for an attractive price—great for salad and fruit lovers as well as hearty eaters! At Coconut Plantation Marketplace, **Aloha Kauai Pizza, Kalika's Noodles** and **Taco Dude** serve excellent take-out. For breakfasts, it would be hard to beat **Kountry Kitchen** in Kapa'a, where our kids have loved the pancakes and 'cheesy eggs' for years, or **Ono Family Restaurant**, which serves hearty family meals.

Al and Don's

There used to be a sign outside boasting 25 breakfast selections. Now it's gone, but no matter. The food was never the real attraction at Al and Don's anyway. The reason to come is the view. From roomy booths next to enormous windows, you can see the ocean, rimmed with ironwoods, stretching out to the horizon. The decor, though nondescript, is pleasant, and the tables are large and comfortable. Waitresses bring coffee immediately, and your order is prepared quickly and served cheerfully. Food is reasonably-priced though not memorable. Pancakes are a trifle heavy, and the corned beef hash, mediocre. Eggs are the best bet, the 'special' with all the trimmings, priced at $3.99.

We had visited Al and Don's only for breakfast, when we could enjoy the restaurant's best attraction—the view! But as an experiment, we sent the four youngsters for a special outing, dinner by themselves. The results were, in a word, mixed. Only one of our four actually ate what was served, and their observations had the compassion and tact one would expect at their ages: the chicken cutlet was like rubber; the chicken stir fry was cold and mushy; the mashed potatoes were sticky; and jello was the best part of the meal. Their parting recommendation (which might well have been reciprocated by management, judging from our oldest child's description of the deportment of our youngest) was "Don't come back." On the other hand, prices are reasonable and, if you time your dinner carefully for before sunset—you might enjoy the view with better luck!

Wailua, Kauai Sands Hotel. 822-4951. Open 7 am - 10 am, and 6 pm - 8:45 pm daily. Credit cards. Map: 1

Barbecue Inn

Where do Kauaians go for lunch? Where can you find a meal which includes soup, a beverage, fresh bread, an entree like a teriyaki chicken sandwich, and dessert for only $6.95? Barbecue Inn doesn't take credit cards, and you can't pay by check, but in this family-owned restaurant you'll find some of the tastiest food and one of the best food values on the island. It has been a local favorite since 1940, when the first generation of the Morishige family opened the doors.

With a comfortable, air-conditioned dining room, Barbecue Inn is the rare kind of place which has something special for just about everyone in the family. The dinner menu offers more than 25 dinners—fresh fish, seafood platter, steak, prime rib — amazingly priced from $6.95–$14.95. Accompanied by soup or fresh fruit, a salad, homemade bread, vegetable, dessert, and a beverage, these dinners are a great bargain. At lunchtime, the entrees are even less expensive, averaging $6.95, but you don't get salad! You do get the chance to try a tuna sandwich so special that it moves into a whole new dimension, for it's made with fresh ahi and served with lettuce and tomato on thick sliced homebaked bread ($3.75)!

Kids will love the cheeseburger ($2.75), which you have to order off the lunch menu even at dinner. Bacon costs 75 cents extra, but it's a small price to pay for a burger which arrives still sizzling on a toasted sesame bun, smothered with melted cheese and garnished with fresh, local manoa lettuce! For only $3.95, kids can order fried chicken, hamburger, spaghetti, or chow mein dinners, seven choices in all, including a beverage, or a grilled cheese sandwich made on delicious homebaked bread toasted crisp and golden. Grown-ups will love the teriyaki steak ($14.95), a good-sized, tender rib-eye with perfectly flavored homemade sauce, or teriyaki beef kabob and shrimp tempura ($11.95). Tempura is light, crispy and delicate, and teriyaki steak skewers tender and tasty.

You will be surprised at the high quality of the "extras" which many restaurants pay scant attention to. Miso soup is superb. Bread is home-made — light, fragrant, and exceptionally tasty. You should also squander a quarter on some homemade "lavosh" which is buttery, almost like shortbread. It's so good, you will want seconds, so splurge on an extra order (or take some out for the beach) for only 60 cents. The fruit cup appetizer is fresh—pineapple, papaya, watermelon, honeydew, and mango—and so wonderful that you'll hope your kids will refuse to eat theirs because there are no canned peaches! The green salad would win no awards for imagination, but you'd be surprised at how much fun the kids have picking out the shredded cabbage and homemade croutons! And everyone will devour the homemade pies—coconut, chocolate, or chocolate cream—pies so light they are almost as amazing as the price: $1.00 a slice, same price as a Coke!

You will see a lot of working people coming off the job, and the portions are so enormous you can understand why. Waitresses are unfailingly cheerful, even when small children decorate the floor with crumbs and ice cubes. All this makes Barbecue Inn a good dinner choice for hearty eaters and hungry families, for anyone who appreciates ordinary food cooked extraordinarily well, as well as some very special treats.

Lihue. 2982 Kress St. (off Rice St.). 245-2921. Closed Sundays. Lunch 10:30 am - 1:30 pm. Dinner 5 pm - 8:30 pm (4:30 - 8:45 pm F, S, Sun). Non-smoking section. Cash only. Map: 1

BeachBoy Restaurant

Are you looking for an all-you-can-eat buffet with bargain prices and even an ocean view? The BeachBoy Restaurant, located in the BeachBoy Hotel in Wailua, offers breakfast, lunch, and dinner buffets at unbeatable prices. The best bargain is breakfast (6:30 am until 10 am), with fresh fruits, cereals, as well as scrambled eggs and hash browns—all for only $6.95 (or $5.95 for seniors and $4.95 for kids 6-12 years). Lunch (11 am until 1:30 pm), with sandwich fixings, salads and fruits, runs a dollar more, and dinner (5 pm - 9 pm) is only $11.95. Hungry eaters will appreciate the four dinner entrees: beef, chicken, fresh fish, and kalua pork, as well as rice and potatoes, while the health-conscious will have fruits and salads to choose from! Kids, who along with seniors have a discount, will love the desserts! The dining room is spacious and attractive, with lots of green plants and large windows looking out past the pool to the ocean. Despite the bargain price, you'll find linen tablecloths! It's filling rather than fancy, and you should come early for the best selection. Before or afterwards, you can take a nice walk (or run) along the shoreline. It's about a mile, roundtrip, with a spectacular ocean view all the way. Less strenuous, but possibly more costly, are the shops at the Coconut Plantation Marketplace! Families might plan a meal after the free hula shows at 4:30 pm Monday, Wednesday, Friday, and Saturday.

Wailua, Kauai BeachBoy Hotel, Coconut Plantation Marketplace. 822-7163. Credit cards. Non smoking section. Map: 1

The Bull Shed

Since 1973, The Bull Shed has been famous on Kauai for offering high quality meals at unbeatable prices. Bull Shed's prime rib is truly special —a thick slice of tender beef, perfectly cooked with a tasty bone (if you ask for it), delicious au jus and fresh horseradish sauce— at $18.95 the best deal for the best portion on Kauai.

Unfortunately, the Bull Shed has also been famous for the long waits due to the no-reservations policy. We have tried hard to beat the system. We have done our best, despite cranky kids and a frazzled babysitter, to arrive before 7 pm, to avoid the traffic jam. Finally, nature has intervened: our children have grown old enough to join us, and our party has hit the magic number of six, large enough to earn a reservation!

A glance at the menu will tell you why the Bull Shed is so popular. Prices are amazingly reasonable, entrees come with rice and the salad bar, and half cost less than $15. Combination dinners are served with a 7.5 oz. tenderloin filet instead of the usual small sirloin. Lobster tail is enormous, a full 12 oz., and perfectly cooked. The wine list is also reasonable, with more than half the primarily California selections costing less than $20, including a Sonoma Cutrer Napa Valley Chardonnay well priced at $20.95. If you choose a white wine, order it right away because your bottle might need time to chill.

The Bull Shed has become a favorite with each member of our family, in itself a small miracle! Our 6:30 pm arrival time is early enough to beat the crowds, and all four children eat everything that is served to them—a rare achievement. Lauren's teriyaki chicken breast ($10.95 or $6.95 child's portion) is always perfectly soft and juicy. Mikey loves the teriyaki sirloin ($15.95), and Jeremy always orders his rack of lamb ($19.95), a large portion, both tender and tasty with a delicious teriyaki marinade. Even better, all four put away huge and healthful-looking salads, picking their pickiest best from the salad bar ($6.95 by itself).

The Bull Shed offers one of the best food values on Kauai in a pleasant dining room, one of the few with an ocean view. Service is friendly, efficient and accommodating, especially our favorite waitress, Lynn. Our favorite table, in a tiny room by itself just a few feet from the edge of a seawall, offers a spectacular view of the waves rolling towards the wall and crashing in torrents of spray. During a storm, the waves splash right against the glass, an awesome sight! Try to come when the moon is full and watch the waves send gleaming ripples through the darkness. If it's warm, be sure to request a table by a window which opens (not all do). Breezes in this restaurant are hard to come by!

Wailua. 822-3791. Dinner 5:30 pm-10 pm nightly. Reservations for parties of 6 or more. Non-smoking section. Credit Cards. Children's menu. Look for the sign (it's small) opposite McDonald's just north of Coconut Plantation Marketplace and turn towards the water. Map: 1

Cafe Portofino

You'd hardly expect to find a gourmet Italian restaurant in a shopping center across from a hotel service entrance! Cafe Portofino offers excellent food, attentive service, as well as an attractive dining room. The hardworking owners, settlers from Italy via a stint in cruise ship food & beverage management, are committed to high food quality and professional service.

The dining room is bright, spacious, and cheerful, the white walls accented with honey–colored wood trim and leafy green plants. Well–spaced tables are covered in linen and set with shining crystal, and the softly upholstered chairs are absolutely wonderful— they swivel and gently rock, and offer excellent lumbar support. Outside, a terrace offers more informal dining, and at lunch you can catch a glimpse of Kalapaki Bay beyond the Anchor Cove Shopping Center.

Your meal will be both tasty and generous, particularly the fresh, homemade pastas, in addition to chicken, veal and fish. Portofino's Italian cuisine is light and healthful, the sauces based on vegetable flavors rather than heavy with cream. Flavorful minestrone is served in a generous portion for a modest price ($3.25). Vegetable lasagne ($13.75) arrives in a huge portion, as festive looking as a wrapped birthday present.

It tastes just as wonderful, the flavors and textures of fresh zucchini and spinach brought together with a wonderful marinara sauce with tasty chunks of tomatoes. Salads are a la carte, a dinner salad costs $4.25 and a somewhat small Caesar, $6.75.

Service is very professional yet friendly, and the seemingly international staff works together with an infectious camaraderie. Everyone seems to care about your dinner, and they're all willing to fetch extra bread or answer questions. The wine list is well selected but expensive (in the section called 'Guiseppi's Favorites' some choices list at $500), with some bargains, like a reasonable vintage Pinot Grigio for $19.

Cafe Portofino meets a real need on Kauai for an Italian restaurant with an attractive setting, reasonable prices, distinctive cuisine, and professional service.

Lihue, Pacific Ocean Plaza, across from Kauai Marriott. 245-2121. Credit cards. Music four nights a week. Lunch 11 - 2 pm M - F; Dinner nightly 5 - 10 pm. Non-smoking section. Map: 1

Dani's

At Dani's, you won't find an orchid on your plate, but if you order eggs, what you do find will be hot, tasty, and filling. Toast and Kona coffee come free with breakfast, though to have real milk instead of artificial creamer will cost you 40 cents, and you can choose from eggs, omelettes, pancakes, and Hawaiian dishes. The ham and cheese omelette is very cheesy and stuffed with ham, though the hotcakes are on the heavy side. The lunch menu offers a wide variety of Hawaiian, American, and Japanese dishes, as well as sandwiches and hamburgers. Prices start at $4.50 and include soup or salad, roll, rice, and coffee or tea.

With prices this low, expect to sacrifice atmosphere. The color scheme is woodgrain formica accented by fluorescent lights, but on the other hand, the large, modern dining room is bright, clean, and comfortably air-conditioned, and the service swift and efficient.

Lihue, 4201 Rice St. Open 5 am - 1:30 pm (1 pm on Sat) Closed Sundays. Credit cards. Non-smoking section. 245-4991. Map: 1

Dragon Inn

Perched on the second floor of a small shopping center on Rt. 56 near Kapa'a, Dragon Inn looks big, bright, and cheerful. Inside, the dining room is clean, if sparsely furnished. The decor may be no more than the

sum of its parts — woodgrain formica tables, green leafy plants, and a red carpet, but the windows frame beautiful Sleeping Giant mountain, the tables are not overly close together, and the food is generous and tasty.

Dragon Inn is a first-rate family restaurant. Waiters are very tolerant of the inevitable whining amid the dining. After listening with a smile to our kids describe what they would refuse to eat if he brought it to the table, our waiter politely revised the orders as they worked out the final details of who would share what with whom. He seemed to know that once he got the egg rolls on the table, the cranky crew would settle down, their behavior following that timeless rule: you can't chew and complain at the same time. And he was right. After egg rolls ($4 .95 for 3), fried won tons ($3.50), the main courses proved as generous as the prices are reasonable. As the kids got down to the work of dividing up everything into precisely equal portions, we adults recognized that we had passed that magical point when everyone's plate has something on it and you know the rest of the meal is coasting.

Silver Flower Scallop soup ($7.25) was delicious and piping hot. The beef and broccoli ($6.75) was so tasty that the short people clamored for a second platter, which we ordered with noodles. It was even better! House chow mein with cake noodle ($8.25) was crispy and tasty, and served with generous chunks of meat. The shrimp canton ($6.75), with eight juicy shrimp, was a perfect balance of sweet and sour.

There is no wine list to speak of, but you can order chardonnay, cabernet, and white zinfandel by the carafe, as well as Chinese beer and all the tea you can hold. Dragon Inn is popular with local families, some arriving with three generations, so come early. If you try Dragon Inn for lunch, you can order a lunch plate with a choice of 12 entrees for only $6.25 or a luncheon buffet for about the same price.

Wailua, 4-901 Kuhio Hwy., in the Waipouli Plaza. Reservations 822-3788. Take-out menu. Lunch 11 am - 2 pm (except Monday). Dinner 4:30 pm - 9:30 pm daily. Credit cards. Non-smoking section. Map: 1

The eastern shore, with Sleeping Giant Mountain . . .

Helicoptering Kauai
Page 86

. . . and the magnificent mountains and valleys of Kauai's western wilderness.

Hiking, Walking, & Beachcombing

The Kalalau Trail into the Na Pali wilderness begins where paved road ends, at Keʻe Beach on the north shore. Page 60.

Reward: The view after climbing the first quarter – mile.

Larsen's Beach, a great spot for beachwalking and shell collecting, even if winter surf is too strong for swimming. Page 31.

Local Flavors

On Wednesdays, at the Kapaʻa farmers' market, the rope drops just before 3 pm! Bananas cost a dollar a bunch . . .

. . . bouquets of heliconia and ginger are only a little more. Page 70.

Snorkeling

Favorite spots (depending on surf and season): Tunnels Beach , Keʻe Beach (summer), Lydgate Park and Poipu Beach (year round). Page 57.

Duke's Canoe Club

Duke's Canoe Club offers just about everything—high quality, reasonably-priced dinners, as well as a generous new salad bar, wonderful nightly Hawaiian entertainment, and a spectacular beachfront location.

If you enter Duke's at beach level, you will ascend a stone stairway carved into an indoor waterfall draped with ferns and trailing flowers. At the top, the dining room is cooled by delightful evening breezes, a perfect spot to look out over Kalapaki bay, watch the setting sun tint the clouds with gold, and listen to wonderful Hawaiian music played by friendly performers who stroll from table to table, offering to play your favorite songs. During one of our dinners, some local guests were moved to dance a graceful hula, to everyone's delight!

Duke's reasonable dinner prices (from $14.95 for chicken) now include a rather amazing salad bar, featuring Caesar salad as well as an array of fresh vegetables and lettuces, fruits, pasta salads fresh-baked banana macadamia nut muffins, and even rice! The salad bar is one of the most generous on Kauai, great for vegetarians! (Salad bar alone: $9.95)

You can choose from several fresh fish entrees ($18-$20) including a tasty teriyaki broiled fresh ahi. You may find some sauces, like the orange-ginger, too strongly flavored and consider ordering them served on the side just in case. Most fish filets (8 to 10 oz.) are already pre-glazed, but we were able to convince the kitchen to find a naked moonfish and grill it plainly, with a wonderful result— the delicately flavored whitefish was soft, moist and delicious.

The prime rib ($19.95) actually stopped the flow of conversation. Nearly 22 ounces, it was so thick that you didn't know where to begin to tackle it. More like a family-size roast, it was a significant dining event, and tender as well as juicy, served underspiced rather than over-salted. Described on the menu as "while it lasts," you might consider reserving a portion when you arrive. Steaks are tender and moist, and the wine list offers some good values, e.g. the low-end Acacia chardonnay ($23).

Everyone in the family will enjoy Duke's, especially walking around the spectacular Kauai Marriott Resort after dinner! Children have four dinner choices, which include fries and the salad bar, for less than $6, and adults can order 'Lighter Fare' (pasta, pizza, or a cheeseburger) for under $10. What comes to your table will be well-prepared, efficiently served, in a setting where you can watch the ocean and listen to wonderful Hawaiian music. That's why you see so many local families crowding the tables! Reservations help a lot, though one section is set aside for walk-ins. Think twice about going in the rain, however, for you'll miss the view when they close the shutters!

In Lihue, on Kalapaki Beach, in front of the Kauai Marriott. Reservations a day in advance (246-9599). Dinner 5-10 nightly. Credit Cards. Park at the Marriott. Non-smoking section. Duke's Barefoot Bar downstairs is open 4 pm to 11:30 for sandwiches, burgers, barbecue plates, ice cream drinks and cocktails. Map: 1

Fisherman's Galley Restaurant

Where can you find the freshest fish on Kauai? If you can't hook up with the fishermen themselves, your next best bet might be the captain of a fishing charter boat. That's the idea behind Fisherman's Galley, which can claim to be 'Kauai's Freshest Seafood Restaurant' because many of its menu offerings come right off the owner's charter fishing boats! In fact, on the walls of Fisherman's Galley you'll see lots of photographs of successful Gent-Lee Charters fishing trips with famous and infamous fishermen (including almost the entire San Francisco 49'ers football team) grinning at their finny conquests! You'll find the fresh fish selections listed on the blackboard, the usual ono and ahi as well as whatever else has been hooked (*and* the date each left the water!), and the waiter will be happy to tell you his personal first choice, and maybe even the fish story to go along with it!

At Fisherman's Galley you'll find one of the best fish dishes on Kauai—fresh island Fish-n-Chips! Wait till you taste ahi deep fried to a golden brown, piled high in a clam-shaped platter, and priced by the number of pieces. At $7.95 for two enormous, meltingly tender filets, as well as a pile of sizzling steak fries, this dish is simply spectacular!

Prices are the same for both lunch and dinner— amazingly reasonable! Start with fresh ono chowder ($2.50), generous with fish and potatoes. For as little as $7, you can sample fresh ono or mahi mahi on a sandwich, the fish perfectly broiled, with no bitter taste from the grill, sweet, tender, and juicy, and attractively served on a sesame bun with fresh lettuce and a bright red tomato slice. For about twice that price ($14.95), you can enjoy a full-sized fresh fish filet. Non-fishy eaters can choose a hamburger ($7.95) sirloin steak ($10.95 for 8 oz.), shrimp, and various combination platters. Almost all the entrees come with a choice of rice, scalloped potatoes or wonderful steak fries.

Fisherman's Galley looks as unpretentious as its name, with a small dining room perched near the road and a new, even smaller dining room in the rear, with a separate torch-lit entrance. Dark varnished wood tables and booths create an informal atmosphere that raises no-frills eating to a decorative motif! The staff is exceedingly friendly. When 13-year-old Lauren requested a grilled cheese sandwich not on the menu, the waitress convinced the kitchen to produce one, golden brown and served with a large portion of fries for the modest price of $2.50.

At Fisherman's Galley you'll find the freshest in local fish, without the heavy sauces or sharp spices that can overwhelm their delicate flavors. If you want to taste genuinely fresh Kauaian fish without spending a lot of money, Fisherman's Galley is for you!

Puhi, just west of Lihue on Rt. 50. 246-4700. Credit cards. Open 10 am to 9 pm M - F and 4 pm to 10 pm Sat. Closed Sundays. Non-smoking section. Map: 1

Flying Lobster

Flying Lobster advertises "a champagne meal at beer prices," its lobster specialty dinners supposedly available at bargain prices. You may discover, however, that your lobster dinner will cost you a lot more than you expect, partly because the menu doesn't feature the same 'rock lobster' tail you find in most restaurants. Instead, at Flying Lobster, you'll find the generally smaller Pacific lobsters, both the 'slipper lobster' which is sometimes in season in Kauai's waters but mostly imported frozen, and the 'spiny lobster' which is larger and more 'seafood-like' in taste. One of these smaller lobster tails won't really fill your plate, and you'll be tempted to order the double tail entree which is considerably more expensive. A single spiny lobster tail, for example, costs $18.50, and two tails run a whopping $27. A single slipper lobster tail is $14, with two at $20. A combination of both will cost $27. Because these tails are smaller than you might expect, even the double portion may not satisfy you.

With a less expensive entree, like barbecued chicken ($14.50) you still get the salad bar, Flying Lobster's best feature, an impressive display of fresh vegetables, pasta and prepared salads, fresh fruits, selected pu pus like fried won tons, and even soup. On Fridays and Saturdays, you can try the all-you-can-eat Prime Rib & Seafood Buffet ($19.95/$10 under 11).

The outdoor dining terrace is lovely in the evening shadows, although white fluorescent lighting somewhat diminishes the romantic effect of the candle lamps. You can enjoy the live music from the cocktail lounge nearby. Service is very friendly, and the wine list is reasonably-priced You might do best to come for the salad bar ($11 for adults), which is becoming a rarity on Kauai due to the high cost of fresh produce flown in from the mainland at sky high prices.

Wailua, Coconut Beach Resort Hotel, Coconut Plantation Marketplace. 822-3455. Credit cards. Non-smoking section. Map: 1

Eggbert's

Once upon a time, when eggs were king, many an enormous omelette was whipped up in Lihue at Eggbert's. Iniki changed all that. Eggbert's closed, and the world moved into synch with a different diet. Now Eggbert's re-opens in a time of low cholesterol chic, when people are counting calories and looking for ways to avoid fat. When you've got 'egg' all over your name these days, you take a hearty risk!

Eggbert's signature omelettes (& you can also design your own) and eggs benedict are priced in various sizes (from $4.25), so you can opt for less yolk, less cost. You can also try tasty banana pancakes with coconut syrup or french toast ($5.95). The lunch menu offers burgers, salads, and sandwiches ($5 to $8).

The new location in the Coconut Plantation Marketplace is great for families, a bright, white dining space with windows on all sides to encourage the breeze. Plastic chairs provide adequate comfort, and blue formica tables have rounded corners, safe at eye level for short persons who like to explore underneath! Service can be a bit on the slow side.

Eggbert's is a good choice for people who like (or need) to start the day with a hearty meal, and though prices may not fit into the bargain range, at Eggbert's you'll find things largely sunny side up!

Coconut Plantation Marketplace, Wailua 822-3787. Breakfast & lunch 7 am - 2:30 pm daily. Smoking on lanai outside. Kona coffee: $1.25. Map: 1

Gaylord's at Kilohana

Once the heart of a 1,700 acre sugar plantation, Kilohana is a special place. Wandering through rooms which have the spacious beauty of large proportions and wide verandas, you can easily imagine the gracious pace of life before airplanes and traffic lights. With the mountains behind and

A rare clear view of the top of Mt. Waiʻaleʻale, the highest elevation on Kauai & the wettest place on the earth. Note the rain gauge which measures the almost constant rainfall.

rolling lawns all around, you can glimpse, even if briefly, a way of life now forever lost. Browsing the shops brings you quickly up to date: trendy clothes and jewelry, and in the Kilohana Gallery, a fine collection of work by Hawaiian artists.

Named for Gaylord Wilcox who built Kilohana, the restaurant has a dining room and veranda looking out over a manicured lawn and garden lush with leafy ferns and brilliant tropical flowers. In the evening, the flagstone terrace is lit with lanterns, and rattan chairs surround comfortable tables decked with white linen and pink napkins arranged like fans. Gaylord's is one of the most romantic restaurants on Kauai, with the kind of setting you'd want to star in if your life were a black and white movie. Candles on the tables flicker softly in gentle breezes, and from your chair beneath the roof you can peek out at stars shining in the velvet sky. As you gaze out at the gardens lit by the moon and stars, you can feel the soft tropical breezes which rustle the leaves. Waiters in tuxedo shirts and cummerbunds move discreetly, anticipating your every desire.

Gaylord's chef has replaced the elaborate preparations and ingenious sauces, with simpler and more consistently prepared entrees. Dinner begins with excellent warm round wheat buns. Sauteed fresh opakapaka (snapper) was excellent, perfectly cooked, both moist and flavorful. Vegetable brochette, served with rice pilaf pleased our vegetarian. Prime rib ($19.95 for 14 oz.) is a good bet, served with lots of au jus. Entrees arrive with rice, potato, or pasta, as well as a vegetable—like still crunchy sugarpeas in the pod and sliced red peppers. Most entrees cost more than $20, and unless you come for "light supper" (5 to 6:30 pm) your least expensive dinner choice is vegetable brochette ($15.95). If you add soup or salad ($3.95), the cost of dining goes up quickly. Gaylord's wine list is now less costly and includes some good choices like Cambria Katherine's Vineyard at $24.

Despite occasional disappointments, the dining experience at Gaylord's can still be wonderful. Waiters are polite, attentive, and professional, and in the quiet courtyard, you escape the usual noisy distractions of clattering trays and banging dishes. Small details get lots of attention: water is served in elegant iced glasses with tangy lemon slices, and coffee cups are watched carefully. If you like to linger after dinner, consider bringing along a sweater, for temperatures can be chilly in winter months.

With such an elegant setting, Gaylord's could develop into one of the island's truly special dining experiences, an image to haunt you when temperatures plunge back home. At this point, our feeling is to order as simply as possible. While in the past we have found our dinners to be of uneven quality, we have heard high praise of Gaylord's lunch, where excellent sandwiches, salads, vegetable platters, burgers and fresh seafood are reasonably-priced ($6.95-$10) and you can look out at the garden in the full splendor of Hawaiian sunshine.

Just west of Lihue, on Rt. 50. 245-9593. Credit cards. Lunch 11 am -3 pm. Dinner 5-10 pm daily. Sunday brunch 9:30 am -3 pm. Children's menu. Non-smoking section   Map: 1

Hamura's Saimin

According to legend, Oahu businessmen have flown to Kauai just to have lunch at Hamura Saimin. To look at the weather-beaten exterior, you'd have your doubts. The tiny building encloses—just barely—twin rectangular counters with stools. A recent face-lift has made the room look cleaner and more like a luncheonette, but now that the kitchen has been moved out of the center and into the back, you can no longer have a ringside seat to watch the cook stir and chop and make things sizzle. The inevitability of change, yes, though some traditions die hard. A sign still warns: "No Gum Under the Counter." Nowadays, our kids check!

On this counter is served some of the finest saimin around, and you come to want to believe the legend about the Oahu businessmen and their expense account lunches. Airfare could certainly be offset with bargain food prices: for $4.25 you get the saimin special—tasty and fragrant soup with noodles, chock full of vegetables and meats. The perfectly flavored won ton soup or won ton min is only $4. To take the saimin out costs 25 cents extra for the container, but it's worth it to escape the cramped little room and head for the beach. Barbecued beef or chicken sticks at $.75 are another find, tasty, moist, and perfectly spiced. Light, homemade manapu, a sweet cousin of the pretzel ($1.50/bag), is a great dessert for kids, while adults can try the lilikoi chiffon pie ($1.25).

When the waitress takes your order, she passes a bowl of the appropriate size and color over the counter to the cook, who inserts the proper mix of ingredients, then covers all with a ladle of steaming broth. If you visit often enough, you begin to appreciate technique, the consumer's as well as the cook's. The truly experienced diners mix hot mustard and soy sauce in their spoons, dipping the mixture into the soup as necessary, and using chopsticks to pull the noodles through.

There's not much variety, but what the cook cooks is very good indeed, and the visit is like a trip into the island's past, a time before tourism brought butcherblock tables and bentwood chairs, air-conditioning and gourmet teas — a time when sticking gum under the counter, though frowned upon, was still possible. So throw away your Bubble Yum before going inside, and try this taste of authentic Kauai!

Lihue, 2956 Kress St. Cash only. M-Sat 10 am - 10 pm. Open (and less crowded) Sundays for lunch. 245-3271. Map: 1

Hanama'ulu Restaurant & Tea House

You could not select a better place to share a really special evening with friends than the Tea House, because this restaurant combines delicious food with the friendliest service on the island, and, as if that weren't enough, a Japanese garden setting to make everything seem just a bit magical. Here you can dine on soft mats at low tables next to the goldfish and water lilies. Children can wander around and count the carp (tell them to be careful; one of our two-year-olds tumbled in!). Local families have been coming to the Tea House for more than sixty-five years! Today they still appreciate superb cooking at reasonable prices, and it's a rare wedding, anniversary, welcome or farewell party that does not take place in one of the tea rooms by the garden. So reserve your tea room several days in advance!

The Miyake family cooks with subtlety and flair, and creates a genuinely special cuisine, with 35 Chinese and Japanese entrees at reasonable prices from $4.75-$14.75. We recommend the won ton soup

($6) as the finest anywhere, generously garnished with scallions, pork, and slices of egg foo young. Children will love the crispy fried chicken with its delicate touch of ginger ($6); the boneless pieces are just the right size for little hands. Also try crispy fried shrimp and teriyaki beef skewers ($7.50).

When our party is large enough, we ask the owner to order a several course dinner. And we are always delighted with the new dishes we discover. Shrimp tempura ($9.75) is spectacular, served on an enormous, beautiful platter, and the taste is just as wonderful, as is the fresh island fish tempura style ($7). Vegetarians will love the vegetable tempura ($6.50) or the crispy tofu tempura ($4) served with teriyaki sauce and green onions. Sashimi is fresh and beautifully arranged, the slices of ahi and ono both slender and fragrant. A specialty, mushrooms stuffed with crab ($5.75), is lighter than many versions of the dish, and very tasty. Chinese chicken salad arrived with lots of chicken, lettuce, crispy noodles, and wonderful dressing.

The sushi bar is becoming a favorite spot to watch Victor's culinary artistry! His salmon skin handrolls are truly special, as he grills rather than bakes the salmon and may even use salmon skins instead of nori to make his wrap ($4.25). Victor's California rolls ($4) feature real crab without mayonnaise, and his signature roll, which he calls the "lava roll," is a huge and amazing creation of smoked salmon, shrimps, scallops broiled together and served piping hot with an avocado sauce ($12).

Reserve at least three days in advance to choose where you dine. Avoid the front dining room where service can be rushed and ambiance nonexistent. You might prefer the teppan yaki room and sushi bar. Our favorite, however, is the tea house by the gardens, where we can listen to crickets sing the songs of evening while stars light up the velvet sky. If mosquitoes like to pick on you while ignoring your friends, don't be bashful about asking for a mosquito coil. The incense smell is great, and it keeps the bugs away.

In twenty years of dining, this special restaurant has never let us down. The cooking is consistently excellent, the prices remarkably reasonable, the service exceptionally friendly, and children are treated with more than usual tolerance by waitresses like Sally and Arlene who genuinely love them. Because this is a restaurant where you should sample as many dishes as possible, and because it is such a special place, we like to save the Tea House for our last night with our Kauai friends, and ask any *kapunas* who might be listening to speed our return! You shouldn't miss the Tea House either.

Hanama'ulu, Rt. 56. Call Sally at 245-2511 for reservations or to arrange special dinner menus. Call in advance to reserve a tea room instead of the front dining room. Credit cards. Full bar. Closed Mondays. Lunch 9 am - 1 pm; Dinner 4:30 pm -9 pm. Banquet facilities. Map: 1

Hanaya Sushi Bar & Restaurant

When you duck beneath the cloth panels at the doorway to Hanaya, you may be surprised to find yourself in a rather crowded room. That is, all four tables may be taken, as may be the nine stools by the sushi bar. Hanaya is popular because prices are reasonable and the food is very tasty. A blackboard will list the day's specials, usually fresh fish. Fresh fish tempura is excellent, very light, very crisp, very tasty, although the julienned carrots and onions which come in the basket are too tiny to be tasty and too tangled to pick up. Ask instead for extra pieces of large vegetable, like delicious sweet potato or zucchini. Teriyaki chicken ($9.55) is mostly meaty, and you may ask if the double breast portion can be halved for a child, for which our waiter charged Lauren only $3. Even her child's dinner included rice and a delicate miso soup served in a lacquer bowl with tofu and green onions.

You'll probably want to sample some sushi since the chef in traditional kimono and head band provides impromptu entertainment. California rolls can be ordered as part of a dinner with tempura ($11.95), the crab salad rolled with avocado inside rice and wrapped with nori. Kappa maki ($3.75), the un-fish sushi, satisfied our finicky eaters with its peeled cucumber center.

Hanaya's decor is an amalgamation. The mean looking guys pictured on kites hanging over the counter are clearly intended to ward off any evil spirits lurking in the bamboo jungle painted on the wall, or to intimidate the giant lobster hanging above the front door. And the tables are certainly unusual, constructed in such a way that almost no person will be able to stretch his legs underneath. If you want beer or wine, stop in at the ABC store beforehand and bring some in!

Hanaya is unpretentious and fun. For a taste of Japan via Kauai, duck under the cloth panels and give it a try!

Kapa'a, 1394 Kuhio Highway. 822-3878. Credit cards. Map: 1

JJ's Broiler

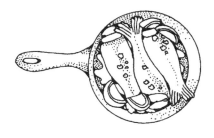

Almost thirty years ago, Kauai's first steak house opened in a refurbished plantation house on the main street of Lihue, then a sleepy town with a single traffic light. Named JJ's after its owner, the restaurant achieved local fame for its specialty, "Slavonic steak", a sliced London broil marinated in a sauce heavily flavored with garlic. When anyone in JJ's was served this dish, everyone else knew it! All that began to change several years ago, when JJ's owners built a new restaurant right on Kalapaki Bay, then added a garish hot pink neon sign to challenge the hotel restaurants just down the beach. Just as the contest was getting interesting, Iniki struck and blew all the dining spots out of business.

Now re-opened, JJ's food and service are uneven. On one visit, the New York steak ($18.95 for 14 oz.) was tasteless and tough, and the prime rib also unsatisfactory. On the other hand, chicken breast teriyaki has been tender and of good size, and the fresh opakapaka cooked to perfect flakiness, though served with a sauce so heavy that we were glad to have ordered it served on the side. The 'macadamia nut rack of lamb' ($21.95) was expertly flavored, though a disappointing cut.

Dinner begins with salad, which is no short subject but the main feature of the evening! What arrives at the table is actually a portable salad bar, a huge bowl surrounded by vegetables and condiments in a lazy susan (by itself, $9.95). Served on large glass plates, the salad is a good distraction from the rather undistinguished bread, which arrives without any plate to hold down the crumbs. Entrees are served with rice and vegetables, some of which seemed rather heavy on onions.

JJ's multi–level design affords each table privacy as well as an ocean view. Above the polished wood tables, in the enormous space of the open beam ceiling, hang actual sailboats. Tables are attractive to look at but could use, for the prices, a cloth or even place mats.

JJ's costs the same or even more than other steak houses like The Bull Shed in Wailua, or Duke's Canoe Club right down the beach, where, in our opinion, portions are larger, the food tastier, and the service more skillful.

Lihue, Anchor Cove Center. 246-4422 Reservations. Dinner 5 pm -10 pm, daily. Credit cards. Non-smoking section. Map: 1

Kalapaki Beach Hut

In the bright blue building right behind Kalapaki Beach, you will find one of our favorite sandwiches on Kauai—fresh ono, cleanly grilled, moist and tender, and wrapped in a soft roll with lettuce and juicy tomatoes — an outstanding way to sample island fish for a reasonable price! You will also find some of the best hamburgers on Kauai. And that shouldn't come as any surprise since the owner, Steve Gerald, originated 'Ono Burger' in Anahola more than twenty years ago. Since then, Ono Burger has achieved near legendary status, a name spoken with reverence whenever fine hamburgers are discussed on Kauai.

Steve Gerald features flame-broiled hamburgers, made with beef or turkey, or even buffalo. Hamburgers are extra juicy, extra tasty, and meltingly delicious. The entry level burger costs $3.75 and comes with lettuce, tomato, and mayonnaise on a sesame bun. Buffalo burgers cost about $1.50 more, but then remember how much less costly they are to your arteries! You can order your burger teriyaki or barbecue style for an additional twenty cents, with cheese for sixty cents or with bacon and cheddar or mushroom melt for about $1. Kids burgers include fries and soft drink for $3.35. French fries are hot and tasty, and you have the choice of vinegar as well as catsup on the tables. Vegetarians can try the veggie sandwich or one of the new salads.

The Beach Hut has become so successful that Steve and Sharon now serve three meals a day plus snacks in between, and you can hardly spend your money more wisely. When you're hungry from playing on the beach — and Kalapaki Beach is one of the island's finest — satisfy your cravings and enjoy the little tower room upstairs for 'ocean view dining.'

Lihue, on Kalapaki Bay, 3464 Rice St. 246-3464. Cash only. Map: 1

Kapa'a Fish & Chowder House

Kapa'a Fish & Chowder House announces its seafood emphasis with its attractive exterior decorated with fishing nets and nautical gear. The bar occupies most of the front dining room, and the 'garden room' in the rear, a peaceful oasis filled with hanging ferns and plants, is the preferable location, though be forewarned that it's also the smoking section.

The specialty is seafood, from both local and distant seas. In addition to more than a dozen seafood entrees, including clams, shrimps, oysters, as well as fresh fish, the menu offers chicken ($12.95), and a 14 oz. New York steak ($19.95), as well as fettucini ($9.95) and six other pastas.

Entrees include choice of steak fries, pasta, rice pilaf or steamed rice, as well as a vegetable, and rolls. Salad is a la carte, as is seafood chowder ($3.95), filled with chunks of fish and vegetables. The wine list is limited though reasonably-priced.

During our visits, we have found the cooking to be inconsistent. The fresh fish entree (most recently $22.95) has ranged from moist and flaky to overcooked and dry. One thing has been consistent, however: overseasoned sauces! Over the years we have learned to ask for our fish broiled or plainly sauteed, so that the filet does not arrive smothered in a sauce which overwhelms its delicate flavor, as would have been the case with the macadamia nut, wine, and garlic sauce we were recently served with opakapaka. Our venture last time from surf to turf was not very satisfactory, as the New York steak was tough, stringy and small.

Given the unevenness of the kitchen's performance, dining at Kapa'a Fish & Chowder House means taking your chances. If you catch it right, you can enjoy a pleasant seafood dinner in the garden room, softly lit with lanterns and candles. But you'll spend top dollar for that dinner, more than you'd pay at the Bull Shed, and amazingly, just about the same as you'd pay at A Pacific Cafe, two nearby restaurants where you can count on an outstanding meal.

Northern Kapa'a on Kuhio Hwy. (Rt. 56). Reservations 822-7488. Credit cards. Dinner from 5:30 pm daily. Specify garden room. Non-smoking section. Children's menu half-price. Map: 1

Kauai Chop Suey

Kauai Chop Suey combines unpretentious surroundings, excellent dinners, and unbeatable prices. The dining room, usually crowded with local families, is clean, bright, and cheerful, with well-spaced tables and fly fans to keep the air moving. The decor is a crisp combination of red and white, accented with red Chinese lanterns and green leafy plants.

The real attraction is the prices. A big tureen of scallop soup ($6.05) is sensational, with a subtly seasoned light broth, tender slices of pork and scallops, and an egg-drop texture. Saimin ($2.95/$4.35) is excellent. The shrimp canton ($6.95) is a perfect balance of sweet and sour, and the shrimps, eight large ones, arrive still crisp from being deep fried and exceedingly tender. Special fried rice (at $6.50 one of the most expensive dishes on the large menu) is indeed special—especially tasty, especially generous, and chock full of delicious roast pork, chicken, shrimp, black mushrooms and crunchy snow peas. In Kauai Chow Mein ($6.95), shrimp, chicken, steak, and char sieu are blended in a colorful combination with broccoli and carrots.

Your level of satisfaction, we discovered, has a lot to do with the service, which has a lot to do with the work load in the kitchen. Even if you see empty tables, the owner may tell you to come back in 15 minutes, and in this way control the pace at which the three chefs have to cook. Once you are seated, you may not see your waitress for a while. That's because, as we saw on our last visit, there was only one waitress, and she was taking orders from all the tables, while two other waitresses served and a couple of busboys cleared the plates. It's not a very efficient system, and it certainly lacks the personal touch, but the prices are amazing, and you can bring along your own wine or beer to make the waiting more pleasant! Think twice, however, about bringing the kids— unless you feed them before you come! To bring food home will cost you 21 cents a box: you pay and you pack! Be warned: your feet must be across the threshold by 9 pm or you will be told, with great politeness, that the kitchen is closed.

Lihue, Pacific Ocean Center. 245-8790. No reservations. Cash only. Take-out 245-8790. Lunch 11-2 pm Tues. through Sat. Dinner 4:30-9 pm Tues. through Sun. No beer or wine, but tea is free. Map: 1

Kiibo Restaurant & Sushi Bar

Kiibo has a pleasant, though small dining room with a clean, though utilitarian decor. Post-hurricane remodeling has brightened the dining room and made it more attractive. Comfortable upholstered chairs surround bamboo colored tables, and brown lattice adorns the white walls. At one end, a low table on rice mats is available to patrons wishing to remove their shoes. Everything is understated, even the air-conditioning!

The menu is actually a photo album of traditional Japanese dishes, You can order tempura a la carte ($1/selection) and select from five different types of fresh fish, chicken, pork, beans, tofu, onion, sweet potato, carrots, even eggplant. On our most recent visit, however, what arrived at the table didn't look like the light and puffy tempura shown in the photograph, but was more like breaded shrimp. Teriyaki chicken was a great success, sweet yet tangy, and both juicy and tender. Sukiyaki appears in a steaming iron caldron, rich and pungent with sauce and translucent noodles.

Priced from $4.75, dinners include miso soup, a bowl of rice and another of sauce, attractively displayed on a square tray. Combination dinners cost more, between $11 and $15. Lunch is a better deal, however, with selections about a dollar less than the same choices on the dinner menu. Lunch is also the better meal; given the cautious size of the portions, dinner might leave you hungry! If you spend a little bit more, you might find a better quality dinner in more pleasant surroundings—for example, at Hanama'ulu Restaurant and Tea House, or Kintaro in Kapa'a.

Lihue, 2991 Umi St. 245-2560. Cash only. Lunch daily 11 am - 1:30 pm. Dinner daily 5:30 - 9 pm. Closed Sundays. Children's menu. Map: 1

The King & I

The King and I is one of those wonderful restaurants you always dream of discovering tucked away in a shopping center, like your child's favorite toy under the socks in the corner of his closet. Well, The King and I really is a dream come true, not only for the diner, but also for the owners, a family who fled Cambodia by boat, settled in Hawaii and trained in Honolulu's famous Keo's restaurant, waiting and saving for the chance to open up on their own.

Surprisingly pleasant and comfortably air-conditioned, the dining room is as modest as the prices. White linen tablecloths are topped with glass in an attractive compromise between attractiveness and utility. A definite step above formica! The dining room becomes more attractive as new paintings or Thai artifacts are added, and orchids give the tables a tropical touch.

But the real attraction at The King and I is the food. For many people, each dish will be an adventure into unknown and exotic tastes. Don't be bashful! The menu is large enough to appeal to a variety of tastes. Everyone will love the spring rolls ($6.25/6) which are crisp and light and wonderfully tasty. Attractively arranged on manoa lettuce with mint leaf and cucumber, and served with a delicious peanut vinegar dipping sauce, the spring rolls are so special that some customers make a meal of several orders!

But it would be a mistake to miss the other dishes that come out of this extraordinary kitchen. Lemon grass soup ($6.95) is served piping hot, with wonderfully fragrant clouds of steam. Shrimps served with a peanut sauce are extremely tender, attractively arranged with shredded cabbage and tomato wedges. Or try the fried rice ($5.95) flavored with tomato, cucumber, and cilantro and garnished with sliced water chestnuts. Don't pass up the Siam Mee Kaob ($5.25), a small mountain of crispy rice noodles, bean sprouts, and scallions, served with a delicately sweet peanut sauce. Sa-teh ($6.25), served with spicy peanut sauce and cucumber dipping sauce, is delicious, whether beef, chicken or the truly amazing fresh mahi mahi ($8.95), crisp and light as a whisper.

Fresh mahi mahi is also available as 'ginger fish' ($8.95), fried crisp and served with a mild sauce flavored with ginger and scallions. Curries are outstanding, and you can select from three. Yellow curry is served with potatoes and onions; colored with saffron, it would be the easiest to identify as a "curry." The green curry takes its color—and flavor—from fresh basil, as well as coconut, lime leaves, and lemongrass. The red curry was the sweetest, flavored with coconut. Best of all, in our opinion, is a curry not on the menu, but the favorite of a Kauai friend—a mild, sweet curry, flavored with peanut and coconut and chock full of tender chicken. You can ask for it as 'Evil Jungle Prince' ($8.95). Don't miss Siam eggplant ($6.50), pungent and wonderful. More than a dozen vegetarian specials range from $5.25 to $6.50. The basil and other spices are grown fresh in Kilauea. Try the special Thai tapioca pudding, which will be more soupy perhaps than the lumpy stuff you may remember from school lunches, and flavored with delicious apple-bananas and coconut. Most wines on the small list less than $20.

The King and I is a special place, a great choice for those times when you find it hard to look at another ahi or ono. You'll love the change of pace, the distinctive cuisine, and the friendly family atmosphere. And when you get your bill, your royal pocketbook will hardly notice.

Wailua, Waipouli Plaza, 4-901 Kuhio Highway. 822-1642. Reservations two days in advance. Non-smoking section. Credit cards. Map: 1

Kintaro

Kintaro's decor is a tasteful harmony of blues, whites, grays and tans in perfect proportion. A fountain set in blue tiles and a sushi bar displaying a beautiful array of sashimi take up one long white wall. On nut-colored wood tables, set with chopsticks in blue and white wrappers, you'll find blue and tan tea bowls, and a striking single flower. Ceiling fans and air conditioning make Kintaro comfortably cool, and subdued Japanese music sets a relaxed mood.

What you choose to eat determines where you sit! Cocktails and pu pus are served in a comfortable, attractive lounge, where you can sip a wonderful chi chi, sample elegant sashimi, or munch on crispy fried won tons from the owner's factory next door. In the same spacious room, you can sit at the teppan yaki tables and watch talented chefs chop and flip and make things sizzle right before your eyes. The ingredients, as you will see when they are presented to you in their raw form, are fresh and of the best quality. The teriyaki New York steak ($18.95) or island chicken teriyaki ($13.95) are tender, tasty and juicy.

If you prefer the reasonably-priced dinners on the regular menu, you might be seated in the smaller dining room, where you are served a small salad of pickled cabbage and daikon. Following delicious miso soup, dinner entrees are presented on traditional sectioned wooden platforms and include rice, zaru soba (chilled buckwheat noodles with a special sauce) and pickled vegetables, along with tea served in a blue and tan pottery teapot. Crispy shrimp tempura with vegetables ($13.95) is feather light and delicious, particularly the green beans! Teriyaki beef made with slices of NY steak is exceptionally tender ($15.95). Beef sukiyaki in a cast iron pot ($15.95) is dark and dusky with translucent noodles, meat, and vegetables. Or try yose nabe ($14.95), a Japanese bouillabaisse.

If you like sashimi, try a combination platter. Ours arrived with six elegantly arranged selections: thin slices of ahi, translucent slivers of ono which were delicately sweet and fragrant, dark strips of pungent smoked salmon, shrimps cooked so perfectly that they seemed to melt as you tasted them, eel astonishingly sweet and tender. Garnished with pickled ginger, this was a sensational palette of tastes assembled with an eye for beauty as well as a taste for harmonies and contrasts.

The sushi bar offers some of the best sushi on Kauai, particularly 'California rolls' ($4.50) with crab and avocado, as well as the 'salmon skin hand roll' ($4.50), in which pieces of salmon are crisped and then wrapped in a cone shaped rice wrapped with nori. Watching the sushi chef's hands move with amazing speed is great!

Children are welcome, as is appropriate for a restaurant named in honor of a legendary Japanese boy hero, and service is polite and, on the whole, unrushed. For more than ten years, Kintaro remains a must if you are looking for delicious Japanese food in a pleasant, comfortable setting.

Wailua, Kuhio Hwy. (Rt. 56). Reservations 822-3341. Credit Cards. 5:30-9:30 pm. Closed Sundays. Non-smoking section. Map: 1

Kountry Kitchen

For years, and despite changes in ownership, the best spot for breakfast on the island's east coast has been the Kountry Kitchen, which serves terrific food at equally terrific prices. The large menu offers delicious eggs, expertly cooked bacon and sausage, as well as several omelette creations, including sour cream, bacon and tomato ($6.25) and vegetable garden ($6.95). You can even design your own omelette by ordering a combination of separately priced fillings. Kountry Kitchen's omelettes are unique—thin pancakes of egg rolled around fillings almost like a crepe—tender, moist, and delicious. Or try wonderful Eggs Margo, a version of Eggs Benedict with turkey instead of ham. Our children usually choose Cheesy Eggs ($6.05) — toasted English muffin topped with bacon and poached eggs and covered with rich, golden cheese sauce, and our babies have all loved the honey and wheat pancakes, which are light and fragrant even when drowning in a small ocean of syrup. Hash browns are outstanding, perfectly golden and crisp pancakes of shredded potatoes, and portions are generous. Kids love the hot chocolate.

This very popular restaurant gets crowded at peak mealtimes; so plan to arrive a little early because tables get taken up very quickly, mostly by regular customers. The waitresses are pleasant and efficient and pour lots of absolutely delicious coffee. Across the street is a park with a sandy beach for walking afterwards.

At lunch you can choose sandwiches, salads and hamburgers priced from $6 to $8. Breakfast beverages include gourmet teas; at lunch or dinner you can order beer and wine. Go early to breakfast—the line may be out the door by 8 am!

Kapa'a, 1485 Kuhio Hwy. 822-3511. Credit cards. Breakfast 6 am - 9 pm daily. Lunch 11 am - 2: 30 pm. Map: 1

Margarita's

Perched right on Kuhio Highway in Wailua, Margarita's is hard to miss. The attractive, rambling green building houses a brightly white dining room with two tiers as well as a wrap-around porch for dining and a bar and lounge. The dining room is spacious and attractive, with green formica-topped tables and rattan armchairs with cheerful red and green cushions. Lots of leafy plants, brass, copper and pottery, as well as interesting black and white photos of old Kauai, decorate the walls. Ceilings are open to the rafters, and fly fans keep the air moving from the patio outside. If you are dining on the terrace, bring some 'Off' and/or ask for a mosquito coil. A friendly donkey from the pasture next door may stroll over to say 'hi.'

The menu is the largest you will find in a Mexican restaurant on Kauai, offering dinners from $10.95, with many entree choices available vegetarian style, as well as a wide variety of less expensive a la carte items. Seasoning is not overly spicy, portions are of reasonable size, and ingredients are of high quality. When you order a beef burrito, for example, you will find chunks of excellent grilled sirloin inside. You can order your chicken or beef burrito for about $8.50 a la carte and pay $2 each for beans or rice, or you can choose the whole package for $11.95.

Margarita's menu has expanded to include fresh island fish. The ahi burrito ($13.95), for example, is sensational, with lots of tender fish as well as avocado, tomatoes, black beans, cilantro and tomatillo sauce. The quesadilla ($6.95) was generous and very tasty. Service is friendly though not always efficient, and the no reservations policy may result in a wait at peak dinner hours.

Margarita's is a good choice for middle-of-the-road, American style Mexican dining in a relaxed and pleasant atmosphere. If order from the a la carte menu, you will be surprised at how little your dinner can cost!

Wailua, Kuhio Hwy. (Rt. 56). 822-1808. Credit cards. Daily 5 to 10 pm. No Reservations. Non-smoking section. Map: 1

Ma's Family, Inc.

Ma's tiny luncheonette is so far off the beaten path in Lihue that you'd probably never find it if you didn't stumble onto it by chance. For more than 25 years, Ma's family has established a reputation for well-priced and well-cooked breakfasts and lunches, and you'll probably find the dozen tables filled with local people on their way to work in the morning or stopping off for lunch.

The few tourists who happen onto it will love Ma's expertly cooked eggs, delicious pancakes and waffles that one of our teenagers described as "about the best." The menu, which is posted on the wall over the pass-through to the kitchen, also lists some Hawaiian dishes, for example roast kalua pig that shredded perfectly for our little ones to pick up with their fingers. Even the toast is excellent. Corned beef hash lovers may find Ma's version too much like a potato pancake, but fried min noodles accompanied by eggs and sausages may open your eyes to new possibilities for breakfast.

Service is fast and extremely friendly in the sunny, spartan dining room. Coffee arrives immediately in a large carafe and the food shortly thereafter. If you don't like canned milk in your coffee, ask for a small glass of the fresh stuff. When you leave, you'll be astonished to find how little your meal has cost you. When three adults and four children can breakfast for less than $25, you feel like popping into the kitchen to give Ma a big hug! And many of our readers agree!

Lihue, 4277 Halenani St. Cash only. Daily 5 am - 9:30 pm. Weekends 12:30 am to 10 am. Coffee or tea are free with breakfast! Map: 1

Mema's Thai & Chinese Cuisine

Can you believe it! Two excellent Thai restaurants within a half-mile of each other in tiny Wailua! Mema's and The King & I are more like 'cousins,' operated by two branches of the same Thai family. There are differences: Mema's features Chinese cuisine as well as Thai; its Thai food is slightly spicier, and the ambiance is more attractive. The newly expanded dining room looks like a garden, with bamboo, orchids, and lots of leafy green plants to provide a colorful backdrop for statues and paintings from Thailand and intricate woodwork in red and gold.

What comes to the table is as tasteful and pleasing as the decor. Spring rolls ($5.98) are wonderfully crisp, attractively served with fresh leafy lettuce and peanut sauce, and can be ordered vegetarian. On the Chinese side of the menu, cashew chicken ($7.95) is delicious and chock full of nuts, and lemon chicken ($6.95) is excellent, very crispy and golden with a lightly flavored lemon sauce. Thai dishes can be hot, so be sure to ask your server which ones match best with your taste! Green curry with coconut milk, lemon grass, kaffir lime leaves, eggplant, and fresh basil $7.95 is truly wonderful and not overly spicy. Red curry ($7.95), served with potatoes and chicken, looks lovely garnished with fresh basil and chopped cabbage, but it may scorch your tastebuds! Fresh mahi mahi satay ($9.25) is a wonderful way to sample island fish! Vegetarians have many choices, and will love the sticky rice ($2.95).

While experts may grumble that no authentic Thai peppers blister the dishes at Mema's, the temperature is up a few degrees from The King & I. With reasonable prices (about $6.95 per dish), lots of variety on the menu, an attractive dining room, and friendly service, Mema's has its own identity — a great spot for a pleasant, relaxing evening.

Wailua Shopping Plaza, behind the Sizzler. 823-0899. Credit cards. Lunch 11 am till 2 pm M-F, and Dinner nightly 5 pm - 9:30 pm. Map: 1

Nanea

So you want to try poi or kalua pig, and experiment with Kauai's ethnic diversity. But you don't want a fancy, expensive luau, and you aren't really attracted to the purplish stuff sold as 'poi' in plastic bags at the supermarket! Well, Nanea is for you! — a perfect spot to taste island-style foods at a reasonable price with exceptionally friendly service.

Nanea's bright white facade catches your eye as you cruise past the row of small shopping centers that have grown up along Rt. 56 in Wailua. Inside, the pleasant green and white dining room is equally clean-looking, and comfortable with fly fans to keep the air moving. The menu offers a range of 'local foods,' that smattering of Hawaiian luau fare and dishes from various Pacific nations. Here's your chance to taste kalua pork (or for the non meat-eaters, kalua chicken) smoked in the traditional way wrapped in ti-leaves ($4), or lomi lomi salmon (S4), luau chicken ($3.75) simmered in coconut milk, ahi poke ($4.25), or chicken laulau ($3.25), braised in taro leaves. Lunch combination plates average $6.25, and the five dinner plates, which feature three of four items plus rice and poi, run $10, and include dessert, coffee/ tea.

Nanea means 'place of relaxation', and is special because it's so family-friendly. The owner, who used to cook at the popular Aloha Diner, gets help from two lovely teenage daughters and grandma's recipes. The two girls make you feel right at home, serving as a friendly team, ready to make suggestions or arrange 'half orders' so you can sample more widely. When our daughter admired the painted spoon which matched her soup bowl, they allowed her to buy it for 2 quarters!

Wailua, 4-939A Kuhio Hwy. Take out: 821-0040. Credit cards. Closed Sundays. Map: 1.

Norberto's El Cafe

Right in the heart of Kapaʻa, Norberto's has served first rate Mexican food on Kauai since 1977. The dining room is attractively laid out on two levels separated by a railing. White stucco walls and woodgrain tables create a setting like a cantina, colorfully decorated with hanging plants, sombreros, and gas lamps. Trophies won by the girls' softball team, coached by Norberto, sit atop a piano, where guests occasionally contribute to the informal atmosphere with impromptu entertainment.

Over the years, prices have not changed much, and almost everything is very reasonable. Margaritas go for $4.00 ($11 for a pitcher), and the a la carte entrees as well as six complete Mexican dinners with soup, vegetable, beans, chips and salsa cost $11.50 or less. Be sure to ask for the homemade chips made with flour tortillas. Guacamole is only $2.50. Nachos ($2.50/small) are generously covered with cheese. When we finished our bean soup ($2), we were asked if we wanted seconds!

The Burrito El Cafe ($9) deserves to be called a house specialty—the tortilla generously stuffed with flavorful beef, beans and cheese, baked enchilada style and topped with guacamole and the freshest red tomatoes and lettuce. On the full dinner menu, the tostada is a huge colorful salad mounded over a crisp tortilla, and the chili relleno ($7.95) is dipped (not drowned) in egg and gently cooked, so that it comes out light, tender and delicately flavored. An El Cafe specialty, enchiladas made with taro ($4) are first rate, the taro leaves, which taste not unlike spinach, providing an island flavor. Almost all dishes can also be ordered vegetarian style. For the some who like it hot, plenty of homemade salsa is on the table to add to your dishes, and the kitchen will say *"Ole!"* to any challenge!

Service is extremely friendly, prices are a few dollars cheaper than other Mexican eateries, and children are treated with tolerance, even when cranky. On our last visit, when the salsa proved too hot for the short people to handle, the waitress immediately brought a bowl of bean soup to our table. As soon as the kids started dipping their chips, all you could hear was happy crunching!

Kapa'a, 4-1373 Kuhio Hwy. 822-3362. 5:30-9:30 pm daily. Closed Sundays. Smoking in bar only. Children's menu. Credit cards. Map: 1

OK Bento & Saimin

In a tiny shopping center in downtown Lihue, this tiny eatery has only five tables, and they don't match. The menu is written on a board, and you may have to pour yourself a glass of water from the dispenser if the place is busy, which it will be if you come at noon when the plate-lunch crowd arrives. While you wait, you can peek through the pass-through and watch the chef take huge portions of saimin noodles, plunge them into boiling water, and lift them out in clouds of steam. Customers drift in, and if no tables are available, they may wait, leaning against the refriger-ated soda case against the wall, occasionally helping themselves to a can, or perhaps inquire politely about an unoccupied chair at one of the tables. You can learn a lot in close quarters; one construction worker a chair away observed that he had eaten at OK Bento & Saimin every day for the past two weeks and never had a bad meal! The decor is spartan, to put it mildly, since the coke cooler and the fire extinguisher pretty much do it all. Fly fans keep the air moving, but their effectiveness has a lot to do with the weather and the body count.

The saimin would be worth any sacrifice, for the broth is fragrant, steaming, and flavorful, and the noodles have just the perfect consistency. When you order, the waitress hands the chef a bowl which she selects from the stacks of different sizes and colors along the wall. You might order the saimin special ($4.45), which comes with diced spam, cooked pork, vegetables, two won tons, and a hard boiled egg, or you might prefer the large plain version with a side order of vegetables. Won ton min ($3.70) is also delicious. Portions are generous, but just remember as the aromas drifting over from the next chair makes you want to opt for the giant portion: any leftovers will have to go into a take-out box, which costs 30 cents!

Lihue, 4100 Rice Street. 245-6554. Cash only. Non-smokers, take your chances! Map: 1

Weathering Kauai

Some days are clear all over the island, but on other days you might have to drive to find the sun. Like all the Hawaiian islands, Kauai's sunny side varies with the winds. Normal trade winds, which blow from the north and northeast, create the lee in the south and west, from Poipu to Kekaha. While the clouds may back up against the mountains and bring showers to the north shore beaches, Poipu and Salt Pond may have sunny skies! However, sometimes the winds blow from the south and west, and these 'Kona winds' create the lee in the north and northeast. The north shore may be spectacular on a day when the eastern and southern shores have rain. To decide whether to go south to Poipu, west to Kekaha or north to Hanalei, listen to the weather report! Or you can call ahead. These merchants have graciously agreed to be your weather tipsters: Brennecke's Beach Center, Poipu (742-7505). Waimea Plantation, Waimea (338-1625). Pedal 'n Paddle, Hanalei (826-9069).

Ono Char Burger (Duane's)

For years, a tiny shack next to the general store at Anahola was famous among local people for delicious hamburgers and fresh fruit smoothies. More tourists heard about the hamburgers, and so the shack, along with Duane's reputation, got larger. Picnic tables were added under the tree, and the menu was expanded. Even if the most recent coat of paint doesn't quite catapult Duane's into the same time warp as McDonald's, the facade is certainly brighter!

Even though Duane has sold the business, the burgers are still delicious, if somewhat smaller than before. They can be made with various cheeses (even blue cheese) or teriyaki style, are priced from $3.95 to $4.95. Children can order hamburgers ($2.50) or deep fried chicken strips and fries ($3.40) that will tempt others to order the adult portion ($6.95). Fries ($1.40) are sizzling crisp.

Service can be slow, particularly at peak lunchtime. Be patient, and pack up your sandwiches (each half will be separately wrapped) and head for beautiful Anahola Beach just a mile down Aliomanu Road. Phone in your order ahead of time if possible!

Anahola, Rt. 6.. 822-9181. Open daily 10 am to 6 pm; Sunday 11 am to 6 pm. Cash only. Map: 1

Sunset in a tidepool mirror

Ono Family Restaurant

Ono Family Restaurant specializes in wholesome, inexpensive family fare. Breakfasts are well-cooked, attractively served, and generous, including some house specialties which are really special. 'Eggs Veggie' is a version of eggs benedict with fresh sauteed zucchini instead of meat. Pancakes were voted "Exc!" by our kids, and the ham and cheese omelette was soft and delicious. Our waitress was very helpful with things like crackers, straws, extra napkins and extra cups for tastes of grown-up coffee—those etceteras of family dining that don't seem essential until they're missing.

For lunch, children's plates are a bargain and include a cup of soup and a beverage. A children's chicken platter ($3.50), for example, includes a leg and thigh baked in a sweet barbecue sauce. Adults will find the hamburgers, ten varieties priced from $3.95 ($2.50/child), on the whole competently cooked, and non-beefeaters will be pleased with the veggie combo sandwich ($4.55) served on wheat branola bread. Buffalo burgers (from $5.25) are more lean and healthful than beef for the cholesterol-conscious, and their distinctive flavor will please some but not others (and unfortunately not our children)! Dinners including soup or salad range from $7.50. You might also try delicious Portuguese bean soup, spicy with sausage, beans and macaroni. French fries are hot and crispy; lemonade is the real thing! Chocolate cream and coconut cream pies ($2.50), though described as 'onolicious,' are heavy, thick and sweet.

The restaurant has a cozy, friendly atmosphere. Wooden booths shine with polish, and many feature a partition which can be removed in order to connect two together and seat a large family like ours. Gold carpeting, pleasant yellow walls with paneling, cheerful curtains, and flowers make the dining room attractive. Family antiques harmonize with a homey assortment of square and round tables. Air conditioning keeps temperatures comfortable.

Although at times service can be painfully slow, everyone is friendly and cooperative. While you wait, children can work on pencil puzzles provided on their menus, and people seem ready to help with each other's restless little ones. On one occasion, when we could not find our waitress to get a glass of water that had suddenly become an urgent necessity, an adjacent Daddy passed over an extra. Just outside the open door, two old timers shared their donuts with our wandering daughter, patted her head as she chewed, and listened politely to her latest fish story.

Kapaʻa, 4-1292 Kuhio Hwy. 822-1710. Credit cards. 7 am - 9 pm except Mondays. Non-smoking section. Closed Sundays at 2 pm. Map: 1

A Pacific Cafe

A Safeway shopping center is an unlikely spot for a gourmet restaurant, almost as unlikely in fact as finding a Safeway shopping center at all on a remote Pacific island. Wherever you would find it, however, A Pacific Cafe would be a special place, because Jean-Marie Josselin is a gifted chef and creates a truly special cuisine, blending the culinary traditions of Europe and the Pacific Rim, while emphasizing the freshest of local ingredients. A Pacific Cafe is a must on anyone's list!

As you enter the air-conditioned dining room, you will see the chefs hard at work behind a tall counter pass-through. That is appropriate, for the kitchen is the centerpiece of this restaurant. A Pacific Cafe realizes Josselin's dream to follow his own inspirations rather than simply implement the ideas of others. Each aspect of the dining experience receives exceptional attention. The plates, for example, are created by his wife, Sophronia. No two are alike in shape or color, and they frame the appetizers and entrees like culinary paintings.

This is a place to venture into new territory. You will be delighted with the ingenious, sometimes whimsical, artistry of each dish. For example, spring rolls ($9.50) arrive on a gaily colored, triangular plate, the crispy halves standing at different heights like a mini citiscape, served in a small lake of sauce garnished with sesame seeds toasted black. Or imagine sashimi served tempura style ($9.50), the ahi wrapped in seaweed, then deep fried and sliced in elegant, dainty medallions, the fish cool in the center, the wrapping crisp outside. Poached scallop ravioli ($6.50) is wonderful, the won ton shaped noodles delicately flavored and the lime ginger sauce delicious. Try grilled Japanese eggplant with goat cheese and chili pepper vinaigrette ($8.50), or a family favorite, Peking duck and shrimp served in a taco with papaya ginger salsa ($9.50). Even an ordinary dinner salad ($4.75) looks like kaleidoscope of colors.

Over the years, we have explored this menu to find even familiar entrees in arresting fashion. Lauren's favorite, rack of lamb, served in four generous, succulent chops, served 'Chinese style' with hoisin sauce ($20.95); she will tell you there is no fat on it. Mikey's favorite sirloin steak is arrayed in lovely slices with fried Maui onions and an excellent barbecue sauce ($18.75). Our vegetarian Mirah prefers Jean Marie's stir fried vegetables, still crunchy-fresh, which he will make upon request. In fact, this kitchen will customize any dish you order, switching preparations or sauces if you desire.

But delicious as these entrees are, the real stars on the menu are the fresh fish, and they are truly magical—sizzling hot, meltingly tender, and

enhanced with wonderful sauces. Try fresh ahi with a Moroccan spice glaze and eggplant puree ($21.95). Wok-charred mahi mahi with garlic sesame crust and lime ginger sauce ($24) is excellent! Jeremy, our family spicy food lover, likes the blackened ono, served with papaya and basil sauce ($22.50). Best of all, certainly the most spectacular, may be the deep fried whole Thai snapper, which arrives standing up and looking right at you, so crunchy and crispy and sweet that you eat it down to the fins and bones ($24)!

Attention to detail makes each aspect of the dinner special. Rice arrives in a bamboo steamer, and even the muffins are out of the ordinary—light, tasty and flavored with herbs. Desserts are delicious and inventive. Chocolate lovers will adore the hot chocolate tart, and Macadamia nut tart with coconut ice cream will please anyone nuts about nuts!

The elegant dining room has a southwestern flair, reflecting the chef's years in Los Angeles. Black lacquer chairs surround the polished wood tables, set with black bamboo placemats, shining crystal, and what can only be described as bonsai cactus. Unlike most restaurants, where the art on the walls is merely decorative, Pacific Cafe's walls seem almost like a gallery, and in fact the 'exhibition' changes at regular intervals. The only disadvantage in the air-conditioned room is the noise. This cafe is really best on an a night when it's not busy, if you can find one! When a restaurant on Kauai makes it to *Sunset Magazine*, you should expect it to be jammed!

Now that Jean Marie has opened a second restaurant on Kauai at Beach House, as well as another on Maui, he splits his time between locations, and you might want to ask who's cooking when you make your reservation. Jean Marie runs such an efficient operation, with such a professionally trained staff under direction of its young manager, Jason, that you may not even notice a difference when he's 'gone to Maui.' But if you can visit when he's in the kitchen, so much the better!

Although Pacific Cafe's a la carte menu may seem expensive, you don't really mind paying for a meal so memorable. And actually, the fresh island fish entrees cost less than at a restaurant of comparable quality like the Hyatt's Tidepools, or the Princeville Hotel's Cafe Hanalei. For this reason, A Pacific Cafe has a loyal following, primarily among local people. On a given night, you might see a housepainter, a real estate developer, and a restaurant owner seated at adjacent tables. Everyone seems to agree that A Pacific Cafe is something special, even four Horowitz children who can't seem to agree on much else! They'll all tell you: Don't miss this one! It's a truly magical dining treat.

Wailua, Kauai Village Shopping Center, Kuhio Hwy. Reservations a day (or 2!) in advance: 822-0013. Credit cards. Non-smoking section. Map: 1

Papaya's Garden Cafe

One of an increasing number of vegetarian eateries on the island, Papaya's is actually a full-fledged natural foods store in the Kauai Village Shopping Center, Wailua. The deli operation offers a wide range of sandwiches and casseroles with the flavors of Mexican, Cuban, Indian, Szechwan, Thai, Greek and Italian cuisines, priced from $4 to $8.95, including 'Garden lasagne,' Spanakopita, and tempeh, fish, or chicken burgers. You can also enjoy espresso, cappuccino, lattes, mochas and teas.

Dine outside on the "patio," more accurately the walkway of the mall, where cheerful white tables are usually occupied by happy diners. The umbrellas come in handy when the rain comes down!

Wailua, Kauai Village Shopping Center, Kuhio Hwy. 823-0190. Open 9 am - 8 pm. Closed Sunday. Map: 1

Panda Garden

Next to the Safeway in the Kauai Village Shopping Center, Panda Garden looks clean and attractive. Tables with white cloths covered with shiny glass tops and set with blue and white china make the white painted dining room look cheerful and bright. Bamboo, favorite taste treat of the panda, is the main the decorative motif. Local people like this place, and the reason may be the combination of reasonable prices with reasonably good food.

Most menu choices are priced between $7 and $9. Won ton soup ($6.25) is hot, delicately flavored, and filled with won tons. Egg rolls ($4.95) are crisp and tasty without being greasy, clearly freshly made. Lemon chicken ($6.95) is deep fried to a golden brown and served with a piquant sauce. Portions are generous, the food tasty, and the service slow, though pleasant and polite. You might wait a long time between ordering and being served, but that's because everything is prepared fresh.

Although Panda Garden has no view, given its shopping center location, the dining room is comfortable and air conditioned, the service pleasant, and the food reasonably-priced and reasonably tasty.

Wailua, Kauai Village Shopping Center, 4-831 Kuhio Hwy. 822-0092. Lunch 11 am - 2 pm except Wednesdays; dinner 4:30 pm - 9 pm daily. Non-smoking section. Map: 1.

The Plantation Restaurant — J.R's

Just a few feet off Rt. 56 in Hanama'ulu, J.R.'s Plantation Restaurant is housed in a historic plantation building cooled by ceiling fans and decorated with sugar plantation memorabilia — machinery parts and tools, horse collars and ox yokes, and even a red wagon wheel hung with lanterns and plants. Candles shine on wood plank tables colorful with tropical flowers, and at the rear, two private booths with black leatherette seats cozy up to a genuine indoor waterfall.

More than two dozen entrees range from $12.95 for chicken teriyaki up to $20.95 for 14 oz. of prime rib, including a 'Hawaiian platter and some vegetarian choices, like vegetable lasagne ($12.95). Dinners include soup or salad, as well as rice, potato, or linguini romano (which, according to our waitress, you can switch for rice if you find it too garlicky). Children under 12 can choose chicken, mahi mahi or pasta for only $9.95, and the boneless chicken breast passed the most stringent "no–yuk" test from the small picky eaters.

For the first course, you get a bowl, which can be filled with either soup or salad of mixed greens. Vegetable soup is excellent, and the green salad is generous and served with tasty dressings. You also get hot french bread, toasted with or without garlic, but the absence of bread plates means that in short order you'll have crumbs skittering everywhere.

The new owner has improved the dining experience. The house specialty prime rib is tasty and tender, served with good au jus, little fat, but no bone, and certainly reasonably-priced at $16.95 for a 10 oz. portion. If you have your heart set on this dish, call ahead to reserve a portion, so you won't be disappointed. Fresh island ahi is moist and tender, though on the small side for the $19.95 price. The small wine list is basic Beringer, the top-priced chardonnay at $18.

JR's Plantation is obviously not the place to order an expensive meal. But prices are reasonable, the dining room pleasant, and the staff friendly.

In Hanama'ulu, Rt. 56. 245-1606. Credit cards. Dinner nightly 5 - 9:45 pm. Early-bird specials till 6:30 pm. Map: 1

ROCCO'S

With its shining double storey windows looking over the central crossroads of Kapa'a town, Rocco's offers reasonably-priced Italian cuisine in a comfortable, informal setting.

Rocco's menu is not extensive, dedicated largely a few to pastas and fresh-baked pizzas as well as several casserole offerings. Many of the choices come with a small green salad, with Caesar dressing available as an 'upgrade.' You can also try minestrone ($3) filled with vegetables and flavorful broth. Fragrant bread still warm from the oven is listed on the menu as 'a la carte' ($2) though we were not charged for our basket. 'White pizza' has a wonderful crust, crisp yet soft, with tasty cheese and a marinara sauce for dipping ($6). Rocco's manicotti, a spinach pasta, is generously stuffed with cheese, though we also found a rather large clove of garlic as well! ($10) In fact, garlic was dominant in almost everything, except for chicken with marsala sauce, which seemed overly sweet.

Service is prompt and polite. The menu does not offer great variety, and garlic is a clear favorite of the chef, but if you are in a hurry for noodles, Rocco's offers fast, reasonably-priced dining.

Central Kapa'a. 822-4422. Credit cards. Open daily for lunch and dinner. Full bar. Non-smoking section. Map: 1

North shore surf can be spectacular during winter months.

Si Cisco's

In the Kukui Grove Shopping Center in Lihue, Si Cisco's has a pleasant dining room, with white stucco walls, green leafy plants, and dark stained wood tables decorated with colorful tiles. Stained glass lanterns provide soft light, and iron grillwork along with murals of south-of-the-border landscapes provide the Mexican touch. In front, the bar is a pleasant, attractive place to enjoy margaritas or sangria. In the dining room to the rear, semi-enclosed booths with straight backed benches line the walls, and because these benches are connected, they can be a problem when the restaurant is crowded. If someone at one table moves down, those seated at the adjacent table move up!

A basket of chips appears quickly, accompanied by both mild and hot salsa, while you consider a menu which is varied enough to have something for everyone in the family to order. 'Specialties' cost less than $10, and combinations just a dollar more. The youngsters in our party, careful readers that they are, pointed out that a plate for sharing costs $2.50 and, while our order was being cooked, devised several ingenious ways to accomplish sharing cost-free! 'Macho Nachos' ($8) arrived on a huge plate, great on the additions (shredded beef, tomatoes, beans, guacamole and sour cream) but weak on the chips. The chimichanga ($9.95) was very good—crispy, moist, with well-flavored beef, and lots of guacamole and sour cream on the side. When asked for details about the fresh mahi mahi specialty ($13.95), the waitress produced the chef, who described the preparation and then sent out a sample! Quesadilla ($4.95 a la carte) was acceptably cheesy, though not memorable; beans and rice were good.

Service varies. It can be just passable or extremely friendly. One final note: we received a take-out container for our leftover rice and beans, and were *not* charged the 50 cents listed on the menu!

Lihue, Kukui Grove Center. 246-1563. Lunch until 4 pm; dinner until 10 pm daily. Non-smoking section. Credit cards. Map: 1

The Sizzler

From the road, the Sizzler's pink neon sign makes a strong statement. Beneath that sign, however, we found a sizzling disappointment! You must stand on line, wait your turn, and then pay in cash while your order is called into the kitchen from the register. With receipt in hand, you hunt for a table, then visit the famous salad bar which costs extra unless you are a senior citizen.

And prices are deceptive. What looks like a great buy on the sign outside (Prime Rib Dinner $10.99) is, according to our waiter, only 8 oz.—not much to look at on the plate, and it's $3.99 more if you add the salad bar. If you add that salad bar charge to the larger prime rib ($17.99), you'll actually pay more ($21.98) than you would at the Bull Shed ($18.95) — which offers a free salad bar and also table service.

The salad bar ($7.99 a la carte) is the best deal in the house. At $3.99, children under 12 have it even better, as that modest price includes even a small beverage. The salad bar offers hot soup, fruits, a completely furnished taco bar with taco and tostada shells, as well as hot pasta.

On a breakfast trip by themselves, our children found the same problems. One morning a helpful waiter offered them fruit from the salad bar when their breakfasts were delayed more than twenty minutes. Another morning, however, the waitress brought the wrong order for one child, and cold eggs for the others. She whisked the eggs back to the kitchen, but the eggs came back reheated rather than re-cooked. At that point, the children told her, with all the grave politeness of short people trying to act tall, that the eggs were as hard as rocks and the papaya slices were hot. When the waitress informed them that eggs could not be returned more than once, she entered our family folklore forever!

At the Sizzler, you have to work for what you eat, and dining is rushed rather than relaxed. You end up, in our opinion, paying too much for too little, and all of it in precious vacation cash. For these reasons, we found the Sizzler, alas, to be a fizzler!

Wailua, Kuhio Hwy. No reservations or credit cards. Breakfast, lunch, and dinner daily. Non-smoking section. Map: 1

Sukothai Restaurant

What? A new Thai restaurant less than a mile away from the two local Thai favorites, King and I and Mema Thai Cuisine? Sukothai tries to find a market niche by offering a larger combination of cuisines: Thai - Chinese - Vietnamese, and, as if that weren't enough of a challenge for the kitchen, Barbecue!

The small dining room is bright and welcoming, decorated in cheerful yellow, with a red carpet and red tablecloths, woven with gold and covered with protective glass. Yellow orchids provide the tropical touch, while roomy rattan armchairs and air conditioning make dining pleasant and comfortable. You will be served a basket of crispy won ton skins as you consider the menu, where most dishes cost about $8. Tom Kar , or coconut and lemon grass soup, is wonderful, presented in a lovely earthernware serving bowl ($7.95). Rice pancakes filled with minced chicken, cut in sections and deep fried, are also delicious ($7.50). Vegetable fried rice is colorful with vegetables ($6.95), and cashew chicken is very tasty. Pad thai, made with rice noodles, is excellent ($8.25). We ran into trouble only when we asked to alter a dish by eliminating or reducing one of its listed ingredients, garlic. Impossible, we were told, because the sauces are prepared in advance. And no way to modify the degree of heat in the 'spicy' dishes, either!

Sukothai tries to appeal to as many people as it can with its varied cuisine, a large undertaking. The main difference is in the responsiveness of the kitchen to individual requests. For that, you could pay the same prices and visit Mema's, or King and I, which will hold the chiles if you ask, and which you might find more attractive.

Kapa'a Shopping Center(near Big Save). 821-1224. Credit cards. Lunch 10:30 am - 3 pm. Dinner 5 pm - 10 pm. daily. Air-conditioned. Map: 1

Sumo Restaurant

In the Kukui Grove Shopping Center, Sumo offers reasonably-priced lunches in a pleasant and attractive setting. The white decor, accented by leafy green plants, looks clean and crisp; shoji screens soften the lighting and mute the traffic noises in the mall.

The menu offers a wide variety of sandwiches, salads, and Oriental dishes. Prices are reasonable, and so is the quality of what you are served. Oriental dishes are hot and colorful with vegetables, though the taste is on the bland side. Combination lunch plates include an excellent miso soup, a better choice than the rather small saucer of romaine that passes for the house salad. You can choose from a wide array of sushi.

Some dishes are surprises, like crispy, tasty chicken wings. Others are more ordinary, including fairly pedestrian sandwiches. Shrimp tempura may seem more like deep fried shrimp in bread crumbs, though it is accompanied by stir–fried noodles with carrots, squash, and green beans and two scoops of rice. Portions are large, and children can choose chicken, cheeseburger, or hot dog with rice or fries and a drink.

While the food may suffer from one–dimensional seasoning, Sumo Restaurant offers a good value for your money in a setting more pleasant than you'd expect in a shopping center. When you're tired of hitting the stores, you can rest your feet without wrestling with your wallet.

Lihue, Kukui Grove Center. 246-0113. Open for breakfast, lunch, dinner daily. Credit cards. Air conditioned. Non-smoking section. Map: 1

Two incomparable views for lunch: Cafe Hanalei, Princeville Hotel . . .
Page 157

Plumeria   *. . . & a picnic at Crater Hill.*
Page 98.

Sea changes

Kalihiwai—our favorite family beach on the north shore. In winter, thundering surf can crash onto the sand (above), while in summer, the ocean can be calm, almost like a lake (below). Page 35.

Lumahai Beach: lovely but treacherous, especially in winter. Page 39.

Windsurfing

Best spots: Anini Beach (north shore) for lessons. Kalapaki Beach (eastern shore) Maha'ulepu and Salt Pond Beach (south shore). Page 58.

Hibiscus

Torch ginger

Island sunsets are especially lovely when reflected on eastern shores.

Tip Top Restaurant

The name Tip Top conjures up certain 1950's type expectations: a clean room for under $20, a square meal for $5. But you're not really sure that you should believe in this any more than you would in the tooth fairy! It is true, though. Since 1916, the Tip Top Motel has served fairly–priced, honest, unpretentious food, and for this reason, is more popular with local people than the tourists who manage to find it on the side street of Lihue.

Even though the legendary Tip Top Bakery is now only a memory, the restaurant is much improved with post-hurricane remodeling— looking more like a restaurant and less like a school cafeteria. The large booths are comfortable, and on hot summer days, you'll appreciate the air conditioning! The real attraction at Tip Top is the prices. Delicious pancakes with macadamia nuts, bananas, pineapples or raisins are only $4.75. Excellent french toast is only $4.50. A ham and cheese omelette or bacon and eggs, accompanied by a scoop of hash browns, costs less than $4, while the price of pork chops, the most expensive item on the menu, is $5.50. While in general the food is well-prepared if unexciting, the homemade pineapple and guava jam is special. Have it on toast, but that's a la carte.

At Tip Top, you won't find the kind of breakfasts you get at Kountry Kitchen, but you won't pay those prices either, and you will feel quite pleased when your bill for six people turns out to be less than $30. It's hot, fast, and filling—perfect for those mornings when you're on the way to the airport and need every ounce of strength to get those bags through the agriculture inspection without misplacing anything—or anybody!

Lihue, 3173 Akahi St. Cash only. Opens daily at 6:45 am. Closed Mondays. Map: 1

Tokyo Lobby

Tokyo Lobby's dining room is attractive and comfortable in an informal way. A red pagoda roof extends over the sushi bar, making it the centerpiece of the room. Black lacquer chairs and tables colored a soft grey make an attractive contrast to the clean white walls, accented with lots of leafy green plants. You may find paper napkins and plastic cups at your setting, but don't despair, for what arrives on your plate may be of higher quality than you'd expect.

The menu offers a wide variety of Japanese appetizers and entrees, and dinners include an excellent miso soup, tsukemono and rice. Chicken curry ($9.95) Japanese style, was a surprise and welcome change for our curry enthusiast, Jeremy, who liked the large chicken pieces served over rice with a thick sauce almost like gravy. Teriyaki chicken ($9.95) is moist and flavorful. Tempura ($14.95) is first rate — light, crispy and filled with vegetables still crunchy and colorful as well as either fresh island fish or shrimp ($11.95). Order tempura in the appetizer portion ($6.95) which contains 5 pieces, and you'll have enough to sample and still have room to try some freshly rolled sushi. California roll, Jeremy's favorite combination of crab and avocado wrapped in rice and nori, is on the small side, but very tasty. Salmon skins, served in a cone shaped nori wrapper, are crispy though less so than at Kintaro.

Service is efficient, for both the staff and the owner work hard to be sure every aspect of the dinner is satisfactory. With prices comparable to smaller, less attractively decorated restaurants, yet food on a level with higher priced eateries, Tokyo Lobby is a good bet.

Lihue, Pacific Ocean Plaza, 3501 Rice St. 245-8989. Lunch & Dinner daily. Non-smoking section. Credit cards. Map: 1

Violet's Place

We might never have discovered Violet's Place except for Hurricane Iniki. Few places were open during our first post-Iniki visit in late 1992, and Violet's Place was a welcome discovery one dreary, rainy lunchtime after a hard morning's shopping at Safeway! What a find! After two bowls of steaming hot saimin ($2.95/$3.75), perfectly flavored and tasty to the last noodle, we enjoyed some first rate club sandwiches ($4.95), with toasted bread, lean meat, fresh tomatoes, as well as a plump, juicy hamburger on a soft sesame seed bun ($3.45). The day looked much brighter – as soon as we polished off the crispy, golden french fries which come with the burgers and sandwiches — as did several other lunchtimes, even when the weather was better!

About a year later, when 13-year-old Lauren chose Violet's Place for her special dinner with mom, the saimin fulfilled all her expectations born of memory, and the fresh ono, which we requested to be stir fried rather than sauteed, turned into one of the memorable meals on Kauai. The vegetables were fresh and still crunchy, and the numerous chunks of ono were perfectly cooked to preserve the delicate flavor and texture of the fish. You'll find Oriental, Hawaiian, Thai, Filipino, and American dishes on a menu large in variety but small in price, with most selections $6 or less. Breakfast choices include homemade pancakes, omelettes, "Molokai sweetbread french toast" with papaya or eggs for less than $4.

Violet's may not look like much from the outside, but don't hesitate to go in and try the carefully cooked meals. With only seven tables and a decor limited to the lavender walls, some plants and a refrigerated case, Violet's is not elegant. But it is clean, comfortable, and friendly, with Violeta herself, a former executive sous chef at the Sheraton Molokai, busy visiting with the customers and making sure everyone is happy. This personal touch is important, as the chef prepares each order fresh, and service can be slow. Those with the wandering spirit can walk to nearby Waldenbooks while the cook is cooking to check out the new titles.

Wailua, Kauai Village Center, 4-831 Kuhio Highway, next to Safeway. 822-2456. Breakfast & Lunch 8 am - 2 pm daily. Dinner 4:30 - 10 pm. Closed Wednesdays. Map: 1

Wah Kung Chop Suey

If you didn't know where to look for it, you probably would never find Wah Kung, tucked away in the interior of Kinipopo Shopping Village across from Sizzler on Kuhio Highway in Wailua. Peek inside the tiny kitchen and watch the cooks hard at work in steam and sizzle. The tiny dining room will probably be crowded with local families who appreciate the large portions and small prices, most around $6. Try excellent saimin ($2.95) or tasty stir fried vegetables ($5.75)! Many people will be waiting for their food to be popped into containers (each costs a quarter), which sit ready for action atop two freezers which seem central to the decor. There's barely enough room left for a few tables, some Chinese decorations, and the handmade signs describing the daily specials. Tables outside on the patio are cooler and more pleasant.

You'll probably be in for a wait, but you can walk around the corner and check out the Korean Bar-B-Q, also crowded with local families, and you can order a portion to go at the same time, or browse the Goldsmith's Gallery nearby for wonderful island-designed jewelry.

Wailua, Kinipopo Shopping Village, Kuhio Hwy. 822-0560. Cash only. Lunch: Tues.-Sat 11 am to 2 pm; Dinner Mon-Sun 4:30 pm to 8:30 pm.

Wailua Marina Restaurant

One of the oldest restaurants on Kauai, the Wailua Marina is a good place to take the family. The large dining room features an enormous mural of an underwater vista complete with stuffed fish and a turtle shell. Weather permitting, ask to sit on the large covered porch decorated with plants and fresh flowers. Cooled by delightful breezes, it looks out over the Wailua River, where boats rock gently in the docks. In the evening, candles light the tables with a golden glow, and the air is soft and fragrant.

A pleasant waitress will probably recommend the fresh fish specials, which are usually delicious. Mahi mahi is carefully broiled, and the fresh ahi stuffed with crab ($16.50) is well seasoned and flavorful. The fresh ono with marina sauce ($15.50) is juicy, tender, and flaky, a generous portion of 2 large slices. If it's in season, try the local slipper lobster, a sweet and tender 6 oz. tail served with a filet of fresh ono ($19) and accompanied with small cups of both teriyaki sauce and drawn butter. The kids preferred the fried chicken ($10) to the relatively dry teriyaki chicken, but they loved the teriyaki sauce on the side for dipping! The roast beef ($15.95/$17.95) was a bit mealy though tasty.

On the dinner menu, most entrees cost less than $15 and include rolls, rice or potato, a salad which can charitably be described as small, and a vegetable, in our case a third of an ear of corn resting on a bed of shredded lettuce with an orchid atop an envelope of catsup! The hot, crispy french fries are considerably better than the somewhat greasy fried rice, although even that's not too bad if you flavor it with some of the kitchen's delicious teriyaki sauce.

To keep prices down, the Marina cuts a few corners, but they're the kind no one really misses if you catch the spirit of the place. The pleasantness of the setting more than compensates for paper napkins and placemats. The salad dressing may not be quite enough for the salad which is not quite enough for the plate, but on the other hand, the rolls with whipped butter are light and fluffy and smell of the oven! If the salad dressing appears in a paper pill cup and the parmesan cheese in the kind of small envelope Lipton's uses for tea bags, just smile, for you can feed the whole family for a reasonable price. Children can chose from ten dinners for about $3 less than adult prices. The 11 wines on the list are not very exciting, but all are priced at $15 or less. Don't pass up the homemade coconut or macadamia nut pies ($2.50).

Prices are up, post Iniki, and the cost of the Marina's fresh island fish dinner is now almost even with the Bull Shed's, where you also have a salad bar. Wailua Marina is still reasonable, however, and you'll come away with a pleasant memory of dining by candlelight, and the lights on the river winking as the dusk deepens into night.

Wailua River State Park, just south of the bridge on Kuhio Hwy. 11 am – 9 pm except Mondays. 822-4311 for reservations. Ask about shuttle service from Wailua area hotels and condos. Map: 1

Waipouli Deli & Restaurant

Does this sound familiar? Your body clock is off. You're fully awake—and starving—3 hours early. You'll never make it till lunch, but you want to spend the morning on the beach and not in some dark, air-conditioned restaurant with poky service!

Well, the Waipouli Deli is for you! Generous portions of tasty food coupled with speedy delivery and unbeatable prices have made the Waipouli Deli a favorite spot on the east coast for local families and increasing numbers of tourists. In fact, although in the past you had to wait for a table no matter when you arrived (there were, after all, only 6 tables), the hardworking Japanese owner has moved her shop to larger, more comfortable quarters to accommodate the growing clientele.

Larger it is, but it still looks like formica city, so don't go expecting orchids on the table! But though short on atmosphere, it's got a "breakfast special" deserving of the name. For $2.99, you get an egg cooked the way you like, two slices of bacon, and two pancakes—perfect for hungry children, not to mention adults. Eggs are expertly cooked, side meats not overly fatty, and pancakes light. On the lunch and dinner menus, there are lots of bargains in American and Oriental food served luncheonette style.

Service is fast, efficient, and very friendly. Children receive smiles, crackers, and once even a pencil and paper for doodling. We were in and out and on our way in less than an hour! If you want to save money and be well fed before the morning slips away from you, this is your place!

Wailua, in the Waipouli Town Center, behind McDonald's. 822-9311 for take-out orders. Open 7:30 am - 9:30 pm daily. Map: 1

Wild Palms Bistro

"It's got tablecloths—so we have to get dressed up!" This observation from the younger set, not quite sure whether to hate having to wash up or to enjoy the prospect of changing clothes for the evening! Wild Palms is an unusual spot, appearing more elegant than you'd expect for its shopping center location in the Coconut Plantation Marketplace. You'll find a good meal for a fair price, with a menu large enough to provide everyone with something of interest, from pasta to poultry, seafood to steaks. Quality is very good even though portions won't overwhelm you, management perhaps having decided to keep prices down by moderating quantity rather than quality.

The pizza bread appetizer, topped with cheese, tomatoes and peppers, pleased all our picky eaters, except that the eaters outnumbered the slices and we had to order a second basket. Sirloin steak ($15.95) was well-trimmed, moist and tender, though small, and the teriyaki chicken ($13.95) was a great hit, a skinless breast perfectly cooked and served with pineapple. Rack of lamb ($16.95) was well prepared and tasty, though again, the portion was on the small side. The child's portion of linguini ($5.95) pleased Lauren with its excellent marinara sauce. Sesame-flavored carrots and potatoes au gratin accompanied the entrees. Mediterranean salad ($6.95) was a great hit with our vegetarian, Mirah, for the fruits and greens seemed perfectly matched with a red currant and baked apple dressing. Cioppino was delicious although both teens who ordered it made a bee line for the ice cream store directly after dinner.

Wild Palms Bistro is attractive, with white stucco walls, lots of green plants, and tables with comfortable rattan chairs. Arched openings let in evening breezes, and the soft light from the hurricane lamps on each table accomplishes the impossible, creating an atmosphere of romance in a spot overlooking a parking lot. If the rosy red light suffusing the bar area seems hokey, try watching the palms grow inside their oversized pots! Service is friendly and efficient, and the servers are cooperative about bringing the extra baskets of bread you may need.

In the Coconut Plantation Marketplace, Wailua. 822-1533. Open daily 11:30 am - 10 pm. Children's menu. Full bar. Non-smoking section. Credit cards. Map: 1

Vegetarian Adventures

Once upon a time, the best you could do on Kauai for vegetarian food was a salad bar, or in a pinch, some vegetable chow mein. Now that Kauai has entered a health-conscious new age, a growing number of vegetarian and natural food eateries are opening in almost each major tourist area. **Papaya's Garden Cafe** in the Kauai Village Shopping Center in Kapaʻa offers breakfast, lunch, and dinner choices, including Garden Burgers, Tempeh Burgers, grilled fish and chicken teriyaki burgers, vegetarian sandwiches, as well as pasta, lasagna, Greek salads, Oriental flavored rice and stir fries priced from $4 to $8.95. Across the Street is **Ambrose's Natural Foods**. In the heart of Kapaʻa town, **Michele's Cafe & Bakery** makes sandwiches, fresh bread, rolls, bagels, and desserts, to take out or eat in. **Aloha Kauai Pizza** in Coconut Plantation Marketplace is ready to experiment with cheeseless vegetarian pizzas and sandwiches. In Lihue, **Kalapaki Beach Hut**'s vegetarian sandwich and salads are tasty.

On the north shore in Princeville, **Hale O' Java** offers a 'vegetariano' sandwich. In Hanalei's Ching Young Shopping Village, **Hanalei Natural Foods** is vegetarian with a New Age flavor. In addition to packaged foods, you'll find sandwiches, including a delicious Greek Wrap ($3.75) with ripe tomatoes, feta cheese, olives, lettuce and shredded carrots wrapped in a whole wheat tortilla. The vegetarian sandwich ($3.50) is one of our favorites, a perfect balance of flavors, and if you like garlic, you'll love the a humus and avocado wrap ($3.75). They may be sold out by noon, so go early! Try taro buns at **Roadrunner Cafe** in Kilauea, as well as vegetarian Mexican take-out with homemade tortillas. **The Farmer's Market** around the corner has a tiny deli which makes salads and sandwiches. **Banana Joe's** and **Mango Mama's** (Kilauea) and **People's Market** (Puhi) specialize in fruit smoothies and frozen frosties.

On the west side, **Hanapepe Bookstore & Espresso Cafe** serves excellent salads and sandwiches (try the 'healthnut'!) in a very pleasant cafe setting. In Waimea, **Waimea Pizza & Deli** serves excellent vegetarian sandwiches and salads.

Pizzerias are also catering to the health food crowd. **Pizza Hanalei** will make pizza with 'tofurella' cheese upon request, and a 'veggie special' pizza on whole wheat as well as white crust. In Kilauea, try **Pau Hana Pizza** for a whole variety of vegetable pizzas with excellent crust. **Brick Oven Pizza** in Hanapepe makes some of the best traditional cheese or 'vegetable' pizza you'll ever find–anywhere!

Salad bars are becoming an endangered species these days, a victim of high overhead. As we go to press, you can still find an extensive one at **Duke's Canoe Club** ($9.95), **Poipu Bay Grill & Bar** ($7/lunch), **Brennecke's Beach Broiler** in Poipu ($6/lunch and $10/dinner), and **The Green Garden** in Hanapepe ($5/lunch; $7/dinner). Also try **Chuck's Steak House** in Hanalei ($8.50/dinner). In Wailua, **The Flying Lobster** ($11/dinner), **The Bull Shed** ($6.95), **The Sizzler** ($7.99) and **Pizza Hut** ($5.99), and the inexpensive all-you-can-eat buffets (breakfast, lunch, dinner) at the **BeachBoy Hotel**.

Some of our favorite vegetarian meals on Kauai are the vegetable curries, stir fries, and spring rolls at both **Mema** and **King and I**, and vegetable stir fry made to order upon request at **A Pacific Cafe**. The taro enchiladas at **Norberto's El Cafe** are wonderful, and **Cafe Portofino's** vegetable lasagne is first rate.

Fast Foods

It still seems odd to see a McDonald's golden arch on this remote island paradise, but in both Lihue and Kapa'a (and inside Wal-Mart!) you can close you eyes as you bite down on a Big Mac and feel like you've never left home! Burger King and Taco Bell at the Kukui Grove Center as well as Kapa'a will keep you from feeling too far away from it all. Pizza Hut delivers (You can charge your pizza to your credit card by phone) and now even Domino's has arrived!

Some local restaurants are swift and tasty alternatives to the national chains for just a small amount more. In Lihue, **Barbecue Inn** has one of the largest, most reasonably-priced lunch and dinner menus on Kauai, and it's air conditioned! Or try wonderful saimin at **Hamura's** or **OK Bento**. **Da Box Lunch** will pack up a picnic lunch (or breakfast!) for you on the spot. Open for breakfast or lunch, **Tip Top** is a Kauai tradition.

On the eastern shore in Kapa'a, **Ono Family Restaurant** offers a bargain-priced children's hamburger platter. Health food lovers should stop in at **Papaya's** for salads, fresh fruits, vegetables, and muffins. Best in the Coconut Plantation Marketplace, in Mikey's judgment, is **Aloha Kauai Pizza**, pizza with crispy crust and tasty sauce; Jeremy prefers **Taco Dude**'s outstanding burrito. **Kalika's Noodles** is a new favorite for saimin. Try **Wah Kung** in Kinipopo Shopping Village for tasty Chinese food, and **Korean Barbecue** next door for spicy ribs and teriyaki beef. A favorite family take-out spot on the eastern shore is **Ono Char Burger** (formerly Duane's) in Anahola. While service can be pokey, the burgers, french fries, onion rings, and fried chicken will seem worth the wait, and you can take your order to nearby Anahola Bay and eat on the beach. Near Kalapaki Beach, try **Kalapaki Beach Hut** and decide for yourself whether Steve's burgers are better than the ones at Ono Burger in Anahola – the business Steve started 15 years ago and sold to Duane! Steve's fresh filet of island ono sandwich is sensational!

In Kilauea on the north shore, near the Kong Lung Store, The **Kilauea Bakery & Pau Hana Pizza** features fragrant breads, rolls, cookies and many varieties of fresh baked pizza. You'll find deli sandwiches at **Farmer's Market** next door, and nearby at **Roadrunner Cafe & Bakery,** tamales, burras, tostadas, enchiladas, sandwiches and salads.

In Princeville, visit **Hale O'Java** for pizza and sandwiches. In Hanalei, try **Hanalei Gourmet** for sandwiches on fresh baked breads and rolls, or have them packed as a picnic lunch. **Subways** now turns out sandwiches from right inside Big Save! Across the street, **Bubba Burgers** fries up burgers within a reasonably short wait. At **Pizza Hanalei,** the homemade crust is crispy and the cheese and toppings generous. Next door at **Hanalei Natural Foods** you'll find delicious vegetarian sandwiches. Try **Papagaya Azul** for Mexican take-out. Or step up to **Tropical Taco's** famous green truck, usually parked just east of the town next to the Dolphin Restaurant on the banks of the Hanalei River.

The inexpensive (around $4) 'plate lunch' with' local grinds,' is a Kauai tradition. Try one at Kukui Grove's **Joni-Hana**, at the lunch counters at the **Big Save Markets**, or the **Dairy Queen** in Lihue, where you can get miso soup and a salad with an entree like boiled akule fish that, according to one reader, "has to be tasted to be appreciated." **Kauai Chop Suey** offers a "special plate" ($4) which is almost enough to feed two, as does **OK Bento & Saimin**. At **Olympic Cafe** in Kapa'a, $5 buys a large mound of crisp cooked tofu stir fry and wonderful rice. The lunch plates at **Dragon Inn** are another bargain.

On the South shore, don't miss **Taqueria Nortenos** for great Mexican take-out in the Kukui'ula shopping center. **Mustard's Last Stand**, just to the west of Poipu, at the junction of Rt. 50 and Rt. 530, offers hot dogs, sausages, hamburgers, and lots of condiments. At "Geckoland Mini Golfpark" next door, kids can putt through 9 holes representing such Kauaian landmarks as "Waimea Canyon," "Sleeping Giant" and the "Tree Tunnel." (9 am -7 pm daily). A couple of miles down the road in Kalaheo you can find great burgers and chicken at **Camp House Grill** and fabulous pizza and sandwiches at **Brick Oven.**

View from the the terrace, Princeville Hotel

North Shore Restaurants

'favor...eats'

Perched on the ocean bluff, several Princeville restaurants have unforgettable ocean views! From **Bali Hai,** you can look out at spectacular Hanalei Bay, and the view from the restaurants at the Princeville Hotel, **La Cascata** and **Cafe Hanalei,** will take your breath away! Try **Cafe Hanalei's** breakfast buffet, excellent lunches, or sunset dinners, and be sure to bring your camera. **'The Living Room'** in the main lobby is a great spot for late afternoon tea or sunset cocktails! The hotel's Italian specialty restaurant, **La Cascata**, has excellent food and a view which is simply amazing, especially if you come early enough for sunset.

In nearby Hanalei, try **Tahiti Nui** for local flavor, or **Cafe Luna** for crispy pizza baked in the north shore's only brick oven. For years, the local favorite for fresh island fish has been the **Hanalei Dolphin**. **Zelo's Beach House** serves excellent salads and a wide range of sandwiches and burgers.

For inexpensive lunches, try **Tropical Taco's** famous fresh fish tacos served from the side of its green truck, parked by the Dolphin Restaurant. **Bubba Burgers** turns out hamburgers and fries, while the **Hanalei Gourmet** next door serves deli sandwiches and inexpensive meals. **Old Hanalei**

Coffee Company serves sandwiches on fresh-baked breads, while **Papagaya Azul** gives Mexican take-out a Hawaiian flavor. Vegetarians can select from salads and sandwiches at **Hanalei Natural Foods**; there's a **Subways** in the Big Save Market; and pizza lovers can try **Pizza Hanalei's** homemade whole wheat crust. Whatever you decide about lunch, don't pass up shave ice at **Wishing Well**, now located in a silver trailer parked near Kayak Kauai.

In nearby KILAUEA, **Kilauea Bakery and Pau Hana Pizza** serves home-baked pizza with imaginative and delicious flavorings. **Casa di Amici** is a local favorite for Italian cuisine, as is the **Farmer's Market** next door for excellent deli sandwiches and vegetarian delights. Just down the street, **Roadrunner Cafe & Bakery** serves delicious breads, rolls, pastries and Mexican take-out with homemade tortillas.

Bali Hai

Imagine dining as the sunset paints the sky all gold and orange above the magnificent angles of the dark and mysterious mountains, turning the ocean almost purple in Hanalei Bay. Sip a cocktail while the cool evening breeze, fragrant with tropical flowers, touches your skin like silk. At the Bali Hai Restaurant, you can find the Kauai of your imagination, the dream of an island paradise that haunts you in the dead of winter.

The dining experience could not be more relaxing, the food brought at a leisurely pace by polite waiters and served at large, elegantly appointed tables, on china painted in colors of the sea. Open to the air on three sides, the dining room's tall ceilings and two-tiered arrangement of tables make the room spacious and, even when full, remarkably quiet. As we lingered over coffee to watch a sudden shower fill the air with shining drops, we felt more at peace than when we arrived.

Hard hit by Iniki, the Hanalei Bay Resort has been completely renovated, with great results for Bali Hai. Finally, the design has taken full advantage of the view so that your line of vision is above the lanai railing, and the tables are angled and set to put each chair in the best position. Even better, off to the right and below Bali Hai, a wonderful salt water pool meanders through tropical gardens. Instead of tennis courts lit for night games, you can look out at the flowers and palm trees and listen to the sound of waterfalls.

Bali Hai's menu features Pacific Rim cuisine, with most of the dozen entrees priced more than $20 and accompanied by soup or salad, rice and vegetable. Excellent spring rolls ($7) are crispy, light, and attractive, served on 'four seasons' lettuce with carrot curls and spicy dipping sauce.

Onion soup ($4) arrives crusted with cheese. Even the dinner salad is generous with local varieties of lettuce and excellent dressing. Our fresh ono ($21) was excellent, moist, flaky, and tender. Fortunately we had asked for the sauce to be served on the side, as both the spicy papaya sauce as well as the butter and tarragon sauce were far too powerful for this delicately flavored fish. Striploin ($26) was tasty if slightly bitter tasting from the grill. Best was 'salmon Bali Hai' ($22.50), a dish which has been on every menu in this restaurant despite changes in ownership and management since we first dined here in 1980. Quality has varied over the years, but in its latest incarnation, the fish was moist and tender in its shell of light puff pastry, accompanied rather than overwhelmed by the spinach, cream and cheese duxelle inside.

Come for lunch and enjoy the view in sunlit splendor! The menu offers salads and sandwiches served with french fries, fruit or cottage cheese. You can also try several salads, including 'sunshine greens' ($5), an array of vegetables and lettuce, and a generous fruit salad with cheeses ($9). The club sandwich ($9.75) features lots of turkey and ripe tomatoes.

Bali Hai has a wonderfully romantic ambiance and unmatched view. Even if the food were terrible, it would still be worth the price of admission. You'll enjoy your evening if you stick to the basics and don't ask the kitchen for fancy footwork. Time your dinner for sunset, have all sauces served in a side dish, and hope for the best!

When making dinner reservations, ask to speak directly with the manager; that way you can avoid arriving at the restaurant to find no record of your call. Should that happen, do not despair. You can discover, as we did, a wonderful walk to a lookout point for the sunset. Head towards the cliff along the sidewalk between the tennis courts. From path's end, you can look down at Hanalei Bay, sparkling with beads of light and turning deep purple as the sun descends. A sailboat cuts silently across the water, the sails filling with the breezes which brush your face and fill your head with the fragrance of evening flowers. The dark craggy edges of the cliffs blend into soft purples and deep blues as the gold and orange sun slowly sinks towards the water, shining more brightly with each second, until flattened into a disk that shrinks to nothing before your eyes. A golden glow remains, burnishing the clouds, polishing the water, then slowly fades into a darkening dusk.

Princeville, Hanalei Bay Resort. Reservations: 826-6522. Credit cards. Children's entrees. Non-smoking section. Breakfast 7 am -11 am. Lunch 11:30 am - 2 pm. Dinner 5:30 -10 pm. Enter Princeville at the main gate on Ka Haku Rd., take the third left onto Liholiho Rd., turn right onto Hono'iki Rd.. Valet parking, or use lot on right. Map: 2

Bubba Burgers

Bubba's began life on Kauai on main street, Kapa'a, with the philosophy that a decent hamburger should not cost *less* than a can of dog food! This idea, and the burger (2.5 oz. of 88% fat-free fresh-ground Kauai beef) caught on, and there's a second Bubba's in Hanalei, equally jammed!

Our children like the "frings" (a portion of fries topped with a couple of onion rings), and the burgers are, to quote the teenage connoisseurs, "O.K. — sorta in-between McDonald's and Burger King." It's fast food, sorta cooked to order, and generally predictable. The indoor dining room in the Hanalei branch has a handful of tables; the picnic tables outside lack something when it's raining, and can be hot when it's not.

Kapa'a and Hanalei 823-0069. 10:30 am - 6 pm daily. Kapa'a location closed Sundays. Cash only. *http://planet-hawaii.com/~bubba/* Map 1& 3.

Cafe Hanalei,
Princeville Resort Hotel

You could not imagine a more spectacular spot for breakfast than Cafe Hanalei, with its panoramic view of a bay that in any weather has the romantic beauty of a fairy tale. Even in the rain, you can watch the mountains peek out from veils of mist like shy princesses. Or watch as the sun's sorcery transforms the landscape from smoky greys into blazing colors—vivid greens and golds, brilliant blues, and on the mountains rising majestically above the bay, the shining silver ribbons of waterfalls. In this land of enchantment, each moment reveals a new mystery, and under the spell of such beauty, you could enjoy breakfast with only a chair!

The breakfast buffet will draw you indoors with its generous display of fruits, juices, and fresh baked pastries, blintzes with sour cream, even an omelette bar where you can have your eggs whipped into colorful and tasty creations right before your eyes. While expensive ($17.50), the breakfast buffet combines an incomparably beautiful setting with delicious food and friendly, polite service. Where else could you find such radiance in the rain?

Or come for lunch, when you can enjoy the view along with an attractive selection of sandwiches, salads, and pastas with an accent of the Pacific Rim. Salad with marinated stir-fried chicken, slices of papaya and tomato served with an orange and ginger dressing is superbly flavored ($13.95). The 12 grain club sandwich with avocado ($13.95) served with Maui potato chips (the authentic kind), pleased the children, as did the 'Junior Burger' accompanied by spiced curly fries, though be prepared for a hefty price for sodas ($2.75). A beautiful salad with fresh ahi, deep fried shrimp, lettuce and rice noodles ($17) is both generous and tasty.

At dinner, the setting sun kindles the sky to flame in orange and turquoise behind the darkening cliffs. Visit the lounge, appropriately called the 'Living Room' first, and enjoy a cocktail while you relax on one of the plush couches in the elegant room, with marble fireplaces and tall shelves filled with books. But who can stay inside at sunset? Outside, the terrace is enclosed by waist high panels of glass, so that you can enjoy the spectacular panorama of Hanalei Bay without a railing to obstruct your view. Boats glide silently; the only sound is the soft music of the waves. Mountains are shrouded in clouds, and the sky turns to gold as the sun slips slowly into the sea, the colors deepening as they are reflected in the tall glass windowpanes.

Later, as Hanalei Bay recedes into the velvet darkness and the first stars appear, walk downstairs to Cafe Hanalei, where the tall windows mirror dozens of dancing candle flames. Tables generously spaced for private conversation are beautifully dressed with damask cloths, elegant china and sparkling crystal and silver. Your server will even address you by name.

All this romance is expensive. Ranging in price from $15.50 (stir fried tofu and vegetables) to steamed Kona lobster ($35.50), the dozen entrees reflect a contemporary interest in the flavors of the Pacific Rim. It would be a shame to miss the fresh fish, however, particularly the fresh caught mahi mahi steamed with ginger and scallions and served in an oriental steamer basket with vegetables ($28.95). Fresh opakapaka is presented like a stir fry, with shiitake mushrooms and Hawaiian sweet potatoes ($27.50). Appetizers are a la carte, the dinner salad an attractive mix of greens, and the papaya chicken soup generous with chicken though somewhat peppery. Be sure to leave room for one of the wonderful desserts, including pineapple macadamia nut crunch with vanilla ice cream, or a superb lilikoi mousse cake with almond rainbow stripes ($5.50).

At Cafe Hanalei, the presentation is attractive, the service friendly, and under the supervision of Rosemary Caldwell, professional.. The best part of a wonderful dining experience remains the setting, which is spectacular enough to make dinner unforgettable. Walk around the hotel afterwards, take the elevator down to the beach and listen to the music of the waves and the melodies in the evening breezes.

Princeville, in The Princeville Hotel. Reservations 826-9644. Open daily. 6:30 am - 9 pm. Theme buffets offered three nights during the week. Buffet prices for children are calculated by their ages. Credit cards. Enter Princeville's main gate and stay on this road for about a mile until it ends at the hotel. Map: 2

Cafe Luna

Gone fishing—Moloa'a Bay

Cafe Luna, the latest Italian eatery on the North Shore, has had three owners since opening in 1995. The most recent, Giuseppe Avocadi, also operates the popular Cafe Portofino in Lihue, and has promised a bold new beginning, complete with a redesigned menu and upgraded service. He will also continue Cafe Luna's unique feature—the only wood burning pizza oven on the north shore! The setting is comfortable; you can dine inside the pleasant dining room, or if you prefer, outside on a spacious veranda which offers a view of the Hanalei mountains and the starry sky. Surrounded by rattan chairs, the wood tables are attractively set, with clever touches like rattan napkin rings. Lots of leafy plants remind you of what makes Hanalei special, and lanterns and citronella candles provide soft lighting. The veranda is roofed in case of rain showers, but skylights let in light at lunchtime or in late afternoon, when you can stop for a snack after a hard afternoon of beaching. If you dine inside, in the small dining room, you'll find tables well-separated for privacy, or you can watch the bustle around the brick pizza oven.

The expanded menu offers a variety of pastas and sauces ($13-$14), as well as poultry, fresh fish, and meat entrees. Steak, veal, or fish entrees range from $18 (linguini with clams) to $22 (rack of lamb). Salad is a la carte ($5). A variety of vegetarian plates includes our favorite from Cafe Portofino, vegetable lasagne ($14.75). Best are the pizzas, ranging in price from $9-$13. Pizza "tre" (three for the non-Italian speakers among us) combines shrimp, papaya and asiago ($12) — wonderful!

Service is friendly, the wine list moderate in size but also in price, and the atmosphere comfortable. Before dinner (or after lunch), you can browse a fascinating collection of pottery, jewelry, artifacts, and works of local artists in the Yellowfish Trading Company adjacent. Non-smokers be warned: The dining veranda is also the smoking section, so there are no guarantees of clean air if you want to sit outside!

Hanalei Town, across Rt. 560 from Big Save. 826-1177. Reservations suggested. Credit cards. Map: 2.

Casa di Amici

It's an out of the way spot for an Italian restaurant—even on Kauai. You'll find Casa di Amici in rural Kilauea, amid sugar cane fields and papaya groves, on the back streets of a former sugar plantation town which still seems closer to Kauai's past than its present. Yet this dining room would be attractive anywhere—with fresh grey and white paint, and sliding glass doors that open to evening breezes. In the candlelight, the dark green tables, rimmed with tan and colorful with red ginger blossoms, look romantic, and the rather spare decor has a charm all its own.

Randall Yates, the chef, has recently purchased Casa di Amici, with great results for the restaurant! Yates, who occasionally strolls the dining room in toque and shorts, can now give free rein to his imagination, and has created such delights as polenta with wild mushrooms and white beans, presented with sprigs of rosemary. Lasagna ($16) tastes fresh and tender. Yates has also retained the best features of the old menu, like Tournedos Rossini ($23), medallions of beef filet tender and topped with foie gras and mushroom caps. Fresh fish ($20) is also excellent, both moist and flaky, though you might ask to have your fresh fish filet plainly sauteed with Sicilian style sauce flavored with onions, peppers, and capers, served in a side dish so you can decide for yourself how much—if any—to use!

Portions are priced for two sizes, either 'light or full,' including pastas ($12 or $15), served with your choice of five sauces, as well as the half-dozen veal, fish, and chicken entrees (from $16 for the light portion of chicken to $24 for the full portion of NY steak). Dinner includes fresh baked bread, either plain or spiced with garlic, as well as rice and zucchini. You might also try minestrone ($5.00), a rich, interesting soup, with a tomato broth, colorful with carrots and still crunchy bell peppers and served in a tall crock to keep it hot. The small antipasto is generous ($10), and 'Mista salad' with three organic lettuces as well as pepper, olives, and tomatoes ($5), is also excellent. Note: since Casa di Amici has no children's menu, at the minimum a child's bowl of spaghetti with meat balls costs $12. The wine list is extensive, with many choices under $25.

Kauai has few Italian restaurants with as pretty a setting as this one, especially when piano music fills the air with melodies. In fact, when the restaurant is jammed, as it often is, some disappointed diners head over to Pau Hana Pizza next door and enjoy the music from the garden tables. Because Casa di Amici is both small and popular, take the precaution of making a reservation well in advance, or come for lunch, after a hard morning at the beach!

Kilauea, Kong Lung Center, on the Lighthouse Road. Music Tuesday through Saturday. Dinner nightly 6- 9 pm. Lunch daily 11 - 2 pm. Reservations: 828-1555. Grand piano music Thursday-Saturday. Map: 2

Charo's

The north shore is an expensive place to run a business. Labor is hard to find; those narrow winding roads and one-lane bridges make deliveries expensive. Adjacent to Hanalei Colony Resort, Charo's has tried over the years to find a menu to satisfy the accountant as well as the customers.

The newest menu— Mexican— has been the most successful. Fajitas arrived on a large platter with chicken, zucchini, carrots, and onions nicely sauteed and generous enough for two to share. When our waiter brought the chopped tomatoes we requested, we could roll some out-standing tortillas. Saffron colored rice and beans are good, though the hamburger was not very tasty and the fries on the anemic side. The menu also includes snack foods, like 'chicken fingers,' five crispy breast strips which Lauren ranks right up there with Burger King's, nachos, and fresh fish. Portions are on the small side, so you might order some extras to round out the plates.

Service can be as variable as the food. Once the hostess was so unfriendly that we wondered if she had been marinated along with the teriyaki chicken, but on our most recent visit our waiter was exceedingly friendly as well as efficient.

Charo's is a pretty place. The setting, tucked into the magnificent Ha'ena coast looking out over the waves, is hard to equal. Dining is very pleasant in two attractive rooms decorated in bamboo and rattan, with abundant ferns and hanging plants. Skylights bring in the sunshine, which gleams on the tile floor and the green tiled tables. (You may even need sunglasses for summertime lunches!) Watch the palm trees sway in the breezes, or the rain drops splash against the glass.

Charo's seems to have fallen victim to the curse of high overhead. Perhaps it is simply not possible to offer reasonably-priced dining so far up the winding narrow road with one-lane bridges, especially when many customers don't want to drive those winding narrow roads after dark! While the Mexican menu is a definite improvement, it's still high on price and small on portions. So if your children are sandy and hungry after a hard morning at the north shore beaches, and if they beg you to pull up in front Charo's, you might just close your ears, pass out the potato chips, and drive a few miles more for lunch at Tahiti Nui or Chuck's!

Ha'ena, adjacent to Hanalei Colony Resort. 826-6422. Non-smoking section. 11:30 - 9 pm daily. Full bar. Closed Wednesdays. Map: 2

Chuck's Steak House

People who live on Kauai seem to like Chuck's in Hanalei even though (or perhaps, even because) it looks more like a mainland restaurant than a tropical island hideaway. When you walk through the door, you could be in Chuck's in West Haven, Connecticut, one of nearly fifty Chuck's which have opened nationwide over the last 25 years.

Prices are reasonable and menu choices extensive. More than 25 entrees range in price from $16.50 (barbecued beef ribs) to $24.50 (11-13 oz. prime rib), including children's dinners (teriyaki chicken, hamburger or barbecued ribs) at $8. Dinners include rice, warm bread and butter, and a visit to the salad bar, a reasonable array of romaine and tomatoes, some fresh vegetables and prepared salads, and excellent dressings, including an outstanding blue cheese. Go early and take some homemade cracker bread to munch on with your cocktails or wine. Be sure to request pacing the dinner, or your entree may arrive when you've barely finished your salad! The wine list is limited in choice but reasonable in price.

Over the years, we have found dinners at Chuck's to be reliably well-prepared. Barbecued beef ribs ($13.75) are enormous, served with a flavorful sauce, and not overly fatty. The New York steak (12 oz. for $24.50) is excellent, very tender and juicy with great flavor and no gristle. The kitchen will prepare it with teriyaki sauce upon request.

Families might try Chuck's for lunch. Hamburgers ($5.95) are a third of a pound and delicious. Our prime rib sandwich ($6.50) though not as well-trimmed as it might have been, was tasty, moist, and miraculously medium-rare, served with a sauce that made it come alive. Club sandwiches are very good, and tuna salad with white meat tuna is first rate ($8.95). With a sandwich order, fries cost $1 extra, and salad $1.50.

Lunches and dinners at Chuck's will be reasonably priced and reasonably good. On the other hand, you don't get anything special either, in food or ambiance. Chuck's offers no views of Hanalei's magnificent mountains or valleys to paint a memory for dark winter evenings back home. Its reputation among local people may have something to do with that. Unlike many of us, who dream of vacationing on Kauai, perhaps they dream of vacationing in West Haven, Connecticut.

Princeville Center, Rt. 56. Reservations 826-6211. Non-smoking section. Credit cards. Lunch 11:30 am- 2:30 pm. 6 pm- 10:00 pm daily. Map: 2

Hanalei Dolphin

The Dolphin has always had the reputation of serving the finest seafood on the north shore. Service is friendly and leisurely in the softly lit dining room, where wooden shutters are raised to let in evening breezes, and lanterns glow pleasantly on polished table tops. The kitchen that Iniki destroyed has been rebuilt farther from the dining room, a large improvement; remodeling has preserved the rustic decor, quaint without seeming contrived.

The small restaurant is almost always crowded, but if you choose a weeknight and arrive around 7 pm, you shouldn't have a long wait. Even better, arrive earlier, leave your name with the hostess, and drive a few blocks to Hanalei Bay and watch the sunset. By the time you get back to the Dolphin, your table should be ready! The Dolphin, if you haven't already guessed, is a favorite destination for our spectacular sunset drives north from Wailua!

Over the past few years, if we have had an occasional disappointing dinner at the Dolphin, we have chalked it up to bad luck in the kitchen. According to our waiter, two and sometimes three chefs alternate during the week, and so the cooking inevitably varies. One night, two broiled fresh ono filets were served partially raw, an error easily corrected. On another visit, the ono (a 12 oz. filet for $24) was perfectly cooked— moist, tender, and flaky—cleanly broiled, with no taste of the grill. The ahi teriyaki ($24 for the larger portion) is always a winner, and it remains one of the most delicious fish dinners on Kauai—juicy, tender, and full of spark. The newest preparation, Cajun style, is also excellent. While fresh

fish is Dolphin's specialty, teriyaki "Hawaiian" chicken ($14/adults; $7/children) received high marks from our kids for taste and tenderness, although New York steak ($18) was small and ordinary.

Most entrees are priced in a regular as well as a smaller, "menehune" portion at about a 40% discount. Dinners include fresh hot bread from Michele's bakery in Kapa'a, and a 'Family Style Salad,' a large bowl of lettuce, cherry tomatoes, bean sprouts, and choice of oil and vinegar, or creamy garlic or Russian dressings. For $10 you can have a "light dinner" of broccoli casserole or seafood chowder, served with salad, rice or french fries, and bread. Seafood chowder (also a la carte for $5), is creamy, steamy, full of fish, scallops, clams and potatoes, and the steak fries are (usually) thick, hot, and crispy.

The wine list is very well-selected, with lots of choices in the moderate range, like a Guenoc North Coast Chardonnay for $23. Even better, our bottle was presented in a bucket filled to the top with water and ice so that the wine was perfectly chilled. We were sad to discover that an old friend on the wine list—the bottle of Chateau Lafitte Rothschild, which survived Hurricane I'wa even when the roof did not — hadn't made it through Iniki and was no longer available for $200. Suddenly, we felt older.

The Dolphin is a local favorite for good reason, so arrive before 7 pm or the line may be out the door and growing by the quarter hour. The setting is pleasant, the seafood usually delicious, service for the most part friendly, and, if you are staying to the south, it's a wonderful opportunity to drive north for the sunset. Just warn the waiter that any overcooked fish will be thrown back, if not into the ocean, at least onto his tray!

Hanalei, on Rt. 560, just past Princeville and the one-lane bridge over the Hanalei River. No reservations. To see who's cooking, call 826-6113. Children's dinners: chicken, steak, or shrimp. A Smoke-free restaurant. Map: 2

The Hanalei Gourmet

For years, on our way to the beach at Hanalei, we have wished for a first rate deli where we could buy sandwiches for picnics on the sand. The Hanalei Gourmet in the old Hanalei schoolhouse features home-baked breads and pastries, wonderful deli meats and salads, fine cheeses, soups, and a selection of gourmet foods and fine wines. Insulated backpacks are available for picnics. Order a sandwich ($5-$6) at the deli counter (or phone ahead), or take a table in the 'classroom' next door, converted into an attractive cafe *cum* bar for those who would prefer to avoid the sand altogether! Entrees and salads cost less than $10. Fans and the large schoolroom windows keep the breezes moving and the temperature comfortable. Note: If you plan to picnic, check each sandwich before leaving. More than once, our bag has contained surprises--or worse, a deficit!

Hanalei Center. 826-2524. Credit cards. Open 8 am to 10 pm daily. Custom picnic baskets. Entertainment 4 nights a week. Map: 2

Kilauea Bakery & Pau Hana Pizza

Some of the most imaginative pizzas on Kauai are created at Kilauea Bakery, whose tiny storefront is almost taken up by display cases filled with varieties of crusty golden breads, a selection of cookies, macadamia nut sticky buns, as well as pizza by the slice at the counter. Don't leave without a bag of bread sticks made from the pizza dough. They have become so popular that they are now distributed all over the island! When you walk in, you may find a pizza made with goat cheese, sun dried tomatoes, and eggplant. Or perhaps one made with feta cheese, olives, zucchini, fresh mushrooms, and tomato slices. The crust, either white or whole wheat, will be very thin and crisp, and you can choose from six different cheeses, including 'tofurella'.

Two tables are crammed under the window, and outside, patio tables with umbrellas protect you from the sun as well as the sudden showers that can threaten to dampen your lunch. Service is friendly. If you want a plain cheese pizza ("without all those things on it") you can call ahead and it will be ready when you arrive! In addition to pizza, you can order a salad made with local organically grown lettuces, and if you are really into health, you can sample organically grown fresh ground coffee drip brewed with filtered water in unbleached filter paper.

Kilauea, Kong Lung Center, on the Lighthouse Road. 828-2020. Open 6:30 am to 9 pm daily except Sundays. Pizza 11 am to 9 pm. Cash only.

La Cascata, Princeville Resort Hotel

A sunset dinner at La Cascata can be one of your most memorable island experiences! Even arriving at the Princeville Hotel is unforgettable. You drive up around a spectacular fountain, and then walk into an enormous lobby, where all along the western wall, giant windows which appear to be seamless reveal the spectacular colors of the cliffs beyond Hanalei Bay. In this wonderful spot is a beautiful lounge called "The Living Room," where you can stop off for a glass of wine or a cocktail (or in the afternoons, enjoy afternoon tea and scones). Comfortable sofas invite you to relax and look out over Hanalei Bay, glistening in the sunlight as the colors deepen to rich gold and orange. Lovely melodies played by musicians add to the witchery of the moment.

Walk down one level below the Living Room, and you will find La Cascata, with an equally beautiful panoramic view of Hanalei Bay. At sunset, you can watch the sky break in brilliant gold and orange waves across the mountains. Bring your camera! Window screens slide open, and you may just capture that unforgettable moment, those matchless colors. The sunset views are more spectacular than the understated decor of the dining room itself, where the soft golden terra cotta color of the walls blends with the quarry tile on the floors to create an informal, comfortable ambiance. Tables widely spaced for privacy are set among arches painted with ivy to resemble an antique Tuscan garden, with picturesque looking chips in the plaster and water stains which are, we suspect, authentic souvenirs of Iniki. Murals provide scenes of Italian landscapes. Candle lamps cast flickering golden light on the tables, dressed with white linen, decorated with tropical flowers in cut glass vases and elegant china, and surrounded with comfortable upholstered armchairs. A singer and guitarist provide pleasant, relaxing melodies.

Foccacio and rolls arrive with a wonderfully light and soft extra virgin olive oil, along with balsamic vinegar and a 'salsa' of fresh tomatoes and basil. This will put you in the best frame of mind to consider the menu, which changes monthly its selection of entrees, pastas, appetizers and soups. Zuppa de pescio is light and delicately flavored, the fish tasty, a better choice than the soup of the day, a rather bland tomato soup ($5). Salads are excellent, both the fresh spinach salad, and the salad of green beans, bell peppers, and sauteed quail with Chianti vinaigrette ($8.75). At least four fresh pastas are available each day, priced according to the size of the portions, ($8 or $14.50). Cannelloni of roasted duck with wilted greens ($8.50 or $14) is delicious, the light, thin crepes filled with slices of duck and still fresh tasting vegetables, the sauce also light rather than thick.

The entrees we sampled were delicious. Fresh island onaga ($28.50) is sweet, moist, a generous portion of three slices, with a touch of mustard, and accompanied by a wonderful spinach and mushroom flan. Fresh ahi ($27), presented on a bed of zucchini and polenta, is perfectly cooked, served with an excellent light sauce and generous portion of penne pasta. The fresh lobster, locally grown on Kona, is tender and moist, served with steamed beans and sauteed red pepper.

Service is polite, pleasant, and professional; every effort is made to be attentive to your needs. If noodles leave your children cold, they may order a cheeseburger or grilled cheese sandwich from the children's menu in the main dining room. If you are not sure about a wine selection, you may be offered a taste before you make your choice from the extensive, and expensive, wine list which contains French, German, Italian and Australian wines, as well excellent California choices. Our standard of measure, Robert Mondavi Fume Blanc, is fairly priced at $23. For dessert, try the lilikoi creme brule with fresh pineapple and strawberries.

When planning your dinner at La Cascata, try if possible to set the time for sunset, when the dining experience is gilded with spectacular colors, particularly in summer months when the angle of the sun allows it to sink right into the sea before your eyes. After dinner, stroll around the hotel, perhaps take a walk down to the beach level and look at the moonlight sparkling on the waves.

In the Princeville Hotel. 826-9644. Reservations recommended. Dinner nightly 6 - 9:30 pm. Non-smoking section. Credit cards. Enter Princeville at main gate and follow this road to the end. Map: 2

Prince Restaurant

With a spectacular panoramic setting amid mountains, rolling fairways, and ocean, The Prince is a great spot for a surprisingly inexpensive lunch or breakfast. The clubhouse for the world-class Prince golf course is designed to impress. The entry is all glass, and through enormous windows you can see all the way to the horizon as you walk downstairs, past the glass enclosed health club, to the dining room. The menu is small, offering fewer than a dozen sandwiches and salads priced around $8, but portions are generous and the choices well prepared. The vegetarian sandwich is stuffed with carrots, lettuce and sprouts, and accompanied by first-rate, crispy french fries. Tangy Chinese chicken salad is filled with crunchy vegetables and a sliced, exceedingly tender grilled chicken breast. The fresh ahi salad is as tasty as it is enormous, the fish perfectly moist and tender, a real delight for the modest price ($8.50).

At the Prince, the view is incredible, the servers pleasant, and the portions generous. For the prices, it's hard to find a more reasonable slice of ocean on seven grain bread!

Just east of Princeville on Rt. 56. 826-5050. Breakfast and lunch daily. Credit cards. Air-conditioned. Non-smoking. Map: 2

Roadrunner Cafe & Bakery

The old bakery on Oka Street, destroyed by Hurricane Iniki, has a whole new look thanks to Dawn and Dennis Johnston. Roadrunner turns out pastries, pies, cookies, and breads, including wonderful taro buns made with Hanalei grown taro. Jeremy loves to poke a hole in the top and fill it with honey! Our favorites are 'coconut rolls,' a spiral Danish pastry filled with coconut and baked toasty brown. Come early for the best pastry selection, or order in advance!

A small dining area adjacent to the bakery features delicious Mexican tacos, tamales, enchiladas, tostadas, and some of the tastiest fresh island fish tacos on Kauai! Tortillas are fresh from the bakery, chips are really crisp, and the spicing is deft and can be customized to your taste. The white painted dining area is decorated with murals and real sand on the floor — just in case you're coming in hungry from the beach and haven't had a chance to wash off your feet! If you like freshly prepared Mexican food with good quality ingredients, Roadrunner is for you!

Kilauea, 2430 Oka St., off Kilauea Rd. Call ahead for take-out. 828-TACO. 7 am - 8 pm M-F; until 8:30 pm on Sat. Closed Sundays.

Tahiti Nui

If you pull up to Tahiti Nui on some nights, the dining room may be almost empty and you'll think you've come to the wrong place. On another night, however, you might not find a place to put your car. Local people have enjoyed Tahiti Nui for years, since Louise Marston first opened the doors and created its special character as a place where tourists can find the authentic "folk" Kauai. As with most attempts to be folksy, the result is a combination of the genuine and the contrived. Spontaneous entertainment is arranged each night; local musicians drop in from time to time, and guests are told with a twinkle that no one is ever quite sure what is going to happen.

Decorated in what can only be described as 'early grass shack,' the small, darkened lounge has touches of the genuinely unique (an inflated blowfish used as a lantern) as well as the genuinely corny (the portrait of the topless Tahitian perched over the cash register). The bar is a favorite spot for local people to talk to old friends over generous drinks. For tourists, it's a great place to meet old timers and hear fascinating stories about the island. Even Tahiti Nui's famous 'family style luau' is more like a local talent show than the typical 'Hawaiian' extravaganza. Entertainment is provided by Louise's family, as well as whoever happens by, usually local performers on their time off, and occasionally even guests!

On the other nights, Tahiti Nui is like any other restaurant — or almost. Post-Iniki remodeling has made the dining room more attractive—woven coconut mats cover the walls, and all six tables have chairs that match, their Hawaiian cloths topped with glass. Progress has its price, however, for you can no longer peek into the tiny kitchen and watch the chef stir and chop and nibble and chat. The menu has been expanded to ten entrees at reasonable prices, from $11.95 (pasta primavera) to $19.95 (12 oz. prime rib), including small salad, bread, vegetable, rice or fries. Vegetarians can also choose a vegetable stir fry or curry ($13.95). Children can eat a hamburger ($6.95), chicken or fish ($7.95). The wine list, small but reasonably priced, offers a Cambria 'Katherine's Vineyard' at its high end for $24.

Dinner begins with a soft garlic-flavored loaf. Dinners are variable, particularly if you come on a luau night when the place is hopping. Soups ($3.95) are usually good, flavorful and generous, as is the generous salad with fresh vegetables ($3.95). New York steak, marinated in a subtle teriyaki sauce, is crisp yet juicy and exceedingly tender, and of good size ($18.95). An extra bonus, it comes with a first-rate baked potato. At our request, the chef prepared the fish stir-fry ($17.95) with fresh ono, which was unfortunately overwhelmed with a sweet sauce and sharp onions. The curry we sampled seemed very ordinary. Best of all may be the prime rib ($17.95 -$19.95), a well-trimmed and meaty slice, roasted with rosemary. Entrees are accompanied with sauteed zucchini, onions and tomatoes. Finish off your meal with homemade cream pies, either macadamia nut, coconut cream, or lilikoi ($3.25).

Lunch, which was always a gamble at Tahiti Nui, has become more predictable. Our children love the huge turkey club sandwich ($7.75) and the wonderful cooked-to-order hamburgers ($5.95)! Fresh fish salad ($8.95) is a great way to sample Kauai's fish. Over the years we have acquired many fond memories of lunch at Tahiti Nui, the time when the waitress served our family, which took up two tables, double baskets of hot, buttery garlic bread for the single order price ($1.75), or the time when the chef offered us all some soup, because she was about to cook up a fresh pot and needed to finish off the day's supply first! Even now, you never know quite what will come your way, like the free refills of soda from the server who thought the glasses were too small!

The 'Family Style' luau, held in the large room adjacent to the dining room, offers great local entertainment and lots of food. It's expensive ($38 or $15 for the show only); the room seems small when full and the doors closed against the non-paying audience! If you prefer the regular menu, you might get more attention if you come on another night.

Like an old friend, Tahiti Nui has grown and changed over the years. But the friendliness has remained. You may look up, between the appetizer and main course, and see Louise pulling up a chair near your table, and, with guitar on her knee, begin to sing 'Hanalei Moon.' At Tahiti Nui, serendipity is always on the menu!

In the heart of Hanalei village. 826-6277 Dinner reservations recommended. Breakfast 7 -11 am; Lunch 11:30 - 4 pm; Dinner 5 pm - 10 pm (except Friday). Call about Luau nights. Nightly entertainment in Lounge. Credit cards. Map: 2

Winds of Beamreach

The name is the same—or almost. For more than ten years, the name 'Beamreach' was synonymous with the most special steaks on the north shore. Then, after Iniki pretty much leveled Princeville, the restaurant folded, was sold, and re-opened under a new name, 'Winds of Beamreach.' The chef is the same, the steaks are ordered, we are told, from the same Wichita supplier, the dining room has the same layout, even some of the staff is the same.

So the dining experience should be the same. Alas, it isn't! The menu is larger, featuring new items like stir fry chicken ($12.95) or vegetables ($13.95), but the steaks are smaller, probably to keep prices down. The signature filet mignon is now an 8 oz. portion ($19.95), and the NY steak is priced in two sizes, $18.95 for 10 oz. and $22.95 for 14 oz.

Dinner begins with warm rolls and a small salad, which seems even smaller when you remember the huge family-style salad bowl which was the trademark of the old Beamreach. Fresh fish is moist and flavorful, but the stir fry vegetables, while tasty, could use more variety and fewer onions. The steaks are competently cooked to order, but no longer special.

Tucked away in Princeville's Pali Ke Kua condominium, the restaurant is pleasant in an understated way, with comfortable chairs and polished wood tables lit romantically with candles, arranged in a two-tiered dining room decorated with original Hawaiian paintings. Regrettably there is no view— the only water you can see is in the apartment swimming pool. But come early for a walk and enjoy spectacular sunsets outside before dinner!

In Princeville. Dinner nightly. 826-6143 for reservations. Credit cards. Non smoking section. Map: 2

Zelo's Beach House

Once upon a time, the old Shell House was a favorite spot for drinking with a little dining. Iniki destroyed all that. Now on the site, Zelo's Beach House has erected snazzy new quarters for dining with a little drinking. The new dining room is much more comfortable, the ceiling open to the rafters creating more air circulation, the tables arranged with greater separation, and the walls themselves opening to the outside through doors rather than windows. The effect is cool California. The dining room shines in cheerful white, blond wood tables and chairs look clean, and behind the counter, you'll see Zelo's trademark, a shining copper espresso machine.

Zelo's offer a varied menu, with most lunch items priced around $8; most breakfast choices at around $5; and most dinner choices around $12. The salads, particularly one featuring fresh ahi, are excellent. Fish and chips is a bit on the doughy side. You'll also find Lion brand coffees and wonderful steamed beverages as well fruit smoothies, croissants and pastries. Of particular note: 'mocha frosted', a delicious chocolate espresso shake with coffee ice cream ($3.95), and 'Grasshopper Pie,' green with mint chocolate chip ice cream in a dark brown oreo crust ($4.95).

Hanalei. 826-9700. Open 7:30 am- 9:30 pm daily. Entertainment some evenings. Non-smoking section. Credit cards. Map: 2

South Shore Restaurants

'favor..eats'

If you're dining on the south shore, you may have a hard time making up your mind! In Poipu, **Brennecke's Beach Broiler** remains a local favorite for the best in fresh island fish, cleanly grilled over kiave charcoal. Reasonably-priced meals include a salad bar, and a view of Poipu Beach. For a spectacular oceanfront setting, particularly at sunset, try the **Beach House Restaurant** near Spouting Horn, now under the direction of chef Jean Marie Josselin, well known for his imaginative Pacific Rim cuisine. In Poipu Shopping Village near the Kiahuna, **Roy's Poipu Bar & Grill** features the signature Euro/Asian cuisine of Roy Yamaguchi. Next door at **Keoki's**, families and hearty eaters will appreciate the large portions of steak and seafood at reasonable prices. At newly re-opened **Plantation Gardens,** you can enjoy a steak and seafood menu, as well as pizza cooked in a woodburning oven. Be sure to request a table overlooking the garden! At **House of Seafood**, you'll find an impressive variety of fresh island fish in creative preparations.

Wherever you dine on the south shore, be sure to stroll through the beautiful **Hyatt Regency Hotel** after dinner, a treat which can be yours for the modest cost of the tip for the valet who parks your car! Enjoy Hawaiian melodies at the cocktail lounge overlooking the gardens and ocean, or stop in at **Stevenson's Library**. Afterwards stroll the hotel's lovely grounds. Or try the hotel's restaurants, either **Tidepools** which serves steak and seafood, or **Dondero's**, which features Italian cuisine. Adjacent to the Hyatt Regency Hotel, **Poipu Bay Grill & Bar** offers wonderful breakfasts and lunches at reasonable prices. The view of the ocean beyond the rolling golf course fairways is wonderful, especially when you enjoy the reasonably-priced and generous sandwich and salad buffet at lunch.

If you're on a budget, visit **Taisho** in nearby Koloa for excellent Japanese food, and try to arrive for the bargain-priced early bird special! Or grill your own steak and seafood at the modestly priced **Koloa Broiler.** For some of the best Mexican take-out, try **Taqueria Nortenos** in Kukui'ula Center, on the road to Poipu. In Poipu Shopping Village, visit **La Griglia** for inexpensive and tasty pasta, sandwiches, and burgers.

But don't stay in Poipu! Take a short drive to Kalaheo and you'll find some wonderful, reasonably-priced restaurants. **Brick Oven Pizza** is a family favorite for the island's best pizza—great crispy crust, wonderful sauce, and generous cheese. The sausage is made right in the kitchen, and service is family-friendly! Just down the road, **Camp House Grill** serves some of the best hamburgers and barbecued chicken on Kauai, and the milk shakes are made with real ice cream in a real milk shake machine! For dinner, try **Pomodoro**, an intimate family-operated Italian restaurant with a level of food and service you'd expect at much higher prices, and **Kalaheo Steak House**, which serves some of the best steaks and prime rib for one of the best dollar values on Kauai!

The Beach House Restaurant

A longtime favorite of both residents and visitors, the Beach House once perched on a sea wall only inches from the waves, a great spot to watch the sun set into the ocean and enjoy dinner in a relaxed and casual setting. In fact, the tables were so close to the waves that when Hurricane Iwa struck Kauai in 1982, the entire restaurant was swept out to sea— leaving only the concrete slab to mark the spot where so many evenings had passed so pleasantly. Even though rebuilt at a more respectful distance from the waves, Beach House was once again destroyed ten years later by Hurricane Iniki, and has now re-opened in the same location, clearly in hopes that the third time is the charm!

At last the quality of the food matches the uniqueness of the setting! Beach House is now under the direction of chef Jean Marie Josselin, whose popular restaurant A Pacific Cafe in Kapa'a has earned high marks for imaginative Pacific Rim cuisine. Jean Marie plans a more Mediterranean flavor for Beach House, and when we visited less than a week after opening, the kitchen, with chef Linda Yamada (formerly of Westin's 'Inn on the Cliffs') presiding, was off to an excellent start.

Dinner begins with a basket of oven-fresh breads — foccacio, herb buns, and wonderful hot sourdough rolls topped with black sesame seeds. On the appetizer menu, you'll find such intriguing choices as clams diced with cashews served sizzling in the shell, or shrimp in Chinese ravioli topped with a chili lilikoi broth ($7.75). Our vegetarian loved her plate of organic tomatoes, no fewer than nine varieties, fresh from a farm in nearby Oma'o. Entrees, particularly the fresh island fish, are equally delicious. Ono is perfectly cooked, the white fish both flaky and tender, and served with a fragrant sauce of ginger and scallions ($22.50). Grilled swordfish is accompanied with a special Israeli couscous, as is the rack of lamb served with a cherry and pinot noir sauce. Grilled striploin with cabernet thyme sauce is first rate ($20), and an ordinary pasta, like penne, becomes special when served with a medley of wild mushrooms ($18.25).

Desserts are delivered daily from A Pacific Cafe, and so if you eat at both restaurants, you'll be able to zero in on your favorites! Be sure to try 'toasted Hawaiian,' a sponge cake layered with macadamia nut mousse, or the lightest of all, pear and chianti sorbet with fresh strawberries.

The setting is truly lovely. Tables are well-separated, arranged in a tiered L–shaped room, where fly fans hum pleasantly to encourage evening breezes. Sliding glass doors open to the evening air and to spectacular views, like surfers catching the waves as the sun sets into the shimmering sea. It's lovely even after dark, as the last light of sunset fades, and you can linger over coffee and watch the waves begin to glisten with moonlight. At Beach House, romance is clearly on the menu!

Poipu, on Spouting Horn Road. 742-1424. Reservations recommended, a day in advance. Request a window table, but be prepared to wait for it. Credit cards. Non-smoking section. Dinner nightly. Map: 3

Brennecke's Beach Broiler

Loyal fans were delighted when Brennecke's re-opened after Hurricane Iniki with a larger menu as well as a new and generous salad bar. One thing remains the same: Brennecke's is still the front runner when it comes to the best, most reasonably-priced fresh fish dinners on Kauai!

In this second-storey restaurant across the street from Poipu Beach Park, you'll find prices reasonable and the atmosphere decidedly informal, so you'll feel comfortable no matter what you're wearing. But the informal ambiance is the result of the meticulous attention to detail which enhances every aspect of the dining experience. The decor, for example, looks very plain — a porch in soft grey and white tones — but everything is spanking clean, the paint shiny and fresh looking, the chairs and grey formica tables immaculate, the flowers in the window boxes bright and cheerful. It's the kind of porch where your child could retrieve a piece of pasta from the floor and put it in his mouth and you wouldn't have to look the other way.

The food receives equal attention to detail. Clam chowder ($2.95) is creamy rather than thick, generous with clams, and delicately seasoned. Teriyaki steak stix ($7.25) are medium rare, tasty, and sizzling hot. Dinner entrees include beef, pasta, and poultry, as well as a host of sandwich baskets and munchies, but fresh island fish is the reason to come to Brennecke's. Your fish, no matter which fin you choose, will be perfectly cooked, crisp on the outside, meltingly moist and delicious inside. The secret to Brennecke's flawless broiling is the grill, designed by owner Bob French and fueled by charcoal of kiawe wood from Ni'ihau. It burns extremely hot and clean, sealing in juices quickly and leaving no aftertaste.

Over the years, we have been delighted with almost every fresh fish we have sampled. Even the old stand-bys, ahi and ono, are cooked so perfectly that they seem extraordinary. Opakapaka, or snapper, could not be juicier or tastier. Grouper, or white sea bass, with a texture somewhat like lobster, is also sensational, flaking easily and gently seasoned. If you are lucky, you will be able to sample the fresh mahi mahi, flaky and soft, unforgettably sweet and garnished with homemade tartar sauce. With the salad bar included, $19.95 is a great price for a great fish!

The dinner menu is larger than ever, including steak, chicken, and ribs, as well as combinations, and even prime rib in three sizes! Dinners include rice or herb pasta, sauteed fresh vegetables, and a visit to a first-rate salad bar, with more selections than you will be able to fit on your plate— all fresh, colorful, ripe, and appetizing. Brennecke's pasta is available as an 'extra' for $2.95 with entree, or as a side order for $3.95. If you're not hungry enough for a full dinner, Brennecke's offers more than a dozen reasonably-priced options, including several sandwich baskets, a huge platter of nachos ($7.95), and burgers ($6.50), even a vegetarian variant. The chicken sandwich is excellent, cleanly grilled and served on a soft bun. Ligea's BBQ beef ribs ($16.95) can also be ordered in an appetizer-sized portion of two ribs, each meaty and meltingly tasty. Or stick with the salad bar, and enjoy seafood chowder with it ($10.50).

The wine list is small, with almost all selections both inexpensive and ordinary, the best a Murphy Goode chardonnay at $23.95. Children can choose from seven dinners, like mini-pizza ($4.95) or teriyaki steak ($7.25) of fresh fish ($10.95), and even have chocolate milk ($1.25) or a grown-up looking fruit punch ($1.50). Kid's burgers, chicken, and fish are very successful, judging from the enthusiasm of six youngsters seated next to our table. At lunch, Brennecke's offers the salad bar as an entree for only $5.75, as well as a wide variety of sandwiches and munchies.

For the best in fresh fish, beautifully broiled and attractively served, it's hard to find a better spot than Brennecke's. The staff is friendly and professional, the dining comfortable and open to evening breezes. Brennecke's may be noisy when full, but it's busy for all the right reasons. Prices are reasonable, and best of all, you can be assured that your money will buy top quality. Since 1983, Brennecke's has been one of the most popular restaurants on the south shore. Be sure to phone ahead for a reservation if you don't want to stand in line, and you might check the fresh fish on the menu and reserve a portion of your favorite in advance!

Poipu, on Ho'one Rd. 742-7588 for the daily fish report, or reservations (necessary). Credit cards. Open 11 am - 10 pm daily. Map: 3

Brick Oven Pizza

Ask just about any Kauai resident where to find the best pizza, and you'll probably hear, 'Brick Oven.' We agree! This family-owned operation in Kalaheo has been one of our most popular stops. And we're not alone, for tourists, as well as local families, have made Brick Oven a favorite ever since it became one of the first to re-open after the hurricane.

Brick Oven had just moved into new, more spacious quarters before Iniki struck, but fortunately the new dining room sustained little damage. It has much of the charm of the original Brick Oven across the street— the cheerful red–checked tablecloths and murals of pizza serendipity — a pizza shaped like the island of Kauai, for example, with "Garlic Grotto," "Mushroom Valley," "Grand Pizza Canyon," and "Port Anchovy." Friendliness is in the air.

But good as all this is, the pizza is even better, as fine as you'll find anywhere. The homemade dough—either white or whole wheat—is simply delicious, crunchy without being dry and with a fluted crust like a pie, shiny with garlic butter. The sauce, in the words of the teenage judges, has "awesome spice, cooked just right"; there is lots of cheese; the Italian sausage is made right in the kitchen, and tomatoes are red, juicy and fresh. Portions are generous and quality unbeatable. A family size (15 inch) starts at $16.25, but you may be tempted to try one of the outrageous special creations described on the menu, the "super" ($11.85/ 10 inch), or one of the delicious looking sandwiches made on fresh baked rolls, priced around $6, or a salad ($3 to $6). You can wash it all down with ice cold beer ($3.35 for 1/2 pitcher) or soda ($3.15/ pitcher). A nice touch - the ice comes in the glasses, not in the pitcher! Kids will love to watch the dough spin into pizza during that hard, hungry time of waiting, especially at peak hours when it's jammed.

At Brick Oven, you'll find a smile and pleasant word for short persons no matter how cranky. When Lauren spilled her coke, our waitress not only wiped her dry but brought her a new glass filled to the very brim! Each child can ask for a ball of pizza dough, which feels so good in the hands that it usually manages to stay out of the hair—all the way home.

Kalaheo, on Rt. 50. Open 11 am - 10 pm. Closed Mondays. Credit cards. A Smoke-free restaurant. 332-8561. Map 4

Camp House Grill

Who would think to look for one of Kauai's best hamburgers in the tiny town of Kalaheo (already sufficiently blessed, one would think, with the island's best pizza)? It's worth the drive to try a Camp House hamburger, 1/3 pound of ground chuck, served in a basket with a pile of some of the hottest, crispiest french fries you have ever tasted, and amazingly priced at $4.95.

If you were able to find Kalaheo, a tiny blip on the line of Rt. 50 going west from Poipu, you would probably decide Camp House Grill looks too much like a greasy spoon, and drive right on by — that is, until you glanced at the parking lot — which is packed — or peeked in at the dining room — which is full. Once you're inside, you'll be pleasantly surprised by the crisp, clean decor: the woodgrain formica tables well-spaced, the blue window frames a nice contrast with whitewashed walls, and even the green plants looking healthy and well-fed. A cheerful waitress will seat you with a smile, no matter how much sand you bring in from the beach, or whether everyone in your party has managed to come up with an even number of shoes.

Though you cut some corners for such reasonable prices, paper placemats and napkins — even paper cups — are a small price to pay for such excellent food and pleasant service. And the placemats with a

drawing of a sugar plantation 'camp house' give hungry kids an opportunity to color, crayons courtesy of management. Another generous touch: sodas are served in a "bottomless cup" for $1.25, and the drinks are served immediately and refilled cheerfully. Better yet, try a milk shake which you can see (and hear) being made fresh at the gleaming silver fountain machine. No soft ice cream made pasty with thickener, Camp House Grill's shake has the genuine texture of ice cream mixed with milk. Mikey knows: it looks just like the milk shakes he makes the in the blender back home! Camp House Grill makes kids feel welcome. Ten-and-unders can eat a "menehune special" cheeseburger or hot dog for only $2.75, while bigger little people can choose from junior burgers ($2.95 for 1/4 pound), fish, hot dogs, and four types of chicken breast sandwiches from $4.95.

Everything is cooked to order, so you might have to wait a bit, but it will all seem worth while once you start eating. Waimea burger ($4.75), otherwise known as a barbecue cheeseburger, is perfectly cooked medium–rare with tangy sauce and great cheese. In a Hanapepe Burger, broiled pineapple and teriyaki sauce make an ideal complement to the beef, Swiss cheese, lettuce, and tomato. Onion rings ($2.95) would steal the show if it weren't already long gone with the french fries. Deep fried chicken ($5.50) comes to you hot, golden brown, and moist inside, a sure crowd-pleaser, more so than the barbecue 'Huli' chicken ($5.95/half) which is on the spicy side. To cool it all off, you can have draft beer, available by the glass, or pitcher for $6.75. Note: a different chef is in the kitchen for the dinner shift, so consistency may vary.

Camp House Grill is clean, cheerful, and sincere. What you see is what you get—and then some extras, including some wonderful home-baked pies to choose from. A deer head and a stuffed rooster look out through the window at what is passing by on Rt. 50. Don't let that be you!

Kalaheo, on Rt. 50. 332-9755 for take-out orders. No non-smoking
section, but tables by a breezy window serve the purpose! Open daily for
lunch and dinner. Map: 3

Dondero's, Hyatt Regency Hotel

Decorated in vibrant green and white, Dondero's is an elegant
restaurant, the showpiece of the lovely Hyatt Regency Hotel. Designed to
capture the more leisurely pace of the 1920's before jet-set timetables
pushed life into permanent fast-forward, Dondero's dining room is
beautiful, with tables attractively arranged on two levels and comfortably
spaced for privacy. Gracefully twining ivy vines painted on the walls
complement a striking design of rich jade green and white tiles, some
patterned with seashells, so that the room seems poised on the edge of a
seaside garden, with large windows and french doors opening to the
terrace. During summer months, when the sun sets around 7 pm, terrace
dining is enhanced with splashes of color from the bougainvillea, and
beyond them the yew trees imported to make the vista more Italianate. At
night, tables set with china and silver are softly lit by crystal lamps with
pleated shades, a golden glow in shades of darkness.

Surrounded by this elegance, as well as the strains of classical
music, you consider a menu which offers more than a dozen a la carte
entrees ranging in price from $21 (chicken with porcini mushrooms) to
$27 (Cioppino), a creation so large that it can be served, if you wish, in
two equal portions. Pastas range from $9 to $12 and can also be ordered
as full sized entrees ($16 to $22). Only two pastas are made fresh,
however, while the rest are "imported." A sign of the times, two choices
in La Cucina Naturele for high fiber/low cholesterol and fat: a vegetable
salad and a whole wheat pasta primavera.

Dinner begins with tiny loaves of light, crispy cheese bread, served
with a deliciously spicy tomato pesto. As an appetizer, pappardelle made
fresh in the kitchen is outstanding, served with two large and tender
scallops, shiitake mushrooms, asparagus, and red peppers, as attractive as
it is tasty. Minestrone, though generous with tomatoes and squash, is not
memorable for its flavor. You might prefer the bean salad, a huge bowl
with lettuce, artichokes, hearts of palm, sundried tomatoes, a great value
and a great taste. Risotto ($12.50/appetizer) is somewhat thick and
garlicky but arrives with excellent vegetables. Of the entrees, fresh
swordfish ($25.50) was surprisingly moist and tender, cooked as perfectly
as fish can be, though marred by the overpowering wine sauce which we

tried to scrape off as best we could. If you order fresh fish, you might ask to have all sauces served on the side! Rack of lamb ($26) is generous, four large chops which are tender but not very tasty. Fresh tomatoes, peppers and squash accompany the entrees.

The Hyatt wine list is expensive, with most selections more than $30 and only a dozen in the range of the $20's, including a Stratford Chardonnay at $28. You'll love the desserts— a smooth chocolate mousse, outstanding tiramisu, and strawberry flambeau with vanilla ice cream.

Dining at Dondero's will be very expensive; even if you limit your order to an entree, appetizer, and coffee, the cost per person will be more than $30. But the hotel comes with the meal! Consider your dinner as a single course in your entire evening. For an aperitif, walk around the lovely hotel and then enjoy a cocktail or glass of wine in 'Stevenson's Library,' one of the most elegant nightspots anywhere, not only because of its gorgeous view, but also its design and appointments. You'll find tables for chess or checkers, even billiards, a huge fish tank, and best of all, comfortable couches for pleasant conversation. After dinner, stroll the hotel's beautifully lit gardens and enjoy the breezes of the evening.

Poipu, The Hyatt Regency Hotel. Reservations a must: 742-6260. Credit cards. Non-smoking section. Free valet parking. Children's menu. Map: 3

House of Seafood

For ten years, The House of Seafood in the Poipu Kai Resort has specialized in fresh fish imaginatively prepared. The two owners, one being the chef, are on excellent terms with local fishermen — a big advantage in winter months when the surf can get very rough for the fishing boats. While other restaurants may have fresh fish in short supply, the House of Seafood will probably be offering as many as eight or nine choices.

Due to the owners' extensive hotel and resort experience, these fresh fish filets will not be simply grilled and sprinkled with paprika. Each will be presented in an imaginative preparation, the creation of the chef as he contemplates what has been hooked that day and decides how best to cook it. You might find fresh sea bass cooked in parchment, fresh mahi sauteed with macadamia nuts, fresh snappers of every hue, or even shark! Most

entrees are priced at $20 or more, and are accompanied by rolls, veg-
etables, and delicious herbed wild rice. Soup or salad are a la carte.

Attention to detail makes each part of the meal enjoyable. Water is
served with a slice of lemon in the glass, and mints accompany the dinner
check. Service is polite and friendly, and you get the feeling that the staff
is genuinely interested in doing the job well. Dinner begins with fresh
baked herb rolls and butter, the creation of a chef who likes to experiment.
If you choose a dinner salad ($5.50), you'll enjoy an attractive mix of leaf
lettuces, enoki mushrooms, water cress and tomatoes served in a large
glass bowl, with fanciful dressings like passion fruit vinaigrette or a
tropical alternative to 'thousand island' made with guava and fresh basil.
Or you may prefer the seafood chowder with taro leaves ($4.50) which is
generous with fresh fish and clams.

You can count on your fish to be generous and perfectly cooked, and
what makes House of Seafood a special place is the variety of interesting
preparations. One of the finest fresh fish we have tasted anywhere, for
example, is fresh ahi flawlessly broiled and served 'luau style', with a
light sauce delicately flavored with taro leaf and coconut. Wonderful!
Also excellent is the sauteed fresh mahi mahi served with orange and
cashew sauce. Or try the more pungent fresh ehu. Sea bass may be
served with a delicious combination of teriyaki, orange, and miso sauce
on a bed of soft noodles, or sometimes with a curry sauce that is too
strong for its delicate flavor. Paella arrives as a huge platter, generous
with clams, shrimp and fish. The vegetables which accompany the entrees
are fresh, carefully cooked and attractively served, like cauliflower with a
light and lemony cream sauce. If you're not sure you'll like the sauce on
your fish, ask to have it served on the side, and be sure to ask for some of
the chef's special tartar sauce with fresh pineapple.

You can spend a lovely evening in the comfortable, quiet dining
room, tastefully decorated with rattan furnishings and lots of leafy plants.
Most tables are near a window, are well spaced for privacy, and attractively set with white cloths and shining silver and glassware. On the well-
selected list, you can find some good wines at reasonable prices, most
priced in the mid $20's, like a William Hill Chardonnay.

At House of Seafood, the personal touch is everywhere. Children
can choose from steak, hamburger, fresh fish and wait until you hear this
entree from a generous and thoughtful management—grilled cheese!
Their dinner includes rice or french fries, vegetable, dessert and a drink.

Because salad is not inlcuded in the price of your dinner, you may
spend more than you would at other seafood restaurants, but in exchange
you get a wider variety of fresh fish and an interesting and imaginative

range of preparations. You also get a quiet dining experience, especially pleasant if you come on a night with a moon. The dining room is open to the night air, and from the darkened room lit by the soft light of candles floating in bowls of flowers, you can watch the last light of evening fade, the pattern of darkness changing with each moment. As stars twinkle through thin filmy clouds, the full moon glows in the deep blue sky, while soft breezes rustle through the hibiscus leaves and crickets sing themselves to sleep.

Poipu, in Poipu Kai Resort. 742-6433. Reservations suggested. Credit Cards. Dinner nightly 5:30 pm - 9:30 pm. Non-smoking section. Map: 3

Kalaheo Steak House

For more than five years, the Kalaheo Steak House has been serving some of the best, most reasonably-priced steaks on Kauai. The small, knotty pine interior is both pleasant and informal, so you will feel comfortable no matter what you are wearing. Plants divide the dining area into two sections, with comfortable booths along the wall and roomy tables in the middle. Fresh flowers and candles create a cozy, even romantic atmosphere.

The restaurant prides itself on the finest of ingredients. Steaks are top-grade Midwestern beef. Bread is baked each day at the bakery across the street. Even the dinner salad is exceptionally attractive, served on a lovely glass plate with ripe tomatoes, white beans and red onions. Choose between a delicious papaya seed dressing, or as a special treat for cheese lovers, a blue cheese dressing made with the genuine article crumbled in a delicious vinaigrette and topped with fresh ground pepper.

The menu offers steaks, seafood, and poultry dinners which include rice or baked potato as well as the salad. Our waitress recommended the New York steak ($17.95) and the fresh island ono (10 oz. for $16.95), and we were pleased with both suggestions. The generous portion of ono was flaky and tender, though you might take the precaution of having the butter sauce served on the side, unless you love garlic. When the steak arrived too well done to be 'medium rare,' the replacement steak was even larger, perfectly cooked, and accompanied by a second baked potato—a steak well worth the wait! Prime rib ($16.95/12 oz.; $22.95/24 oz.), was both tender and tasty. Entrees are cooked with little salt, a nice feature.

Service is friendly and efficient, and prices are extremely reasonable, with teriyaki chicken ($12.95) at the low end of the entrees. The wine list is small and fairly priced, with a Guenoc Chardonnay right on the mark at $16 and most wines less than $20. Or choose a cocktail or a Miller on draft, served from the bar which occupies the front of the building.

The Kalaheo Steak House is one of the best values on Kauai. You'll be pleased with your dinner, especially when you get the bill and find that two can dine in style for less than $40, or for less than $60 if they have the most expensive bottle of wine on the list! If you are staying in Poipu, it's an excellent alternative to high-priced hotel food, and if you are staying on the eastern shore, it's well worth the drive. The no-reservations policy makes planning difficult, but you might consider reserving a portion of prime ribs as a way of taking a stab at a table!

Kalaheo, 4444 Papalini Road. 322-9780. Credit Cards. A smoke-free restaurant. Dinner nightly 6 pm - 10 pm. Map: 3

Keoki's Paradise

At Keoki's you might feel as if you've wandered onto the set of Gilligan's island. Tables are arranged on several levels around a wandering lagoon, where taro grows among the lava rocks, and you can even spot a frog or two resting among the lily pads. Green plants hang everywhere, and the night is filled with the sound of crickets. Wooden tables are roomy and rattan chairs comfortably upholstered. Ask to be seated outside, where dining is cooled by evening breezes and you can watch the light of evening fade and the sky turn luminous with shining stars. If a shower threatens to douse the table, waiters will raise the awnings!

One of the most successful restaurants on the south shore, Keoki's offers reasonable prices as well as an atmosphere of South Pacific chic. In times of normal tourism, long lines of hungry diners begin to form at about 7 pm, so even with a reservation, expect company when you arrive!

To the right of the entrance is a bar and lounge, serving pu pus, nachos, and burgers, as well as Mexican specialties from a Seafood and Taco bar where you can watch the chef chop, saute, and stuff burritos. His stainless steel grill, he modestly claims, is 'clean enough for surgery!' Come early and grab one or the half dozen tables near the bar, and you can make an inexpensive dinner of these Mexican treats.

Keoki's main dining room features a reasonably-priced, extensive menu offering fresh fish, chicken, steak (sirloin only) as well as a huge 26 oz. portion of prime rib ($19.95) aptly named 'the Flintstone Cut', available only "while it lasts"—so you might want to phone ahead and reserve a portion when you reserve your table! Entrees include salad, rice, and fresh bread. Many cost about $10, and for about $6, children (even adults) can choose a burger or chicken sandwich. Children's full dinners are reasonable, $4.50 for a hamburger or $8.95 for chicken breast.

Unfortunately, the dining room doesn't serve any of the delicious looking tacos you might have seen being assembled at the Taco Bar on your way in. As a substitute, we tried 'summer rolls,' ($6.95), a sushi roll with crab, vegetables and avocado, which was still partially frozen in the center. (The spicy Thai dipping sauce arriving with it was delicious, however, and great with the fish entrees, so be sure to ask for some on the side!) Some may find the fish chowder ($3.95) overly thick and salty, and the salad which comes with the dinner is one choice and one choice only – a sharply seasoned Caesar salad with too much cheese, too many crou-tons, and the limpness of bulk preparation. You might try asking for romaine lettuce with oil and vinegar!

The dinner menu usually features several fresh island fish. On our most recent visit, the fish entrees were available only pre-marinated, however, and so we could not order the fish cleanly broiled, which we prefer after years of finding sauces and marinades to be of varying quality. The fresh–baked opakapaka ($18.95), which our waiter recommended, was moist, generous, and fragrant with basil. Fresh ono was flaky enough but a bit small and overwhelmed with a strongly flavored wine and caper sauce which should have been left on the side (or in the kitchen!). The prime rib ($19.95), truly enough for two, was moist and tender though a bit bland. A sign of the health-conscious times, Vegetable Lasagne ($9.95) with spinach, peppers, zucchini, Maui onions and three cheeses is a delicious entree choice. Koloa barbecued pork ribs were not as tasty as we expected, with the sauce seeming to be an afterthought rather than a part of the cooking process. A better choice was teriyaki sirloin, carefully marinated and very tender. Entrees are accompanied by an adequate herb rice and vegetables, or you can have baked potato ($2.50), though only one of our order arrived in time for dinner! The small wine list features a reasonably-priced Chateau St. Jean chardonnay. Try hula pie ($4.95), for which Keoki's is justly famous—an oreo crust with macadamia nut ice cream, chocolate sauce, and whipped cream.

Keoki's attracts a large clientele because of reasonable prices and reasonable cooking. Service is friendly, though geared to the masses, so you may have to stand up to catch your waitperson's attention. Be prepared to enjoy what comes your way rather than trying to customize your order or change the way the kitchen prepares it. Don't expect the kitchen to excel in subtle seasoning, and stick to simple dishes. Keoki's is a good choice for the truly hungry, for how can you go wrong with all that prime rib, and for those who love the truly hokey, for you can giggle during dinner under those fake Polynesian torches about which Hollywood script you would most like to be acting out in Keoki's Paradise.

Poipu, in Poipu Shopping Village. 742-7534 Reservations a must, and be prepared to wait even if you have one! Credit cards. Dinner 5:30-10 pm nightly. Seafood & Taco Bar 4:30-midnight.

The Koloa Broiler

The least expensive steak house on Kauai, the Koloa Broiler has devised a unique solution to the problem of overhead. Diners not only help themselves to salad, baked beans, and bread, but even cook their own entrees on an enormous indoor grill. A glass case at the entrance contains the menu in its raw form: mahi mahi (previously frozen) ($9.95), barbecued chicken ($9.95), top sirloin ($11.95), beef kabob ($9.95), fresh fish, and a hamburger ($7.00), with prices the same for both lunch and dinner, except the hamburger is $1 less. The waitperson will bring your selection to you raw, recite a few cooking instructions, and then you're on your own!

While this approach has obvious advantages, it is not foolproof. Hopping up and down to check the progress of your meal is hardly relaxing, and sometimes conversation distracts the attention you need for careful cooking. You end up being responsible for the quality of your dinner, so you can hardly send it back if it turns out raw or burnt. A few tips: you might try marinating your steak in the Italian salad dressing while you enjoy a cocktail. And despite instructions to the contrary, removing the foil wrapping from the chicken or fish in the final moments of cooking enhances the flavor. While your entree cooks, you can also toast some buttered bread.

The dining room is large and plain. Decorated with a few hanging plants and whirling ceiling fans, it has all the ambiance of a converted storeroom. And in certain spots, the fragrance of the grill is unmistakable. (This is one place where a non-smoking section is practically impossible!) But the real attraction here is unbeatable prices. It's a change of pace from the usual restaurant experience, and if you're on a tight budget, you won't find a more satisfying way to spend your evening or your money.

In the heart of Koloa. 742-9122 Credit cards. Children's dinner: hamburger/cheeseburger. 11:00 am to 10:00 pm daily. Full bar. Map 3

Piatti at Plantation Gardens

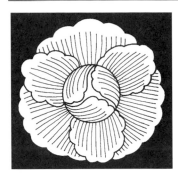

For more than 20 years, the lovely Moir Gardens have provided an especially romantic setting for a restaurant—a beautiful old plantation home, where you can dine outside on a veranda cooled by evening breezes fragrant with tropical flowers, and see water lilies glow in moonlit ponds like night-blooming stars.

Piatti is the newest resident of the old plantation home and by far the most elegant. China and crystal sparkle in candlelight on crisp linen cloths. At the same time, the decor is understated, so that the gardens, lit with subtlety and flair, draw the eye outside to a landscape brushed with shades of darkness. The dining room glows softly yellow and pink in the evening, like a plumeria blossom. At Piatti, romance is on the menu!

The newest link in a chain of highly successful west coast Italian restaurants, Piatti brings to Kauai an Italian cuisine with a touch of nouvelle California. Fresh vegetables abound, sauces are light, pasta fresh, spicing judicious. Herbs, spices, greens, even eggplant, are picked fresh from the restaurant's gardens. Crusty bread still warm from Piatti's brick pizza oven arrives immediately, along with a dish of signature garlic and basil olive oil pesto which your server will invert, with a flourish, onto a serving plate. Purists might prefer the extra virgin olive oil served in a decanter as a more subdued complement to Piatti's delicious foccacio baked with fresh mushrooms. The wine list offers both variety and depth, featuring the best as well as some of the lesser known California vintners, in a reasonable price range. For connoisseurs, there is a reserve list.

The extensive menu offers tempting choices at every price, with excellent pizzas and fresh pastas from $9.95, more than a dozen salads and antipasti from $5, and entrees ranging from lamb, veal, beef, pork, to chicken and seafood ($12.95 - $22.95). Vegetarians will love the variety of fresh vegetables (from $3.50) which can be ordered as a platter ($11.95). Appetizers are inventive, for example 'porcupine shrimp' wrapped in crispy, thin fried noodles, crunchy and very tender ($9.95). 'Mista salad' of fresh island greens is generous as well as crisply fresh ($6.95). Caesar salad can even be ordered in a single serving ($5.95), and white bean soup is light and tasty ($4.95).

Entrees are artfully arranged and well-prepared. Fresh island snapper is both flaky and tasty, though if you prefer the pure taste of fish, you might order the sauce served on the side ($23.95). Fresh ahi is northing short of spectacular— moist, tasty, and generous. Cannelloni ($13.95) made with fresh pasta, is light and flavorful, though perhaps more suitable for a traditional "secondi" role than a full entree if you are really hungry. Homemade pappardelle pasta served with shrimp and home-grown arugula is excellent ($18.95). If you like spice, you'll love the rotisseried chicken, whose herb crust makes a significant statement ($16.95).

Waitpersons are discreet, polite, and efficient, and every effort is made to make the dining experience pleasant and memorable. South shore Kauai now offers many dining options, and if you are looking for a romantic setting combined with first rate Italian cuisine and service, Piatti is for you—especially on a night when the moon is full!

In Kiahuna Resort, Poipu. Reservations 742-2216. Request the veranda. Credit cards. Open daily noon - 10 pm. Take-out orders, FAX 742-2216.

Poipu Bay Grill & Bar

Where can you enjoy a delicious lunch, with great sandwiches and an excellent salad bar, in a comfortable air-conditioned dining room with a spectacular view? You'll find it hard to beat the Poipu Bay Grill & Bar for value and enjoyment. The dining room is spacious and beautiful, with enormous windows looking out over the rolling green fairways of the Poipu Bay Golf Course, studded with palm trees. You can even see sand dunes and beyond them the ocean waves smashing against the rocky cliffs in bursts of brilliant spray. Tables are well separated, ceilings high and airy, and an elegant carpet with a leafy design creates a tropical mood.

For all this comfort and beauty, prices are surprisingly reasonable. The lunch menu offers a variety of sandwiches, including an exceptional hamburger — 'the 19th hole' ($8.95)— a half pound of beef, ground right in their own kitchen, served with apple smoked bacon, the sweetest imaginable fried onions, sauteed fresh mushrooms, and lots of melted cheddar cheese. The fresh ahi sandwich is one of the tastiest on Kauai, especially when served with teriyaki sauce and fresh pineapple. The best deal may be the sandwich and salad bar ($8.95 for adults and $6.95 for children), a generous spread of cold cuts and breads, including croissants and onion rolls, as well as an extensive array of fresh vegetables, fresh island fruits, and prepared salads, including pasta and potato salads, tuna salad, even pork fried rice! There's also a kettle of first rate soup!

Breakfast is equally wonderful, with complete meals reasonably-priced from $3.95 to $9.95 for steak & eggs. The garden omelette ($6.95) is a light almost crepe-like skin of eggs fully stuffed with green peppers, mushrooms, tomatoes, and Maui onions. The cheese omelette is hot, tasty and covered with perfectly melted cheese. Potatoes are crisp, and bread is served with excellent jam.

Poipu Bay Grill & Bar is located in the golf clubhouse at the Hyatt Regency Hotel in Poipu although the golf club is not operated by the hotel. With a wonderful view with good food, Poipu Bay Grill & Bar may be the Hyatt's best kept secret, though probably not for long!

Poipu, adjacent to Hyatt Regency Hotel. 742-8888. Breakfast 7 am - 11 am. Lunch 11 am - 5:30 pm (Sandwich/salad bar until 2 pm). Coffee: $1.50/ carafe. Non-smoking section. Credit cards. Do not confuse with Roy's Poipu Bar & Grill. Map: 4

Honeymoon, Kauai

Pomodoro

Once upon a time, two hardworking brothers from Italy arrived on Kauai via New York City, where one found a wife, and opened the island's first Italian restaurant. Over the years, as Casa Italiana grew into a success-ful restaurant, they imported the island's first pasta machine from Italy. As time went by, other restaurants, including the specialty restaurants in the big hotels, began to order their pasta, and so they sold Casa Italiana and became full-time purveyors of fine noodle creations.

But long hours with eggs and flour were just not as interesting as working with people. A true New Yorker, Gerry missed all those midnight hours in the restaurant, the seven-day workweeks, the temperamental customers and frazzled servers. So the family sold the pasta company and opened Pomodoro Restaurant, and Gerry is once more in her element, bustling from table to table keeping her diners happy.

Pomodoro is both attractive and small, with only ten tables, all of which will probably be occupied when you arrive. The dining room, filled with leafy green plants, is clean, comfortable, and informal. Service can be slow because everything is prepared to order, but prices are reasonable, with pastas from $8.95, and the most expensive dishes, the veal specialties, at $16.95. If you add a salad or soup, both of which la carte, the price goes up by about $4. Children can eat spaghetti for $5.95 or ravioli for $6.95, as well as small portions of selected entrees.

Food quality remains as high as ever. Minestrone ($3.50) arrives in a large bowl generous with noodles, beans, and still crunchy vegetables. Bread is served with extra virgin olive oil and balsamic vinegar instead of butter, sign of the healthful times. On the other hand, fresh fish is on the menu only as an occasional special, and four of the nine entrees are veal! Pasta primavera is excellent, the fresh zucchini, carrots, tomatoes, green onions tossed in what is almost a light and flavorful vegetable broth. Pomodoro's salad of mixed greens ($3.25) looks beautiful with purple and green spinach as well as various fresh organic lettuces, the kind your child may refer to as "weeds." The kids will love the manicotti, thin crepes generously stuffed with cheeses ($12.95), as well as the ravioli ($9.95), the soft pillows stuffed with ground beef or riccotta cheese, and even served with tasty meatballs ($11.50). Chicken cacciatore ($14.95), a skinless breast, is very tender. Pomodoro's sauces, especially the marinara sauce and the Alfredo cream sauce, are light and flavorful without being overpowering. Homemade foccacio is hot and tasty, and as we discovered, delicious with any leftover marinara sauce. Lasagne ($13.95) is excellent For dessert, try spumoni ice cream cake.

For excellent Italian cuisine at modest prices, Pomodoro is a good choice, and worth the drive just west of Lihue to Kalaheo, a tiny townlet which is fast becoming a center for dining, with the island's best pizza, as well as an outstanding steak house, great hamburger joint, and now an excellent Italian restaurant.

Kalaheo, Rainbow Shopping Center. 332-5945. Children's menu (under 12). Credit cards. Dinner nightly. Non-smoking section. Map: 3

Roy's Poipu Bar & Grill

Roy's is 'dining theater' at its best! From the time you arrive (and you'll probably have to wait, even with a reservation), you're part of a performance. No matter where you stand, you'll feel like you're in the action, as waiters whoosh by, leaning like skiers into the turns in the pathways between tables, steaming plates in hand, perhaps even an inverted chair. Given Roy's long, narrow layout (it occupies converted souvenir stores along one arm of the Kiahuna Shopping Center), each step, each turn counts, as servers maneuver through what amounts to an obstacle course of patrons and supply stations. You wonder if there should be a traffic light—or at least a stop sign!

The kitchen takes up a long slice of the restaurant, or it could be equally accurate to say that the dining room takes up a long slice of the kitchen! For at Roy's the cookery is the main act, and the kitchen is

center stage, just behind a wall of glass from the nearest tables. So the best seats in the house are only inches away from the gleaming chrome and tile workspace, where chefs and servers hustle and bustle as if performing in a silent movie starring Charlie Chaplin. Watch one chef weigh pizza dough on a small scale, spin it expertly into a crust and pop it into the tiled oven, while another adorns plates with colorful greens and vegetables, and a third flames pasta dishes in seeming defiance of fire safety rules. In a constant stream, servers enter the in-door, scoot along a narrow pathway picking up plates, and emerge from the out-door, while the executive chef surveys it all, smilingly serene, in his baseball cap.

At Roy's, the pace is fast bordering on frenetic, and the amazing thing is that with all this volume and activity, what emerges from the kitchen is carefully crafted and delicious. Since most entrees can be ordered in appetizer portions for about half the price, you should sample as many dishes as possible! Try potstickers flavored with lobster and miso sauce ($6.95), or delicious ravioli of shiitake mushrooms and spinach served in a creamy sauce of sundried tomatoes and riccotta cheese ($6.95). Spring rolls ($6.50) are light and crispy; 'Hibachi salmon' ($8.25) is about as tender and moist as fish can be, and risotto cakes made with vegetables ($7.95) are crisp, light and wonderful. Don't miss Roy's pizza, the crust both chewy and soft, though you'll be hard pressed to choose from options including eggplant, roast duck, grilled chicken, or an eyecatching creation of goat cheese and shiitake mushrooms topped with a small mountain of lettuce tossed in warm balsamic vinaigrette ($7.50). Entrees are equally tempting. Crispy Thai chicken is served with sticky rice, green beans, and almonds in a wonderfully light spicy sauce ($14.95). Fresh fish is memorable, like baked fresh salmon served with a delicious balsamic and cabernet sauce flavored with pancetta and onion, or fresh mahi mahi in a ginger-flavored crust ($21.95). A homey dish like pot roast with mashed potatoes becomes a showpiece when served in a pungent apple, ginger, and pineapple sauce ($15.95).

To keep prices reasonable, Roy's is organized for volume. The staff is highly trained and the tasks diversified: one waiter takes your order, another serves bread and water, and food is delivered by runners. This system works well for the most part but is not foolproof, as some parts of our order arrived late, one never appeared at all, and sometimes dishes come so fast that there is no time to appreciate the presentation. The kitchen was out of five items by 8:30, and custom ordering, we were told, requires the prior consent of the chef! Vegetarians may end up with few options besides salad, as the menu offers no dairy-free pasta or pizza.

Roy Yamaguchi opened his first restaurant in 1988 on Oahu, where he still spends most of his time, and he has successful restaurants in Maui, Guam, Tokyo, and now Pebble Beach, California. They feature the same Euro-Asian cuisine, the same system, even the same wines, as Roy has arranged with some of California's finest vintners to bottle 'Roy's Sauvignon Blanc' (Chalone, $28), 'Roy's Chardonnay' (Au Bon Climat, $38), and Roy's champagne (Iron Horse Vineyards, $39). Each Roy's combines the 'signature Roy Yamaguchi style' with the personal stamp of its resident executive chef. While the left-hand page of the menu contains selections generic to all Roy's, for example, the right-hand page describes the creations of the Poipu Roy's executive chef, Mark Segawa-Gonzales.

If you were to imagine the ultimate in fine restaurants, you might envision your table as a peaceful island, where discrete waitpersons present each course unobtrusively, and the only sound you hear is the delicate tinkle of silverware and china. Well, Roy's breaks all these rules. You won't find a quiet table in the house, and you are never alone, for the plan, in the words of our waiter, is to 'attack the table' with a barrage of attention — serving and clearing, offering fresh baked rolls or ice-water, sweeping away crumbs from the granite-topped table or just asking how you are enjoying your meal. The essence of Roy's is interactive dining! You're part of the performance, and everyone on the staff seems to be enjoying the show. And it's this almost electric energy, as well the truly delicious food, which makes Roy's a unique dining experience on Kauai.

Poipu, Poipu Shopping Village. 742-5000 Reserve well in advance. Nightly 5:30 pm - 9:30 pm. Non-smoking section. Credit cards. Map: 3

Taisho

In the heart of Koloa Town, Taisho offers well-prepared Japanese cuisine at reasonable prices. As you walk into the somewhat dark interior, you will be asked what you would like to eat. Sushi customers are sent through the dining room to a small, colorful room in the rear offering hand-rolled varieties as well as fresh-cut sashimi.

In the somewhat sparsely furnished dining room, service is quick and friendly, and the menu offers a variety of well-priced Japanese specialties. Dinners include an excellent miso soup and rice, and entree choices include fresh fish ($11.95), meat, and chicken. Tempura ($13.95) is excellent, particularly the fresh fish like mahi mahi, which is light and delicate and absolutely delicious. Chicken stir fry ($11.50) is served in an enormous portion, with lots of fresh carrots, zucchini, sweet onions, and mushrooms. There's not much on the wine list, but soda arrives in cans which are inexpensively priced at $.80.

Sushi is attractively served on fish-shaped glass plates. The chef likes to make his rolls with wasabi, however, so specify if you prefer to add it yourself. Spring rolls ($5) are hot, crispy, and tasty. The best deal is the early bird special dinner (5 pm until 6:45), which for about $10 includes a teriyaki entree with selected sushi.

Old Koloa Town, across from the Post Office. 742-1838. Dinner 5: 30 - 9:30 pm. Closed Sundays. Cash only. Map 3

Taqueria Nortenos

When you drive by the Kukui'ula Center in Poipu, you often see a jammed parking lot and a small cluster of people on the sidewalk. This congestion is due to Taqueria Nortenos, which serves some of the best, most sensibly priced Mexican food on Kauai.

You'll have to wait on the take-out line by the tiny kitchen, (For those in a rush, there's an 'express window') and while you're being driven crazy by the wonderful aromas, you can calculate the price of your selections. The menu offers meat or vegetarian burritos, tacos, and tostadas at modest prices ($2-$4) with fillings and toppings priced separately. If you worry about fat in your diet, you can skip the sour cream and not pay for it! Beans, rice, and sauce come free, and inexpensive extras like tomatoes or onions will be cooked right inside your burrito or taco. Nachos are generous with cheese and plenty of everything, and you'll find both fresh corn and flour chips. Guacamole is chunky with avocados. Your beef burrito will be filled with huge chunks of tender and tasty shredded beef, and covered with cheese, in a portion so large you will be hard pressed to clean your plastic plate. Spices are mild, with plenty of hot sauce available. Take-out, or eat at picnic tables in the tiny (& dark) self-serve dining room.

Poipu, Kukui'ula shopping center. 11 am – 11 pm, Mon-Sat. Wed: 11 am till 5:30 pm. 742-7222. Map: 3

Tidepools

Hyatt Regency Hotel

Nestled at the bottom of the cliff in the center of the lovely Hyatt Regency Hotel, Tidepools combines an elegant ambiance with expertly prepared fresh fish. To get to Tidepools, you walk down from the hotel lobby, a spectacular marble perch built into the cliff and overlooking the sea. At the base of the cliff, clustered near the edge of the hotel's wandering waterways, is the restaurant, a 'village' of connected Polynesian style huts, each housing an arrangement of tables and covered with a thatch roof of indeterminate sun-faded color.

The dining room is comfortable, spacious, and attractive. Parquet-topped tables with cloths of Hawaiian tapa design are well spaced for privacy (there's not a bad table in this restaurant), and lit with candle lamps glowing golden in the evening light, reflected in the blue wine and water glasses. Dinner begins with a delicious fresh-baked seven-grain loaf, served warm and ready to slice on a breadboard.

A new menu offers fewer choices than in the past. You can still choose fresh island fish, either poached with organic Kauaian herbs, sauteed with lilikoi lemon basil, plainly grilled or even blackened, but sadly, you can no longer choose the signature preparation, 'Tidepools' fresh mahi mahi baked on a slab of kiawe wood and served in a frame of braided bread. Purists may order fish (and even beef) simply pan seared; you'll find this *'Cuisine Naturelle'* listed on the menu in calories as well as dollars! Those who don't care for the finny set can choose from lamb, chicken, prime rib and steak ($18-$25) as well as three Japanese entrees ($18- $32). Vegetarians have few choices on the new menu, and the plate of vegetables we requested turned up as an extra large serving of the zucchini and carrots which accompany the regular menu entrees!

At Tidepools, portions are reasonably generous, presentation attractive, service polite and unhurried, and every aspect of the evening designed to make your evening pleasant, down to the oversized cup for your coffee. For hotel fare, you can't expect much more than this! Children may choose from selected entrees at half-price. Prices are high, but the hotel comes with the meal! Be sure to explore the lovely grounds, walk along the ocean and find one of the hammocks just a few feet from the sand, lie back, listen to the sound of the waves, and look up into the bowl of stars. Or enjoy an after dinner drink in the informal comfort of Stevenson's Library, one of the most special after-dinner spots on Kauai.

Poipu, Hyatt Regency Hotel. Dinner nightly. Reserve a day in advance. 742-6260. Complimentary valet parking. Non-smoking area. Credit cards. Map: 3

Tomkats Grill

Housed in a covered veranda at the rear of the historic Koloa building, Tomkats offers informal, open-air dining at reasonable prices. About a dozen tables with cushioned rattan chairs cluster on the plank floor, and just beyond the railing is a small quiet garden, fringed with red ginger, where a small fishpond is home to goldfish tuned in to 'Hawaiian time,' moving slowly enough to entrance the twelve-and-under set. Tomkats courts families, as the supply of high chairs and booster seats indicates, and features a special "kittens" menu with PBJ ($2), hamburger or grilled cheese ($2.50). There's serendipity in the sculptures of cats looking yearningly at painted fish, and hanging plants seem to grow in harmony with Hawaiian melodies, or the occasional faster beat of country and western music. The open air dining is pleasant, with fly fans gently encouraging breezes, and even in a sudden shower this sheltered spot is peaceful, the rain beating a muffled tatoo on the tin roof. A full bar is adjacent, though not intrusive to diners.

The menu offers a wide range of sandwiches, burgers, and large, first-quality salads; "Tomkats' Nibblers" and several dinner entrees round out the menu. Sandwiches are carefully prepared and attractively served in baskets piled high with french fries. The Turkey club on rye ($6.50), with avocado as an extra ($1.25) was first rate, as was the Cobb Salad ($6.50). Portions are generous and service is friendly. The all-day hours make Tomkats a convenient stop after the beach, when some of your party may be hissing with hunger!

Central Koloa. 742-8887. 11 am -10 pm daily. Credit cards. Take-out available. Map: 3.

Westside Restaurants

'favor...eats'

In Hanapepe, the **Hanapepe Bookstore and Espresso Cafe** serves wonderful vegetarian dishes, as well excellent sandwiches and coffee drinks. Nearby, the **Green Garden Restaurant** is a Kauai tradition for 'island style food' — a cuisine reflecting the multi-ethnic heritage of the island—Chinese, Japanese, Filipino, and American. A salad bar at a modest price, as well as famous lilikoi chiffon pie, make this a great choice for lunch! After lunch (or before!) visit beautiful Salt Pond Beach Park, one of our favorite family beaches. **Sinaloa** serves Mexican dinners, featuring tortillas made fresh in its own kitchen! In Eleele, visit **Toi's Thai Kitchen** for inexpensive, and delicious, Thai food.

In Waimea, on your way to (or back from!) Polihale or Koke'e, be sure to stop in at **Wrangler's** for an outstanding hamburger platter, as well as excellent sandwiches, salads, and chicken. **Grove Dining Room** offers tasty food in a lovely gardenside setting for a romantic evening.

The Green Garden

There has been a Green Garden Restaurant for about as long as Kauai has been called the Garden Island. A local legend, it has been owned and operated by the same family since 1948, its reputation based on generous portions and inexpensive prices. The menu features American, Japanese, and Chinese dinners, many priced around $5. Even at lunch, meals include several courses as well as a beverage. Service is fast and very friendly at the long, ranch style tables, and although the dining room may look and sound more like a high school cafeteria than a garden, you certainly get full value for your money. Where else could you find a hamburger platter with fries, a salad, dessert, and iced tea for under $4? At $5.50, the fresh ulua tempura or shrimp tempura are also bargains. For children, club sandwiches are about $4, and grilled cheese only $1.95— remember: this price includes salads plain enough for picky eaters, lots of fries and a drink! The newest feature, the salad bar, offers a generous assortment of fruits, vegetables, and great dressings for the amazing price of $5 at lunch and $7 at dinner. Combine it with a bowl of soup, priced in three sizes, the 'medium' at $2.80 easily large enough to be a 'large'!

The Green Garden's pies would stand out at any price, and we recommend them all—the chocolate cream pie is a child's favorite treat, and the coconut cream pie has a light flaky crust filled with marvelously light egg custard topped with toasted coconut. Macadamia nut cream pie is equally delicious. The lilikoi chiffon pie, for which the Green Garden is justly famous, has the lightest texture imaginable and a taste of passion fruit that will arouse your taste buds.

The Green Garden is terrific for large families on small budgets. Children are treated with tolerance, and the staff is exceptionally friendly. The Green Garden also serves dinner, with most of the same entrees priced about $1 higher than lunch.

Hanapepe, on Rt. 50. Reservations suggested for dinner. 335-5422. Open daily except Tuesdays: 9 am - 2 pm and 5 pm - 9 pm. (Opens 8 am Saturdays and 7:30 am Sundays) Credit cards. Map: 4

The Grove Dining Room

Along the beach in Waimea, the Grove is at the center of a restored sugar plantation turned resort, a complex of refurbished cottages once occupied by plantation workers. The restaurant is temporarily closed, although buffet dinners are offered each weekend, catered by Wrangler's

Hanalei Bay's strong winter surf

Restaurant, in the original plantation house, a spacious building with tall ceilings, large windows, and a lovely wraparound porch. Entertainment by local Hawaiian musicians makes dining very pleasant. The dining operation is in the process of change, and may be different when you visit, so call ahead to find out what's cooking!

Waimea, 9400 Kaumualii Hwy. 338-2300. Map: 4

Hanapepe Bookstore & Espresso Cafe

Rustic Hanapepe looks like a black & white movie set, with the Bookstore & Cafe as the setting for the main scene. Books aren't the only

---

'800-Kauai Treats'

Papayas   Akana Farms   (800) 572-7292
10 pounds of Kilauea papayas shipped via federal express (about $40). Deliveries on Fridays; order by Tuesday (p.72)

Tropical flowers   Kauai Tropicals   (800) 303-4385
Box of beautiful ginger, colorful ti, heliconia shipped via federal express (from $40). Order 3 days in advance (p. 74)

item for sale, and you will be delighted with delicious breakfasts and lunches, and you may come back for the dinners served only on Thursday, Friday, and Saturday nights.

This is vegetarian cuisine with an island flair. You'll find scones flavored with passion fruit ($2.50) as well as a changing menu reflecting the chef's daily fancies. The tiny restaurant seats only 6 parties. Paintings by local artists fill the clean white walls with color. Lots of leafy plants provide the green and growing look, and the clean white formica tables are set with fresh flowers. Dominating the dining area is the gleaming tiled counter, a remake of the original 1940's curved lunch counter of the Igawa Drugstore, and now the home of the espresso bar, where you can enjoy Larry's excellent espresso and capuccino, including first-rate iced mocha.

Meals are attractively presented and very tasty. 'Kelly's Best', a garden burger made from oats, carrots, cottage and mozzarella cheese, is served on a cracked wheat roll with bright red local tomatoes, lettuce and a tasty spinach spread. Accompanied by an excellent potato salad, it's well priced at $6.75. Vegetable fritatta ($7.75) is stuffed with red and green peppers, zucchini, squash, mushrooms, mozzarella and topped with local tomatoes. Ask Chris to describe the pasta of the day ($6.75). Ours featured fresh local vegetables with a light, delicious creamy tomato sauce. One of our favorite sandwiches on Kauai is the "healthnut" sandwich ($5.25), spread with homemade humus and served open faced so that we could assemble it ourselves, selecting just the right proportion of tomatoes, lettuce, sunflower sprouts, cucumbers and onions.

On Thursday, Friday and Saturday nights, the dining room turns Cinderella-like into a lovely black and white cafe, with soft lighting and live music, where you can enjoy dinners created by Greg Forker (chef of the Waiohai Hotel's Tamarind until Iniki destroyed it). He may devise a vegetable lasagne with spinach, gorgonzola, and riccotta ($16.95), or pasta primavera with a marinara sauce of tomatoes and sundried tomatoes, which we found lighter and more tasty. Entrees can be accompanied with vegetables, fresh from the farmers' market, a wonderful option! Appetizers include puff pastry with zucchini, with a watercress, basil pesto or a salad elegantly adorned with a fan of tomato slices.

The dining area and espresso bar take up only about half of the room, so while your meal is being cooked, you can browse through the eclectic collection of art, jewelry, souvenirs, and fragrances, most created on Kauai. In one of the more interesting touches for a Ladies Room, we found a plant growing in a fixture usually reserved for men! Afterwards, you can wander the main street—it won't take you very long—stopping by the Kauai Fine Arts Gallery, Uncle Eddie's Angel Store, and at the end of the street, the Taro-Ka chips factory—you'll love those chips!

Hanapepe, 3830 Hanapepe Road. 335-5011. Open 8 am - 2 pm. Closed Mondays and Tuesdays. Dinners Thursday, Friday & Saturday 5:30-9 pm. A smoke-free restaurant. Credit cards. Map: 3 or 4

Sinaloa Taqueria

Painted in hot pink, turquoise, yellow and vivid green, Sinaloa gives the term 'south of the border' a whole new resonance! The dining room certainly makes a vivid statement; the walls are painted like a technicolor jungle, with a leopard prowling through Mayan ruins, even a parrot flying across a painted ceiling! Dinners are also vivid, up a few degrees from other Mexican eateries on Kauai. Friends from southern California who are Mexican food aficionados, view Sinaloa's cuisine as the most authentically Mexican on Kauai.

The creation of a 'Mexicano' Los Angeles lawyer bored with his practice, Sinaloa is a family project, and the tortillas produced in the factory behind the restaurant have become so successful that some of the relatives have moved to Honolulu to handle the marketing and distribution! You can buy Sinaloa tortillas in most food markets on Kauai. They make great chips, and so at Sinaloa, the nachos are excellent, filled with cheese, beans, tasty guacamole, sour cream, and green onions ($6.95). Burritos stuffed with shredded beef or chicken are also first rate, as was the chili relleno and the 'Friday night special pork.' Entrees are accompanied with rice and a cup of beans which almost all of us found too spicy The gracious hostess, however, found us a milder version as a substitute.

At Sinaloa, service has the friendly pride of a family operation. Prices are reasonable, with dinners between $10.95 and $13.95. The kitchen prides itself on using only fresh tomatoes, as well as chiles direct from Mexico! Everyone seems eager to please, and the atmosphere is so relaxed that you will feel comfortable no matter what you are wearing. Chances are, your evening will be spent pleasantly, with tasty food and reasonable prices.

Hanapepe, Rt. 50. 335-0006. Credit Cards. Open 3 pm until 9 pm except Wednesdays. Map: 4

Toi's Thai Kitchen

You can't get more underground that Toi's Thai Kitchen! Once housed in a large carport semi-attached to a bar called 'Traveler's Den' in sleepy Kekaha, Toi's used to consist of a half dozen formica dinette sets, some with card table chairs. As word of Toi's magic spread, more people came, and eventually Toi's moved to more spacious quarters in a shopping center in almost-as-sleepy Eleele. Your first job is to find it, huddled between Big Save and Dairy Queen. The dining room is pretty bare, the painted cinderblock walls decorated by white lace curtains around the windows. A few plants try valiantly to liven up the decor, assisted by fresh anthuriums on the dozen formica tables.

No matter the appearance of the dining room, what comes out of the kitchen is delicious. Toi's has developed a loyal clientele who have spread the word, attracting newcomers who can't believe their eyes when they arrive—and shake their heads when they leave.

We arrived for lunch one afternoon, hungry and sandy from the beach. After a brief look, we might have turned right around had it not been too late to go anywhere else! In Thai Saimin ($4.95), fresh white flat noodles float in a gently spiced broth colorful with vegetables, several varieties of bean sprouts, and lots of tender chicken. Beef saimin has a stronger, more pungent flavor. Spring rolls are crisp, served with fresh lettuce, mint leaves, and a zesty peanut sauce ($6.95). The hot yellow curry pleased Jeremy, our spice enthusiast. Pad Thai ($7.95) was another wonderful dish, the tender chicken and fresh Thai noodles sweetened with coconut milk and fresh basil. Fresh eggplant sauteed with tofu and huge fresh mushrooms was a marvelous contrast, both pungent and spicy ($5.95). Everyone loved Thai fried rice ($7.95), so colorful and tasty that it was devoured to the last grain. Be sure to try Toi's Temptation, a sweet curry made with your choice of chicken, beef, pork, or fish simmered in coconut milk and flavored with lemon grass, lemon and basil leaves, and served with either potatoes or pineapples. Those who prefer American food can try hot, crisp french fries ($1.50/$3), or sandwiches and burgers priced from $3.40 to $5.

We were astounded that our hungry family of six could feast for less than $40. You won't find Toi's Thai Kitchen listed in the yellow pages, and the sign is pretty hard to see. Part of the fun, however, is the adventure of the hunt!

Eleele Shopping Center on Rt. 50. 335-3111. Lunch 11-2:30 pm except Sundays. Dinner 5:30-8:30 pm daily. No non-smoking area. Cash only.

The ruggedly beautiful Na Pali coast can be seen by helicopter or boat.

Wrangler's Restaurant

There's good news at Wrangler's! Completely destroyed by Iniki, Wranglers' new dining room retains the outlines of its historic building, where you expect to see Matt Dillon stroll in at any moment, but inside, everything has been rearranged to be far more comfortable. The dining room is more spacious, with ceilings open to the rafters, fly fans to keep the air moving, large windows for light. Tables are roomy and well separated, and arranged on two levels for quiet and privacy. A veranda outside in the rear offers open air dining, and there's even a private room for larger parties. The decor retains its plantation flavor, with saddles and tack from the Hawaiian cowboys, the paniolos.

Even better is the new menu. Some old favorites, like the 'Wrangler Burger,' remain, but you'll find a new emphasis on the healthful. You can choose from a wide range of salads, sandwiches, 'Mexican Lunches' with soup or salad, Spanish rice and beans, or Plate Lunches with Korean chicken or tasty fresh island fish, as well as the chef's 'cook-off' winning Portuguese Bean soup. The 'Wrangler Burger' is one of the best on Kauai, a juicy half-pounder on a sesame seed roll, with lettuce and tomato, served with lots of fresh, crispy, piping hot steak fries — the real thing. And with soup or salad, this two-handed burger is remarkably priced at only $7.95.

Service is very friendly, and those too restless to sit while food is prepared can explore Wrangler's shop, which features lovely items from local artists, including Hawaiian quilts, dolls, and stuffed animals. Deborah Tuzon of Waimea weaves placemats and jewelry of lauhala, and Caz, on the staff, creates wonderful sunflower barrettes and headbands of colorful woven plaid paniolo cloth. If you're on your way to Koke'e or to Polihale, you'd be hard pressed to find a better spot than Wrangler for victuals. Waimea is a historic town. Right across the street from Wrangler's is the Waimea Hawaiian Church, circa 1820, where Hawaiian language service is held at 8:30 every morning!

Downtown Waimea, on Rt. 50. 10:30 am - 9 pm daily. Closed Sundays. Credit cards. Non-smoking section. Map: 4

Espresso Kauai

North Shore: In the Princeville Shopping Center, try *Hale O'Java* for coffees, sandwiches, & pizzas as well as tropical flavored gelato. In Hanalei, *Old Hanalei Coffee Company* serves delicious coffees and sandwiches, as does *Zelo's Beach House*. In Kilauea, you can sample coffees and pastries at *Kilauea Bakery* and at *Roadrunner Cafe*.

Eastern Shore: At *Border's Espresso* you can sip coffee and discuss the latest books at what is fast becoming the 'in' spot on Kauai! *Coffee Tea & Tee* combines coffees with Italian sodas and also shirts. *Michelle's Bakery,* main street Kapa'a, serves coffees, sandwiches, salads, baked goods, vegetarian creations, even tamales. *Papaya's Garden Cafe*, Kauai Village Shopping Center in Wailua, offers coffees, vegetarian deli entrees, salads, and sandwiches, with self-serve dining on the patio. *Cafe Espresso*, Coconut Plantation Marketplace, Wailua, serves pastries, sandwiches, soups, coffees, teas.

South & Western Shore: *Hanapepe Bookstore & Espresso Bar,* main street in Hanapepe, has wonderful coffees, vegetarian salads, sandwiches, pastas. Lunch daily, Dinner served on weekends in a pleasant cafe. *Kalaheo Coffee Co. & Cafe*, on the main street in Kalaheo, serves coffees, pastries, breakfast & lunch.

Suggestions From Our Readers

The Patlers of Mill Valley, CA share their "special afternoon with Daddy" : walking the beach at Hanalei Bay, crossing over to the Waioli Mission grounds to swing and shoot baskets, and ending up at the Wishing Well for the best shave ice! Macadamia nut ice cream over shave ice is a favorite, as is lilikoi.

Polihale Beach on a very rainy day is not a good idea, according to the Franks of Edgewood, Kentucky. "We mired our car in the muddy cane road and were lucky to be pushed out by some plucky Wyoming tourists!" This advice is true of all Kauaian dirt roads.

The Dawsons of Los Angeles suggest a visit to the Waioli Mission House and Church in Hanalei. Sunday services are conducted in Hawaiian as well as in English, and the very friendly family atmosphere is evident in the announcement at the top of the Sunday Bulletin: "Our *keikis* are apt to wander during church. They do this because they feel at home in God's house. Please love them as we do." Call 826-6253 for information.

About Secret Beach, Donna Madden of Orinda, California writes "Either you kept a secret from us, or the beach kept its secret from you, because it is sometimes a nude beach. We were surprised when we got to the bottom of the path and ran into a man with long bond hair wearing nothing but a guitar." Each to his own music!

L J Huffman of Lihue recommends the fresh ono sandwich at Kalapaki Beach Hut as the 'island's best.'

Siragan Bengoian took the Kauai Bus from Wailua to Kilauea for 50 cents, then paid another quarter to go all the way to Ha'ena! You can't beat the prices! Buses run frequently. Call 241-6410 for the regular schedule.

Rosemary McCann of New York City recommends Angeline Locey's Hawaiian lomilomi massage as one of the best things to do–anywhere!

A special mahalo to Charlie, Rebecca, Jim, Craig, Mish, Aunty D, Kathy, and *all* my friends on *Compuserve's Hawaii Forum*, especially Linda (if ever a wiz there was!) for great suggestions and advice! Our cyberspace encounters (of the third kind!) are always lively & informative!

Index

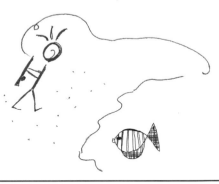

Order Form

Please send the
Kauai Underground Guide to:

I enclose $9.95 plus $2 shipping and handling.
(For orders of 2 or more books, shipping is free)

Papaloa Press

362 Selby Lane, Atherton CA 94027

FAX (415) 364-3252

Email: kauaiguide@hotmail.com

http://www.hshawaii.com/kvp/best_kauai_guide/

Eastern Shore

Restaurants

Kilauea
1   Casa di Amici, 160
2   Roadrunner Cafe, 168

Anahola
3   Duane's Ono Burger, 135

Kapaʻa
4   Kapa'a Fish & Chowder, 123
5   Kountry Kitchen, 129
    Hanaya, 121
    Olympic Cafe, 134
6   Rocco's, 141
    El Cafe, 132
    Ono Family Rest, 135
7   Sukothai, 143

Wailua
8   Dragon Inn, 111
    King & I, 126
    Nanea, 132
9   A Pacific Cafe, 136
    Papaya's, 139
    Panda Garden, 139
    Violet's Place, 146
10 Waipouli Deli, 149
11 Margarita's, 129
12 Bull Shed. 109
13 Kintaro, 127
    Mema, 131
    Sizzler, 142
    Wah Kung, 147
14 Flying Lobster, 115
    BeachBoy, 109
    Wild Palms, 150
    Eggbert's, 116
    Al & Don's, 106
15 Wailua Marina, 148

Hanamaʻulu
16 Hanama'ulu Tea House, 119
    JR's Plantation, 140

Lihue
17 OK Bento & Saimin, 133
18 Duke's Canoe Club, 113
    JJ's Broiler, 122
    Cafe Portofino, 110
    Tokyo Lobby, 145
    Kauai Chop Suey, 124
19 Barbecue Inn, 107
    Ma's, 130
    Hamura Saimin, 118
20 Kiibo, 125
21 Sumo, 144
22 Gaylord's at Kilohana, 116

Beaches

Ninini Beach, 23
Kalapaki Beach, 23
Hanama'ulu, 24
Lydgate Park, 25
Wailua Bay, 25
Kealia Beach, 26
Donkey Beach, 27
Anahola Beach, 28

Hotels

A   Coconut Beach Resort
B   Islander on the Beach
    Kauai Beachboy
C   Kauai Sands
D   Kauai Resort Hotel
E   Outrigger Hotel
F   Marriott, Kauai Lagoons

Kauai's main traveled roads: Rt. 56 (Kuhio Hwy) goes north from Lihue to Wailua, Kapaʻa and Anahola. Rt. 56 curves to the west towards Kilauea and then Princeville.